Prentice-Hall, Inc. Englewood Cliffs, New Jersey 07632

LEROY S. FLETCHER
University of Virginia

TERRY E. SHOUP
University of Houston

Introduction to engineering

including FORTRAN programming

Library of Congress Cataloging in Publication Data

FLETCHER, LEROY S
    Introduction to engineering.

    Includes bibliographies and index.
    1. Engineering.   2. FORTRAN (Computer program
language) I. Shoup, Terry E.,   joint
author. II. Title.
TA145.F53   620'.004'2   77-24142
ISBN 0-13-501858-7

10 9 8 7 6 5 4 3 2 1

Printed in the United States of America

Prentice-Hall International, Inc., *London*
Prentice-Hall of Australia Pty. Limited, *Sydney*
Prentice-Hall of Canada, Ltd., *Toronto*
Prentice-Hall of India Private Limited, *New Delhi*
Prentice-Hall of Japan, Inc., *Tokyo*
Prentice-Hall of Southeast Asia Pte. Ltd., *Singapore*
Whitehall Books Limited, *Wellington, New Zealand*

To
Nan and Betsy

Contents

Appendices

With the increasing importance of technological developments in everyday life, the importance of engineers and scientists also has increased. As problems become more complex and diverse, the engineer and scientist must develop skills in problem-solving techniques which are independent of the type of problem. In order to equip themselves to handle effectively the problems they confront, engineers must develop an understanding of problem solving and computational techniques.

This textbook has been prepared as an introductory engineering textbook for first-year students in engineering and engineering technology, to provide some background and practice in the formulation and solution of engineering problems. The book introduces the wide range of opportunities in the field of engineering and offers instruction in the formulation of problems, the International System of Units (SI), engineering analysis, use of computational tools, and FORTRAN programming for use in more complex calculations.

Because of its basic nature, the text does not treat its subjects in great depth. References are provided, however, for students who would like to pursue any of the subject areas in more detail. Numerous problems are provided at the end of appropriate chapters to give the student practice in

P reface

applying the skills that have been learned. The practice in solving problems is essential to the development of a firm understanding of engineering problem solving and computational techniques.

The material is divided into three sections, as it might be presented in an undergraduate course. In the first section, Chapter 1 describes engineering and introduces the various disciplines with their unique areas of interest and educational requirements. Chapter 2 describes some of the various opportunities open to engineers, and points out the engineer's professional responsibilities.

The second section of the book deals with problem solving, engineering analysis, and computational tools. Chapter 3 introduces problem solving, describing how engineering problems are formulated in order to facilitate solution. Chapter 4 introduces the International System of Units (SI) and discusses the base units and derived units as well as their use in engineering problems. Dimensional analysis is also reviewed. Chapter 5 develops techniques for data analysis, including statistical, graphical, and numerical methods. Chapter 6 describes the scientific pocket calculators and how they operate, and points out ways in which these calculators may be used in engineering problem solving. Chapter 7 describes the digital computer, the concept of its operation, and how the digital computer has become the mainstay in the solution of engineering problems.

The third section of the textbook provides instruction in FORTRAN programming. Chapter 8 discusses the fundamentals of programming, including the use of constants, variables, and expressions. Chapter 9 explains the basic FORTRAN statements, including control statements, I/O statements, and specification statements. Chapter 10 describes the use of subprograms as a means for solving complex engineering problems.

This textbook is based upon a first-year introductory engineering course developed and taught at Rutgers University. Particular thanks go to R. H. Page for challenging us to be innovative and for his support and encouragement during the development of this course. Thanks are also due C. E. G. Przirembel who team-taught this course with us.

Throughout the development of the course and resulting text, a number of people contributed constructive ideas. We are grateful to the students involved in the course for their receptiveness to innovation in the classroom. Particular thanks for assistance in reviewing sections of this manuscript are due to many people, especially R. H. Fletcher, L. R. and R. A. Merz, G. Burnet, A. Gianniny, E. J. White, J. E. Cox, and J. Skrypa.

L. S. F.
T. E. S.

Offshore drilling. (*Courtesy* Tenneco, Inc.)

Engineering is a challenging profession for young men and women. It is a dynamic, creative, and exciting profession which combines the fundamentals of mathematics and science with the skills of the scientist and craftsman to meet the material needs of our ever-changing world. More specifically, engineering is an applied science which deals with the planning, design, construction, testing, management or operation of facilities, machines, structures, and other devices used by all segments of society. Indeed, the results of engineering invention touch virtually every aspect of our everyday lives. Spectacular feats of engineering and science, such as interplanetary space probes, make newspaper headlines. Yet most engineering accomplishments, although they receive little publicity, touch us far more directly: computerized checkout systems, satellite communications, modern medical diagnostic techniques, and food processing.

The engineer is an adventurer, an innovator, a builder, and, above all, a problem solver. He or she is seeking better, simpler, quicker, and more economical solutions to the problems that plague our world. The engineer may devote efforts toward better housing, cleaner air, economical transportation systems, better health care systems and facilities, new energy generation systems, improved agricultural production, safe and reliable products, or a myriad of other challenges. In short, the engineer transforms scientific and mathematical principles into systems, processes, and goods for industrial and personal use.

It is important to note that few engineering accomplishments have been achieved by individual engineers, nor exclusively by engineers of a single discipline. Engineers generally work together, and often with those trained in other disciplines.

The potential engineer must be challenged by unsolved problems, must be curious about the composition of things and how they work, and must have both an interest and ability in mathematics and science. Equally important, engineers must be concerned about the safety and health of others, the environment, and the social implications of the solutions they provide. The engineer must work for and with people, as well as things.

Engineering is a profession which draws men and women from diverse backgrounds to play significant roles in a broad range of technical and administrative fields. It provides, as well, a basic education for living in the latter years of the twentieth century.

1.1 Origins of engineering

Engineering is an ancient profession. Those who designed and built the pyramids and aqueducts of ancient times surely performed tasks which today would be classified as "engineering." Yet the designation of "engineering" probably first occurred in the latter part of the eighteenth century. Napoleon, famous for his military expertise, developed plans for bridges and roads required for his conquests. His "military engineers" supervised the design and construction of bridges, roads, and forts. At about the same time, the term "civil engineer" was used in England to designate those who supervised the construction of buildings and other structures needed for peacetime activities. The profession of engineering, then, was first directed toward public projects and was firmly based in the field we know as civil engineering.

Labor-saving inventions in England between 1750 and 1850 were a part of the Industrial Revolution (Figure 1-1). Through this period there evolved a new breed of engineer—the civil engineer interested in machines. The use of steam power for manufacturing and locomotion encouraged the development of new materials, machines, and transportation systems. In this way, mechanical engineering emerged as a new field of engineering.

By the latter part of the nineteenth century, chemicals were used increasingly in all phases of industry. The chemist, working closely with the

Figure 1-1 Schematic of an eighteenth century ore crushing and refining facility. (The Diderot Encyclopédie; *courtesy* Alderman Library, University of Virginia.)

engineer, contributed to the growth of industries associated with the processing of chemicals, fuels, and synthetic products. Thus the field of chemical engineering evolved.

Also in the late nineteenth century, Maxwell demonstrated that electromagnetic waves travel through space. Edison noted that when electricity was passed through a small filament, it would glow. The harnessing of electricity brought about a new revolution. The development of electrical generating and distribution systems, communications, and electronics became the domain of the electrical engineer.

From these original branches of engineering, many new fields have evolved as technology has developed. Engineering as a profession is indeed a product of its history, yet it permits the growth and development of new subdisciplines and interdisciplinary programs. The main foundation of engineering education, that of problem solving, provides the engineer with an ability to assess problems and develop techniques for solving them, despite continuous changes in our needs as well as the manner in which we define and state our needs.

Engineering education in the United States began in 1802 with the basic rudiments of military engineering at the U.S. Military Academy. Rensselaer Polytechnic Institute was chartered in 1826 to offer education in architecture, business administration, engineering, and science, and granted the first engineering degrees in 1835. Since that time, the field of engineering has expanded to many institutions and a wide variety of engineering programs.

1.2 Science, engineering, and engineering technology

Engineering and science include a great many diverse subject areas. A major portion of the industrial work force is involved in tasks related to engineering. This work force, which incorporates a wide range of educational backgrounds, includes scientists, engineers, technologists, and technicians. These different job categories are distinguished by the direction and duration of the formal technical education each requires.

The *scientist* studies the basic laws of nature and their effects on materials. Scientists use systemized observation and experimentation to examine a specific concept in the context of existing theories and principles. The objective is to develop an orderly description of the natural world. The scientist generally has pursued his education past a bachelor's level, and often to the Doctor of Philosophy degree. Emphasis of study has been devoted to mathematics, the basic sciences, and the philosophy of science.

Engineering is applied science. The *engineer* has "a knowledge of the mathematical and natural sciences gained by study, experience, and practice which is applied with judgement to develop ways to utilize, economically, the materials and forces of nature for the benefit of mankind."* The engineer is a problem solver, using knowledge and ability to devise or improve the solution to technological problems. The engineer is concerned with learning why a system or concept operates and how it might be directed toward useful, beneficial products. Engineering education prepares one for the practice of engineering at the professional level. These studies usually culminate in a bachelor's degree but may continue toward advanced degrees. Emphasis is generally placed on the basic sciences, mathematics, engineering sciences, design, and the application of these fundamentals to problem solving.

The *technologist* is concerned with "that part of the technological field which requires the application of scientific and engineering knowledge and methods combined with technical skills in support of engineering activities; it lies in the occupational spectrum between the craftsman and the engineer at the end of the spectrum closest to the engineer."† The technologist participates in the organization and management of engineering projects through coordination of the work force, materials, equipment, and facilities for the project. In addition, the technologist participates in the planning, construction, and operation of engineering facilities. The technologist's higher education consists of a four-year program emphasizing methodology, as well as physics, algebra, trigonometry, materials and processes, and specialized technical electives. The program culminates in a bachelor of engineering technology degree.

The *technician* also applies engineering knowledge and methods in support of engineering projects. Specialized skills and training in practical techniques are important to the work of the technician. The technician is a specialist in methodology devoted to the accomplishment of practical objectives. The technician pursues a two-year educational program with emphasis on practical techniques, culminating in an associate degree in engineering technology.

1.3 Engineering and engineering technology degree requirements

Curricula leading to degrees in engineering and engineering technology are established by each college or university. The profession establishes criteria

* Engineers' Council for Professional Development, 43rd Annual Report, September 30, 1975, EC 9-1/76.
† ECPD, 43rd Annual Report.

for accreditation of these curricula through the Engineers' Council for Professional Development (ECPD). The Council was founded in 1932 for the "promotion and advancement of engineering education with a view to furthering the public welfare through the development of the better educated and qualified engineer, engineering technologist, engineering technician, and others engaged in engineering or engineering related work."* In order to achieve these objectives, basic educational requirements and guidelines were developed with the participation and support of the professional societies representing the various major disciplines in engineering. These criteria were established as the minimum educational standards for institutions granting engineering or engineering technology degrees. The criteria are revised from time to time, to reflect the changes in both scientific knowledge and society's needs.

Selected representatives of the profession under the auspices of ECPD periodically visit each university or college offering engineering degrees. These visitors review the curriculum, faculty, and facilities to assure that the educational program and degree requirements are consistent with the current ECPD guidelines. Because of the guidance given schools by ECPD, a person graduating from a university or college with an accredited engineering or engineering technology program is assured that his education will provide him with the basic skills necessary for employment.

The accrediting process considers a number of factors related to each engineering program and its environment. Major considerations include the quality of the instruction offered and the breadth and depth of knowledge which the student gains in an engineering program. In addition, the competence and size of the faculty, the laboratories and other teaching facilities, the acceptance of former students by the profession, and the commitment of the institution to engineering and/or engineering technology also are considered by the accrediting panel.

The accreditation process, then, assures the student and the public that the engineering and engineering technology programs meet minimum standards. This process also provides recommendations to the university or college for improving its educational programs.

Engineering programs.† The engineering programs may be accredited at the bachelor's (basic) level, the masters (advanced) level, or both. At the bachelor's level, the curriculum for engineering is expected to include

---

* ECPD, 43rd Annual Report.
† ECPD, 43rd Annual Report.

approximately two and one-half academic years of study in mathematics, science, and engineering, consisting of one-half year of mathematics beyond trigonometry, one-half year of basic sciences, one year of engineering science, one-half year of engineering design, and a minimum of one-half year of humanities and social sciences. Although all accredited engineering programs incorporate this basic curriculum, each institution and department has further degree requirements equivalent to one additional year of study. These required courses are selected to implement the educational objectives of students and/or their institutions.

*Engineering technology programs.** Degrees in engineering technology programs may be awarded at the associate level (two years) or at the bachelors level (four years). Graduates of the two-year program are termed technicians, while those completing four years are termed technologists. The educational program should include at least one-half academic year of basic sciences and mathematics including algebra, trigonometry, and the rudiments of calculus, an equivalent of one year of technical courses, and approximately one-fourth year of nontechnical courses, including communication, the humanities, and social sciences. Again, each institution has additional criteria for obtaining degrees in engineering technology.

Many different accredited programs exist at many different institutions. Programs in some of the traditional branches of engineering such as civil, mechanical, chemical, and electrical engineering, may be found at most institutions. Other accredited engineering programs in more specialized fields may be found at various colleges and universities throughout the nation.

1.4   Traditional engineering programs

Four engineering disciplines have maintained their traditional identities even as engineering has evolved and grown. These traditional disciplines, all with a large number of accredited degree programs, are civil engineering, mechanical engineering, chemical engineering, and electrical engineering. Each of these programs has unique characteristics and requirements, as well as a specialized focus.

* ECPD, 43rd Annual Report.

Civil engineering. The oldest of the traditional branches of engineering, civil engineering is primarily concerned with the public domain.

Civil engineers are builders, involved in the planning, analysis, design, and construction of large-scale structures such as bridges, tunnels, airports, pipelines, roads, dams, towers, ships and models, and buildings for commerce and industry (Figure 1-2). They are concerned with public safety and

Figure 1-2 Civil engineers plan and supervise the construction of a new industrial plant. (*Courtesy* International Minerals & Chemical Corporation.)

services such as water purification and supply systems; solid waste and waste water treatment systems; highway, rail, and water transportation systems; urban planning and environmental control. Civil engineers are concerned with the impact of their projects on the environment and the public, and they attempt to coordinate public need with technical feasibility. Civil engineering deals with three major areas: *structures and foundation systems, transportation and urban planning,* and *water supply and waste disposal systems.*

In the structures area, civil engineers are concerned with the static and dynamic forces of nature, geology, and properties of materials. They deal with forces exerted on structures, techniques for construction, and the management of large construction projects. The towering World Trade Center in New York, the picturesque Golden Gate Bridge in San Francisco, and the massive Grand Coulee Dam in Washington are but a few of the diverse challenges which have been met by civil engineers, together with architects, geologists and many others.

In the area of transportation and urban planning, the civil engineer is concerned with mass transportation, efficient use of people-moving systems (Figure 1-3), highways, airport systems, pipelines, land use planning, site

Figure 1-3 Engineers were instrumental in the development of the light rail vehicle now used for urban mass transport in Boston. (*Courtesy* The Boeing Company.)

planning, and traffic engineering. Civil engineers, for example, have been actively involved in the design and construction of the Alaska pipeline, of new guide-rail transportation systems for urban use, of the vast interstate highway system, and of the increasingly popular PUDs (planned unit developments) throughout the nation. The transportation and urban development problems of today, as well as those of tomorrow, require new ideas and new approaches to meet ever-changing needs.

In the area of water supply and waste disposal systems to improve and control the environment, the civil engineer is particularly concerned with creating a better physical environment in which to live. Emphasis is placed on ecology, filtration, biological problems, waste treatment, and water systems. The civil engineer will play a significant role in the development of solid waste energy generation systems and techniques for purification and reuse of waste water.

The curricular requirements in civil engineering include the basic engineering requirements described previously, as well as specific courses related to the field of civil engineering. Some of the courses generally studied include structural theory, fluid mechanics, material properties, soil mechanics, environmental engineering, concrete and metal design, transportation engineering, construction engineering, and economics. Technical electives are directed toward special areas and might include water quality management, structural optimization, new construction materials, urban mass transit systems, and foundation engineering.

Mechanical engineering. Perhaps the broadest of the engineering disciplines, mechanical engineering is concerned with the application of science and technology in the solution of the countless problems facing our increasingly complex world.

Mechanical engineers are innovators, developing devices and systems to perform useful services. They are involved in the conception, planning, design, analysis, testing, production, and utilization of facilities, systems, and machines. They are concerned with the production and use of energy, with combustion processes, environmental control, thermal pollution, noise pollution, air pollution, materials processing and handling, the design of transportation vehicles and propulsion systems, and the safety of products. The field of mechanical engineering may be divided into two major areas: *thermosciences* and *design.*

In the thermosciences area, the mechanical engineer is concerned with thermodynamics, fluid mechanics, and heat transfer—the behavior of solids, liquids, and gases—in engineering applications. Emphasis is placed on energy conversion systems, energy analyses, the design and development of engines and propulsion systems (Figure 1-4), and the use of energy.

The mechanical engineer is involved in energy-related projects such as the performance testing of new solar collector systems, the integration of solar heating and cooling systems into new buildings, analysis of the efficiency of coal or gas fired boiler-turbine-generator systems for electricity generation, the design of heat exchangers for ocean thermal energy conversion systems, and the development of windmills for power generation. Mechanical engineers have been instrumental in the development of combustion systems and of precipitators and washers for the effluents of these systems. They are also concerned with efficient environmental control in

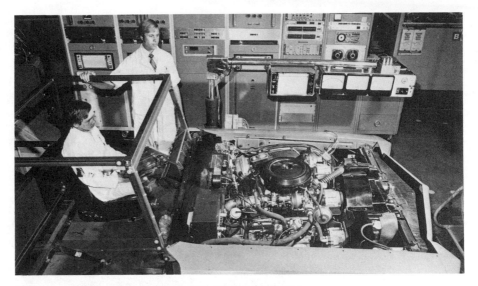

Figure 1-4 Mechanical engineers direct the performance testing of new engines such as the staged combustion compound engine. (*Courtesy* General Motors Research Laboratories.)

buildings, including heating, ventilation, air conditioning, and humidity control. The increasing demand for all forms of energy, while conventional supplies diminish, provides a tremendous challenge to creative mechanical engineers (Figure 1-5).

In the design area, mechanical engineers are concerned with the development of new and improved labor-saving devices and machines. They work toward the development of devices to transmit and control mechanical power for useful purposes. Emphasis is placed on machine design, mechanisms, kinematics, and automatic controls. Mechanical engineers, for example, have had a hand in the design of such diverse commodities as automobiles, typewriters, wheel chairs, and ball-point pens. They have also been instrumental in the development of machines to produce these commodities for the marketplace.

Applied mechanics, often found in both mechanical and civil engineering programs, deals with the application of the physical laws governing forces, motion, energy, and deformation of materials. Subject areas include dynamics and vibrations, biomechanics, applied mathematics, theoretical mechanics, and the analysis of high-speed systems.

The curricular requirements for specialization in mechanical engineering may include elementary partial differential equations, applied thermodynamics, fluid mechanics, mechanical control systems, heat transfer,

Figure 1-5   The development of new energy sources, such as synthetic natural gas, involves mechanical engineers. (*Courtesy Mechanical Engineering,* ASME.)

machine analysis or design, solid mechanics, and engineering economics. Technical electives or specialties might include in-depth studies in solar energy systems, propulsion systems, kinematics, HVAC systems (heating, ventilating, and air conditioning), air pollution control, internal combustion engines, heat power, machine and control analysis, power plants, and direct energy conversion.

Chemical engineering.   The field of chemical engineering deals with the practical application of chemical processes in the development and refinement of materials and products. It is characterized by a study of substances and processes which change in composition or energy content.

Chemical engineers have led the way in the development of synthetics, plastics, and fibers—so common in our everyday lives. They plan, design, and analyze large-scale systems involving chemical and physical changes in organic materials, exotic metals, paints, pharmaceuticals, rubber, paper, detergents, nuclear fuels, energy conversion, environmental protection, food processing, biochemistry, biomedicine, and so on. They develop new chemical compounds and materials, energy conversion techniques, and efficient chemical manufacturing facilities. Chemical engineering may be divided into two major areas: *chemical processes* and *molecular systems design.*

In the chemical processes or large-scale process area, emphasis is placed on systems such as petroleum refining, plastics manufacturing, food processing, pharmaceutical manufacturing, wastewater treatment (Figure 1-6), and the processing of petrochemical feedstocks. The chemical engineer

Figure 1-6   Chemical engineers assist in the development of water treatment systems such as the twin module brine concentrator. (*Courtesy* The Boeing Company.)

has played a significant role in the development of substances ranging from nylon to styrofoam, shaping them into thousands of useful forms from sailboat riggings to hosiery to coffee cups. The process chemical engineer is concerned with system dynamics, equilibrium and transport processes, and separation processes. Particular emphasis is placed on the effect of chemicals on the environment.

In the area of molecular systems design, the chemical engineer is concerned with immobilized enzymes, molecular sieve catalysts, reverse osmosis membranes, and other systems designed to enhance large-scale processes (Figure 1-7). The chemical engineer is constantly striving to develop new techniques for the production of commodities including food-

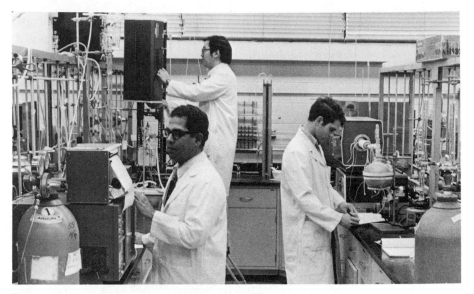

Figure 1-7 Chemical engineers develop new techniques for the thermochemical production of hydrogen from water. (*Courtesy* Institute of Gas Technology.)

stuffs, pharmaceuticals, and cosmetics. Interaction by chemical engineers with both chemists and biochemists contributes to the improvement of molecular designs.

Curricular requirements for chemical engineering emphasize organic chemistry, physical chemistry, transport processes, chemical engineering kinetics, process synthesis and design, and process dynamics and control. Technical electives might include subjects such as complex variables, vectors and tensors, physical metallurgy, biochemical engineering, polymers and enzyme engineering, energy conversion, and environmental studies.

Electrical engineering. Electrical engineering deals with electrical phenomena and everything operated by electricity; it deals with communication and navigation systems, computer and control systems, power systems, electronic devices, and instrumentation. Electrical engineering is a science involving electrons, magnetic fields, and electric fields, all invisible phenomena which are used to perform labor-saving tasks.

Electrical engineers have spearheaded the miniaturization and development of electronic components, notably computer systems. They apply their knowledge of electricity and electronics in the planning, design, and development of new facilities and systems, including biomedical electronics and instrumentation, satellite communication systems, digital and analog computers, meteorological instrumentation, fuel cells, lasers, power systems, and decision-making systems. The field of electrical engineering may be broadly divided into the study of *power* and *electronics*.

In the power area, emphasis is placed on the generation, storage, control, transmission, and distribution of electrical energy. Efforts focus on the design and development of more efficient electrical machines, motors, and controls, as well as the development of electrical applications for

Figure 1-8 Electrical engineers are involved in the development of new and refined medical instrumentation such as the heartbeat monitor. (*Courtesy* General Electric Research and Development Center.)

domestic use. The photovoltaic or solar cells which generate electricity for satellites in orbit, as well as other space vehicles, were primarily the product of electrical engineering research. Knowledge obtained through this research is now being directed toward the development of improved solar energy electricity generation systems.

In the field of electronics, the electrical engineer has become involved in the design, fabrication, and analysis of new materials and devices in the area of solid-state and integrated circuits for digital and analog computers, control systems, and calculators. The miniaturization of components has led to refined and more accurate instrumentation systems, suitable for medical purposes (Figure 1-8), more in-depth studies of natural phenomena, the monitoring of critical chemical and biological processes, and improved meteorological analysis. Miniaturized computers have been developed for purposes ranging from inventory accounting to navigation systems. (Figure 1-9). In communications, digital phone links, computer-to-computer processing, and information display are important concerns of the electrical engineer. The electronic systems for transmitting the vital signs of ill or

Figure 1-9 Electrical engineers develop new navigation systems. (*Courtesy* Sperry Marine Systems.)

injured persons to the hospital for evaluation have greatly improved emergency health care. Satellite communication systems make it possible to view by television events which are occurring half a world away. Electrical engineers have developed communication and decision-making systems so refined that it is possible to remotely operate scientific experiments on other planets.

Curricular requirements in electrical engineering include courses on vectors, complex variables, networks, circuit analysis, magnetic components, lines and fields, electric machinery, communication engineering and transients, as well as electrical laboratories. Technical electives may include in-depth study of linear feedback systems, pulse circuits, electronic circuits, microwave devices, high-frequency energy conversion, fields, digital computer design, biomedical engineering, and electromagnetics.

1.5   Other engineering disciplines

In addition to civil, mechanical, chemical, and electrical engineering, there are other major branches within the profession of engineering. Among these are materials science, aerospace engineering, industrial engineering, nuclear engineering, and agricultural engineering.

Materials science. The field of materials science is broadly concerned with the behavior and properties of materials; their development, processing and production; and their efficient use in various applications. In all branches of materials science, knowledge of both the micro- and macroproperties and characteristics of materials is important so that materials developed will meet the requirements for applying them, whether for structural or special use (Figure 1-10).

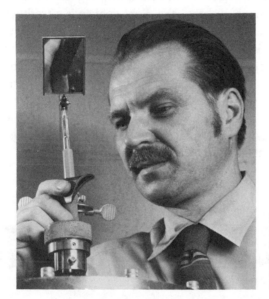

Figure 1-10 Materials engineers are instrumental in the development and analysis of materials such as new alloys for high temperature turbine blades. (*Courtesy* General Electric Research and Development Center.)

Materials science is a combination of several of the basic sciences, including polymer chemistry, ceramics, metallurgy, and plastics. It deals with the properties and uses of both metals and nonmetals. Since most minerals and fuels are nonrenewable natural resources, the field of materials science is concerned with optimizing the use of these materials and developing new or synthetic materials. In view of the continuing depletion of natural resources, new techniques must be developed to economically extract more materials and fuel with minimum energy consumption and disturbance to the environment.

Areas of emphasis include materials processing, physical metallurgy, materials production, high-temperature techniques and applications, metals, alloys, process metallurgy, polymers, fibers, and synthesis.

Aerospace engineering. The field of aerospace engineering includes both aeronautics and astronautics, and deals with almost every aspect of both manned and unmanned flight—from light planes to satellites to deep space probes to other planets. Since the Wright brothers' original flight at Kitty Hawk, the field of aerospace has grown rapidly and expanded to travel through space. From the rapid advance of technology necessary for these achievements have come "spin-offs" that benefit our everyday lives—from medical diagnostic techniques to minicomputers.

The aerospace engineer is concerned with flight vehicles, from conception to takeoff or launch, whether the flight vehicle is a traditional aircraft, a ground effect vehicle, a vertical takeoff and landing aircraft, a missile, or a spacecraft. (Figure 1-11). The aerospace engineer uses his skills to improve air transportation systems. He works with others to launch and operate satellites for world weather studies, navigation systems, earth resources studies, and remote sensing of the earth's surface characteristics.

The emphasis in aerospace engineering, is placed on aerodynamics, propulsion systems, fluid mechanics and gasdynamics, aeroelasticity, structures, celestial mechanics, trajectories and transfer orbits, guidance and control, acoustics, and instrumentation.

Figure 1-11 Aerospace engineers develop a new concept in Short Take-Off and Landing aircraft (STOL). (*Courtesy* The Boeing Company.)

Industrial engineering. The field of industrial engineering is particularly concerned with the development of systems which optimize the use of people, materials, machines, and equipment (Figure 1-12). These systems are applied to industries and services as diverse as transportation systems, hospitals, communication companies, medical centers, retail merchandising, education systems, banks, airlines, and the manufacturing industries.

Figure 1-12 Industrial engineers are involved in the development of assembly line systems for maximum efficiency, such as this new system for flash baking pizza crusts. (*Courtesy Mechanical Engineering*, ASME.)

The industrial engineer is concerned with improving productivity in the most economical manner possible, not only by optimum use of machines and materials, but also through efficient use of manpower. In many cases the work involves the use of computers, and the modelling or simulation of a problem to ascertain the most efficient layout or procedure.

In industrial engineering, areas of study include operations research, statistics, probability, and computer techniques. The focus of research is on systems, economics, business, accounting, and finance, as well as facilities design and layout, production control, scheduling theory, inventory systems, materials processing, and cost prediction.

Nuclear engineering. The field of nuclear engineering centers on the energy derived from the atom (neutrons, protons, and electrons) and its production and useful application in fields such as medicine, science, agriculture, and industry. Nuclear energy is used to produce power (Figure 1-13), and nuclear propulsion systems are used in ships and submarines, with substantially less atmospheric pollution than traditional power generation sources.

Nuclear engineers are concerned with the interaction of radiation with matter; the design, development, and operation of nuclear facilities; and the

Figure 1-13 Nuclear engineers have developed fuel rods composed of hundreds of fuel pins loaded with slightly enriched uranium pellets for use in the generation of power. (*Courtesy* Atomic Industrial Forum.)

use of radioactive materials. Although much of the effort in the past has been directed toward the fission reactor, nuclear engineers are becoming more involved in the development of energy from thermonuclear fusion. The generation of energy through fusion would make available a larger energy source than is now provided by fission reactors and fossil fuel generation facilities. In addition to the generation of power, the nuclear engineer is concerned with the application of radiation in the diagnosis and treatment of disease, the processing and preservation of food, space propulsion and power supplies, scientific measurements, and the acceleration of atomic particles.

Areas of emphasis in nuclear engineering studies include radiation measurements, interaction of radiation with matter, radioisotopes, reactor physics, fusion reactors, reactor design, materials for nuclear applications, and radiation safety.

Agricultural engineering.   The application of engineering principles to the farm and food production industries is called agricultural engineering. It involves both the physical sciences and the biological sciences. The constant demand for increased food productivity from the farm industries, caused by the increasing world population, necessitates the optimization and mechanization of the "horse and plow" (Figure 1-14). The field of agricultural engineering is one that is directed toward the basic needs of all—the production and processing of food and of fiber products for clothes.

Figure 1-14 Agricultural engineers participate in the development of new machinery to improve farm productivity. (*Courtesy* Deere and Company.)

Agricultural engineers are concerned with the design, development, and improvement of farm machinery and equipment, animal handling and shelters, produce harvest, storage and processing, as well as the development of farm land, irrigation, drainage, and erosion control systems. They work to develop new and improved farming techniques and facilities, to solve problems posed by waste disposal and pollution, to replenish agricultural lands and forests, and to deal with the problem of the expansion of cities over primary agricultural lands.

The agricultural engineer is also involved in studies of soil-plant-machine systems, agricultural structures, unit processes for biological materials, land and water resources, environmental systems analysis, and energy conversion for biological systems.

Interdisciplinary programs in engineering. There are other specialized branches of engineering which are directed toward more specific science-, service-, or industry-related fields. Generally these more specialized branches draw upon interdisciplinary interests, combining the basic curricula of two or more major fields of engineering. These branches of engineering, most of which are accredited at one or more institutions,* include architectural engineering, biomedical engineering, ceramic engineering, construction engineering, engineering mechanics, engineering physics, engineering science, environmental engineering, geological engineering, manufacturing engineering, marine engineering, mineral engineering, mining engineering, ocean engineering, operations research, petroleum engineering, sanitary engineering, systems engineering, textile engineering, and transportation engineering.

1.6 Summary

As the realm of scientific and technological knowledge has burgeoned over the past two centuries, so, too, has the engineering expertise which applies this knowledge and encourages this scientific revolution. Once concerned primarily with military and civic matters, engineers today deal with a diversity of challenges not even dreamed of a few decades ago.

The field of engineering has room and need for new engineers with a wide variety of interests and training. Many educational paths—from two-year technology programs to advanced doctoral studies—may lead to an exciting and productive career in the broad field of engineering.

* ECPD, 43rd Annual Report.

The accomplishments of engineers over the past several decades are too many and too pervasive to list. From the testing of Martian soil to the development of freeze-dried coffee, engineers have worked wonders. Future contributions and achievements will be limited only by the talents and vision of tomorrow's engineers.

REFERENCES

BEAKLEY, GEORGE C. and H. W. LEACH. *Engineering: An Introduction to a Creative Profession*, Second Edition. New York: The Macmillan Company, 1972.

Engineers Council for Professional Development: *43rd Annual Report.* New York: ECPD, 1975.

GLORIOSO, ROBERT M. and FRANCIS S. HILL, Jr. *Introduction to Engineering.* Englewood Cliffs, N.J.: Prentice-Hall, Inc., 1975.

KONZO, SEICHI and JAMES W. BAYNE. *Opportunities in Mechanical Engineering.* New York: Universal Publishing and Distributing Corp., 1971.

KRICK, EDWARD V. *An Introduction to Engineering: Methods, Concepts, and Issues.* New York: John Wiley & Sons, Inc., 1976.

SMITH, RALPH J. *Engineering as a Career*, Third Edition. New York: McGraw-Hill Book Company, Inc., 1969.

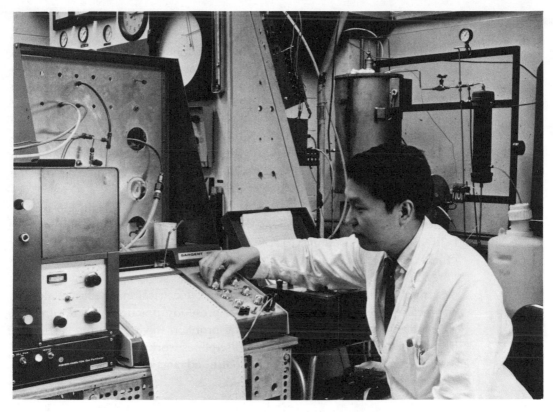

Engineer at work. (*Courtesy* Institute of Gas Technology.)

Engineering
as a profession
2

The profession of engineering is often thought of as a single field. In fact, however, it is an extremely diverse profession, both in areas of concern and in tasks performed. Although it is true that most engineers are problem solvers, they operate in a variety of different ways using a variety of different technological disciplines. In the previous chapter, the different disciplinary branches of engineering were discussed. Within each of these disciplines are a variety of job functions. This chapter will describe these different job functions and explain how they relate to the professional role of the engineer.

The professional satisfaction derived from an engineering job usually comes more through what the engineer does (job function) than through the field in which it is done (disciplinary field). For simplicity, engineering "function" may be thought of as a noun that is modified by a disciplinary "branch" adjective. Thus, for example, we see engineering activities described as mechanical engineering design, electrical engineering sales, or chemical engineering research. As it is presently practiced in industry and government, the process of engineering problem solving is often carried on by teams of engineers from different disciplines working together in a shared job function to contribute to technological advancements that benefit mankind.

2.1   Engineering job functions

The array of engineering job functions shown in Figure 2-1 can be thought of as an activity spectrum through which an idea may be transformed from basic knowledge into a useful product or process. As with a spectrum, the division between function areas is not clearly defined, and considerable overlap can exist. The research, development, and design functions are concerned with the initial stages of implementing an engineering idea, whereas production, operations, and sales deal with the final realization of that idea as a useful, saleable product or process. Thus, the engineering job spectrum runs all the way from concern with abstract ideas to work with intricately detailed hardware. Paralleling and supporting the spectrum of engineering endeavor are two additional functional areas—management and education—both of which are essential to the continuation and successful operation of the broad spectrum of engineering jobs.

Research.   As its name implies, this function area is concerned with the exploration and discovery of new principles and new technologies for

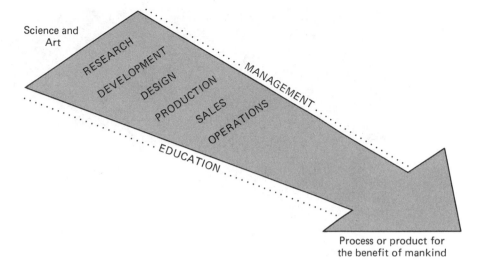

Figure 2-1   The spectrum of engineering jobs.

satisfying the world's needs. In this job category an engineer often performs studies using the basic laws that govern the physical principles of the universe. New materials, new processes, and new techniques may be developed to expand the technological resources available for the solution of a particular engineering problem.

The work of the research engineer differs from the work of the research scientist primarily in the ultimate objective or application of their work. The research scientist seeks to discover basic truths in order to expand scientific knowledge about the universe. On the other hand, the engineering researcher seeks to discover basic knowledge with a view toward eventual application of this discovery to new products or processes (Figure 2-2). The same research discovery made by a scientist and an engineer may be utilized quite differently, since the engineer seeks to apply the discovery for the benefit of the consuming public.

Since research engineers may explore uncharted technological territory, they must be careful, methodical, and well educated in their areas of expertise. Since they must have a deep understanding of basic sciences, engineering researchers often have one or more advanced degrees.

Development.   Once a research engineer has made a basic discovery that appears to have potential, the next step is to develop this discovery into a process or product that is technologically efficient and economically profita-

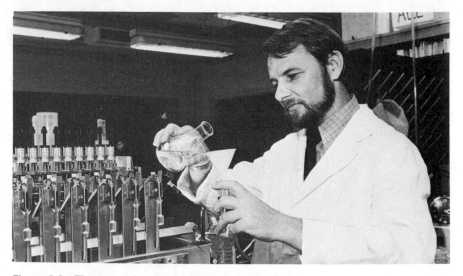

Figure 2-2   The research engineer seeks new principles and new technologies for satisfying the world's needs. (*Courtesy* Office of Information, University of Houston.)

ble. This is the job function of the development engineer (Figure 2-3). The development engineer often makes use of real and mathematical models for study, improvement, and testing. Since the functions of the research engineer and the development engineer are so closely related, many organizations list these two types of personnel in a single combined category known as research and development, or "R & D."

Of course not every input to the development engineer comes from research. Often an existing product or process will be returned from service to the development engineer. The developer will then analyze and test the product with a view toward improvement of its form and function. In this way, products are upgraded and refined to meet the strict competitive demands of the consumer in the marketplace.

To perform their job well, development engineers must have a thorough understanding of the basic tools of engineering analysis and an ability to recognize the economic factors of construction and distribution. They must be able to work with test hardware, and to suggest what changes would provide a worthwhile improvement in a product or process.

Design.   The design engineer provides the best possible communication link between the generation of ideas and the production of hardware. The designer will join groups of usable ideas to create the components necessary for the fabrication of an engineering system (Figure 2-4). Responsibilities

Figure 2-3 The development engineer seeks ways to make a process or product technologically efficient and economically profitable. (*Courtesy* United Engineers & Constructors, Inc.)

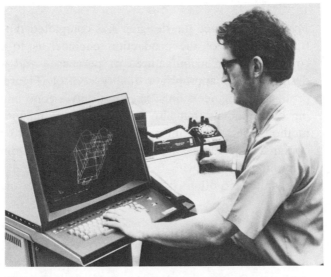

Figure 2-4 The design engineer uses the techniques of computer-aided design to develop a new engineering system. (*Courtesy* McDonnell Douglas Automation Company.)

include the calculation of strengths, determination of fits, enumeration of parts required, selection of materials, and production of drawings and other details for a complete description of the object or process to be manufactured.

As is true for most engineering endeavors, the design process often produces many suitable answers to a problem. When this occurs, the designer's task includes a search for the best possible solution from among those available. One of the most interesting challenges in the design function comes through the iterative nature of this selection process. Since a slight design change at one point in a system often influences the behavior of many other components, the designer may have to perform a large number of calculations to predict the new performance. The design engineer often works closely with both the development engineer and the production engineer.

The talents desirable for a good designer include the ability to create, to visualize, to economize, and to communicate. The design ability of an engineer usually is enhanced as the engineer becomes more experienced and can bring previously successful ideas and experience to bear on a new problem.

Production.   Once the designer has completed the drawings and specifications, the job of the production engineer is to see that the parts and components are manufactured or purchased and assembled as they were designed, with appropriate quality control (Figure 2-5). For this reason, production engineers must have not only a good understanding of engineering fundamentals, but also a knowledge of manufacturing and fabrication methods. Since they must translate drawings into marketable products or systems, they must be able to visualize in a three-dimensional way and must communicate well with the design engineers and the staff of technicians, mechanics, and others in the work force who perform the hands-on fabrication.

Sales.   One of the most important links between the engineering idea and its eventual acceptance by the technical or business consumer is the sales engineer. Contrary to the door-to-door, high-pressure salesman of bygone days, the engineering salesperson is often sought after for his or her specialized knowledge and services, to assist in the decisions associated with new facilities and systems. The engineering salesperson generally communicates the technological properties, capabilities, and economics of the product or process to other professionals (Figure 2-6). The challenge is to see that the product or process best meets the needs of the consumer.

Figure 2-5 The production engineer sees that the engineering product meets specifications. (*Courtesy* General Motors.)

Figure 2-6 The sales engineer must communicate the engineering properties of his product to other professionals. (*Courtesy* McDonnell Douglas Automation Company.)

The sales engineer must have a thorough understanding of basic engineering principles in order to understand the limitations of the product and to suggest how the product or process can be applied in the most efficient way. Clearly, the sales engineer must acquire a good understanding of the customer's requirements, as well as of the product being sold. The sales engineer represents the company to the public. In many industrial organizations, the sales engineer also functions to feed back information to the research and development areas by suggesting what new products are needed.

Operations.   In the modern industrial environment, there exist many complex systems that need specific care and maintenance. The supervision of this task is the function of the operations engineer. In this task of caring for the equipment used for manufacture, the operations engineer often works closely with the production engineer. In addition, the operations engineer is often the primary engineer consulted when additions or modifications are being considered. In this job function, particular emphasis is placed on planned preventive maintenance, time and motion study, plant arrangement, systematic replacement, new equipment set up, safety, and a host of other interrelated concerns (Figure 2-7).

Figure 2-7   The operations engineer is concerned with the arrangement of materials for plant use. (*Courtesy* Exxon Company, USA and Chaparral Steel Company.)

Because of the diversity of problems that can occur in plant operation, the operations engineers must have a very broad knowledge of the principles that apply to engineering equipment and operations. They must be able to work well with both people and machines.

Management. Because of their abilities in problem solving, engineers are frequently asked to assume leadership roles in industrial organizations. Engineers generally are best equipped to manage technical tasks because of their basic understanding of science and engineering (Figure 2-8).

Figure 2-8 The engineering manager combines the skills of modern management and engineering principles. (*Courtesy* Office of Information, University of Houston.)

In his capacity as manager, the engineer is concerned with the optimum use of engineering resources to solve a particular problem. Frequently the engineering manager must make decisions and establish policies that involve time, equipment, labor forces, and financial resources. Much of the actual responsibility for the successful completion of engineering tasks lies in the hands of the engineering manager. Because of the importance of both engineering knowledge and management knowledge used in this function, many engineering managers have sought graduate degrees in business administration, accounting, law, personnel relations, or other areas in addition to their undergraduate training in one of the engineering disciplines.

Education. Perhaps one of the first engineers that a student will encounter is the engineering educator. This job function is particularly rewarding for the person who has the desire to help others learn about engineering problem solving. Most engineering educators have advanced-level degrees as well as some experience in industrial or research activities (Figure 2-9).

Since they are highly educated specialists in their teaching areas, most educators are also involved in research. This involvement satisfies a dual purpose. It not only provides a service to the profession by advancing the state-of-the-art, but it also keeps the engineering educator aware of the most recent technological advances, thus providing a background resource for classroom use. Most universities require teaching faculty members to do independent research and to publish their results.

Figure 2-9　The engineering educator must meet the challenge of a changing knowledge base. (*Courtesy* NCR Corporation.)

Entrepreneurial engineering.　The engineering job functions which have been described pertain primarily to the larger engineering employers, such as the large industrial and research organizations, the federal and state governments, and, to a lesser extent, educational institutions. When self-employment or small business is the chosen endeavor, job functions may be less well defined. The establishment of a successful consulting or contracting firm, whatever the choice of engineering discipline, requires some degree of proficiency in all of the preceding job function areas, as well as in business. Self-employment as a consulting or contracting engineer presents an attractive challenge to those who wish to let their abilities provide the direction and scope of their job functions.

Engineering as a background for other professions.   Undergraduate training in engineering can provide an excellent foundation for further studies in other nonengineering areas. The reason is simple: an engineering education teaches one to be a problem solver. The need for an ability in problem solving is clearly not limited to scientific fields. Undergraduate engineers can and do use their training as a basis for initial preparation in such diverse fields as medicine, law, politics, business management, accounting, journalism, and education. Perhaps no other basic area of study can claim to be so universally useful.

2.2   The engineer as a professional

Although the term "professional" means different things to different people, there are certain characteristics that may be attributed to a vocation or occupation which requires specialized training beyond a high-school education. Some of the more general characteristics that might be ascribed to a profession such as engineering are:

1. Members are highly trained in a specific area;
2. Members engage in continuing education for self-improvement;
3. Members conduct their activities in accordance with accepted standards of ethics;
4. Members exercise their responsibility to society and their profession through public service;
5. Members have an organized structure for the promotion and oversight of their profession.

Specialized training.   Without question, the engineer is a highly trained specialist, with a background in the fundamentals of science and mathematics, as well as engineering. In colleges and universities, engineering is usually regarded as one of the more challenging curricula available to an entering student. With a fairly regimented program of studies leading to the bachelor's degree, the student develops experience and skill in applying the fundamentals of engineering to the solution of problems. The field of engineering requires considerable training and effort to become the specialist or professional who embarks upon a career as an engineer. The engineer's scientific training should be combined with training in the communication of ideas and solutions to the public with integrity and responsibility.

Continuing education. The accomplishments of science and engineering are continually changing and advancing the knowledge base from which the engineer works. The engineer who neglects continuing education and self-study will soon find that the knowledge base gained during undergraduate study is no longer sufficient to meet job obligations. This is especially true for the engineer who must perform in a technological environment that changes rapidly. Fortunately for the engineer, the undergraduate training provides a foundation in engineering fundamentals upon which continuing education may be based.

Engineering professional societies provide special programs, seminars, workshops, conferences, and a large number of publications devised to encourage and enable the engineer to keep up-to-date. Most colleges and universities also have active, ongoing continuing education programs offering special courses in timely engineering topics. By voluntarily availing themselves of these self-education opportunities, engineers can keep themselves up-to-date and can also acquire valuable interaction with other members of their profession.

Ethics and canons. Ethics involves the behavioral concept of what is right and what is wrong. Without established standards of behavior, the world would be a troublesome place in which to live. For example, imagine the chaos that would result on the highways if there were no established rules for driving on one side of the street, or imagine the perils of the business world if transactions were not completed with mutual trust and good faith. Both of these illustrations serve to emphasize the need for clearly defined rules of ethics whenever people interact. Clearly no profession can exist in isolation. Most professionals interact with others who rely on their services to fulfill a need. This is especially true of engineering.

Ethical problems arise when two desirable aims are in conflict. The gasoline engine is without question a device that has saved millions of people from back-breaking labor and countless hours of inconvenience. Using the gasoline engine, the automobile provides comfort and convenience, yet every year this same device causes many traffic deaths and contributes to the pollution of the air we breathe. Nearly everyone wants to enjoy the benefits of technological progress, but few people want to accept the responsibility for the hazards that this progress brings. Engineers have enormous potential for doing good, but they also have enormous ethical responsibility for human safety (Figure 2-10).

In the engineering profession there are a number of well-developed ethical codes and canons which have been devised by engineers and

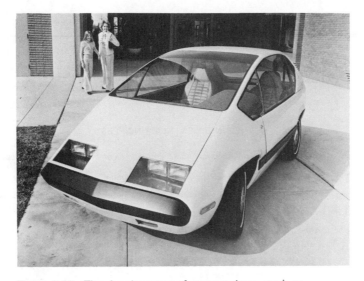

Figure 2-10 The development of new products, such as this electric town car, requires both engineering skill and ethical responsibility. (*Courtesy* Copper Development Association, Inc.)

engineering societies in order to establish a degree of integrity and respect within engineering. Several of these codes and canons have been adopted by major engineering societies as the code of ethics for their professional membership. The "Code of Ethics for Engineers" adopted by the Engineers Council for Professional Development (ECPD) is perhaps the most generally accepted engineering code of ethics in use today.

All of the codes and canons of ethics that are available to guide the engineer deal with the relationship of the engineer to his employer, to his client, and to the public. These fundamental principles provide the engineering profession with uniform guidelines for its activities. In taking the initiative voluntarily to adhere to these ethical codes of the engineering profession, the engineer adds respect, dignity, and prestige to the profession.

In addition to the voluntary code of ethics, most states have engineering registration laws designed to protect the public from unqualified persons claiming to be engineers. Although the laws differ from state to state, most states require the engineer to pass a written examination, show evidence of engineering competence, and agree to abide by the state-approved code of ethics. The examination portion of the registration process usually consists of two parts. The first part concerns engineering fundamentals that are common to all disciplinary branches of engineering. The second part concerns professional practices and is more discipline-specific.

CODE OF ETHICS OF ENGINEERS

THE FUNDAMENTAL PRINCIPLES

Engineers uphold and advance the integrity, honor and dignity of the engineering profession by:

I.   using their knowledge and skill for the enhancement of human welfare;

II. being honest and impartial, and serving with fidelity the public, their employers and clients;

III. striving to increase the competence and prestige of the engineering profession; and

IV. supporting the professional and technical societies of their disciplines.

THE FUNDAMENTAL CANONS

1. Engineers shall hold paramount the safety, health and welfare of the public in the performance of their professional duties.

2. Engineers shall perform services only in the areas of their competence.

3. Engineers shall issue public statements only in an objective and truthful manner.

4. Engineers shall act in professional matters for each employer or client as faithful agents or trustees, and shall avoid conflicts of interest.

5. Engineers shall build their professional reputation on the merit of their services and shall not compete unfairly with others.

6. Engineers shall associate only with reputable persons or organizations.

7. Engineers shall continue their professional development throughout their careers and shall provide opportunities for the professional development of those engineers under their supervision.

Approved by the Board of Directors, October 1, 1974

Nearly all states have provisions for an "Engineer-in-Training" (EIT) status which allows a person to take a written examination on engineering fundamentals at the time of graduation from the undergraduate engineering program. Although the EIT offers no legal rights or privileges, this system of examination is a convenience to new graduates since it allows them to take the fundamentals portion of their registration examination at a time when the material is fresh in their minds. Under this system the engineer may take another examination later in his career in order to complete the registration process.

Although the laws from state to state are different, most states provide what is called "reciprocity." This means that an engineer who is registered in one state may become registered in another state provided his present registration is based on a procedure that is equivalent to or more rigorous than that of the new state.

Although it is possible to work for an engineering firm as a nonregistered engineer, a court of law generally will not recognize an individual as an engineer unless he or she is registered. In many states it is against the law to advertise oneself to be an engineer unless one is registered. In addition, there are certain engineering jobs involving public safety, public health, and public welfare that cannot be performed by unlicensed persons. It is likely that professional registration in the future will be even more important since it is often regarded as a measure of technical competence. For this reason every young engineer would be well advised to seek registration as quickly as possible after graduation.

Public service. Many engineers, like other professionals, go beyond the exercise of their employment responsibilities by voluntarily contributing a portion of their time and expertise for the benefit of their local communities and the improvement of their profession. This may take the form of participation in local government, either by running for election to a public office or in an advisory capacity (Figure 2-11). Engineers also voluntarily contribute their time for the improvement of their technical/professional community through professional society activities. Some engineers assist in an advisory capacity to both the state and federal governments, serving on panels, commissions, and committees directed toward the technological aspects of government actions. Often, engineers become involved in public service to assure that the goods and services being offered to the public meet the state guidelines and codes. In this way, the technical community contributes to decisions that affect the quality of our lives.

Figure 2-11 Engineers may volunteer to assist in the solution of local problems such as rush hour traffic congestion. (*Courtesy* The Texas Business Executive, Texas A & M University.)

In the area of public service, the engineer is concerned with the impact of products and processes in the consumer marketplace. Every engineer is responsible for assuring that the product or process produced through his or her efforts is durable and reasonably safe for its intended use. Engineers, then, are responsible to the public for their actions.

Engineering organizations. Several hundred engineering societies or related groups are presently in existence for the basic purpose of serving the technical and professional needs of the engineering profession. These organizations operate primarily through the dissemination of information. Numerous personal advantages can be derived from membership in these organizations and by participation in their programs. Among these are the regular receipt of educational journals and periodicals, learning of the latest advances in the field at society meetings and conferences, and, most importantly, the opportunity to interact with professional colleagues.

Among the many engineering societies, there exist five major societies referred to as the "founder societies":

1. American Society of Civil Engineers
2. American Institute of Mining, Metallurgical, and Petroleum Engineers
3. American Society of Mechanical Engineers

4. Institute of Electrical and Electronics Engineers

5. American Institute of Chemical Engineers

In 1904 these societies founded the United Engineering Trustees, Inc., which now occupies and operates a headquarters building in New York City, housing a number of engineering societies and an excellent library facility known as the Engineering Societies Library.

Most engineering societies require that their members meet high standards of conduct for membership. Although most engineering societies are organized along special activity or disciplinary lines, several general engineering organizations include the whole engineering spectrum. One of the largest of these is the National Society of Professional Engineers, which concerns itself with the image of the profession.

2.3 Summary

Engineering is a diverse field, with a wide range of opportunities and responsibilities. Engineers are problem solvers, applying their knowledge and abilities to problem areas ranging from basic research and development to marketing and sales. The engineer is a professional, responsible to the public for the technological advancements that benefit society as well as the effects these advancements have on the environment. As a professional, the engineer should contribute to the technological decisions which shape our way of life. There is a challenge, then, to develop our abilities as problem solvers, to meet the objectives and goals of the engineering profession.

REFERENCES

BEAKLEY, G. C. and H. W. LEACH. *Engineering: An Introduction to a Creative Profession*, Second Edition. New York: The Macmillan Company, 1972.

Engineers Council for Professional Development: "Engineering: Creating a Better World." New York: ECPD, 1970.

Engineers Council for Professional Development: "Make Your Career Choice Engineering." New York: ECPD, 1974.

GLORIOSO, ROBERT M. and FRANCIS S. HILL. *Introduction to Engineering*. Englewood Cliffs, N.J.: Prentice-Hall, Inc., 1975.

KEMPER, J. D. *The Engineer and His Profession*. New York: Holt, Rinehart and Winston, Inc. 1967.

RHINE, S. H. and D. CREAMER. "The Technical Manpower Shortage: How Acute?" National Industrial Conference Board, 1969.

WOODSON, T. T. *Introduction to Engineering Design.* New York: McGraw-Hill Book Company Inc., 1966.

Wind energy (*Courtesy* NASA.)

Engineering problem solving

3

The solution of engineering problems is both exciting and satisfying: to discover that it is possible to assimilate information, formulate a specific question or problem resulting from that information, and then determine an answer that satisfies the question and stands the test of time.

In most engineering problems, there is a need to arrive at an answer in terms of numerical values, to determine the magnitude, volume, or size of some parameter or mathematical expression needed to satisfy the question or problem under investigation. As a result, it is necessary to calculate various parameters to arrive at numerical solutions. Usually, both the formulation of the problem and the resulting solution require some form of computation.

Solving engineering problems is an art, a combination of skill and experience, and may be developed with a good basic understanding of problem solving techniques. In general, this technique consists of recognition and formulation of the problem, selection of a model with appropriate assumptions, establishment of a plan of attack within the limitations of the problem, and determination of a solution that will satisfy the problem and its limitations. This chapter discusses the manner in which engineering problems may be formulated and solution methods by which answers may be obtained.

3.1 Engineering problems

Perhaps the first step in the recognition and formulation of an engineering problem is the establishment of some criteria for determining what may be defined as a problem. A problem is generally a question based on factual data from which the solution may be determined by the application of engineering methods (Figure 3-1). Often it is necessary to establish the basis of the factual data before determining the question to be answered or the problem to be solved. A schematic of the guidelines appropriate for the formulation of a problem statement is shown in Figure 3-2.

There are numerous questions that we may ask about a problem. Frequently, these questions are based on partial information or incomplete data sampling practices. If we had access to all of the pertinent facts, then it would be easier to determine the primary question or questions that need to be answered. The review of basic information to sift out the important factors, and the interpretation of this information becomes the basis for recognizing the problem.

Joe Padget, an engineer recently graduated from college, has developed a small device for use in automobiles to improve performance. He has been

Figure 3-1 Development of a system to service satellites in earth orbit is a real engineering problem. The Space Shuttle has been designed to accomplish this mission. (*Courtesy* NASA.)

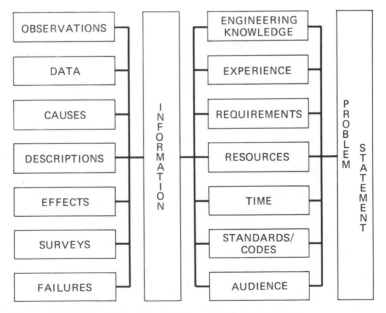

Figure 3-2 Schematic of guidelines for formulating a problem statement.

granted a patent for this device, called a fuelmiser, and has decided to build these units in his garage while holding down his regular full-time job. He has some machine shop equipment in his garage and can modify his design to fit the availability of material and his limited garage space. He incorporates his business, Padget's Gadgets, Inc., and starts to make plans for production. He purchases 69 irregularly-shaped sheets of carbosteeloy, a newly developed material with properties suitable for fabrication of the fuelmiser. He has also secured a market for his product in a nearby town.

Obviously engineer Joe Padget faces a number of problems as he plans for the production of the fuelmiser. First, he needs to determine the pertinent facts: the number of fuelmisers that can be made out of the material at hand, the time required to manufacture the parts for the fuelmiser, the amount of time available for work in the garage, the availability of additional materials, and so forth. It should be pointed out that all facts pertaining to the subject at hand are not necessarily pertinent to the formulation or the solution of his problems. For example, he does not need to know the color of the fuelmiser or the day the fuelmiser is made, and so forth. This information, though pertinent to the situation, is superfluous to the formulation and solution of the engineering problems that he will encounter.

In order to evaluate the basic information pertaining to a scientific puzzle, it is essential to have a thorough understanding of scientific fundamentals associated with the problem area. It is necessary to develop a background of knowledge in various scientific areas through reading, study, and individual investigation. This is the very purpose of an engineering education. This knowledge, combined with a review of the basic information pertaining to the problem, permits recognition of the important questions involved and helps the problem solver develop a skill in the solution of problems which will become sharper and keener the more it is practiced.

Engineer Padget must have knowledge of the fundamentals associated with the manufacture of the parts for the fuelmiser in order to define adequately the totality of his manufacturing dilemma. He must know the basics of design for optimum strength, reliability, and simplicity of manufacture and service, the machining practices for optimizing manufacturing time for each fuelmiser, and so on. He must also know the material properties, machineability, and range of applications of the carbosteeloy from which the fuelmisers are to be made. He must be concerned with product inspection and quality control. Padget's basic engineering knowledge and experience will assist him in formulating the most important questions to be raised and in identifying areas warranting additional attention.

The critical step of formulating the questions also depends on the audience for whom the question is to be answered. Of whom will the question be asked? How will the answer be used? What is the level of understanding of the person or group who will use the information? The audience must be considered because an answer that is meaningful to some may be so technical as to be meaningless to others.

> Clearly engineer Padget wants the questions raised and answered for himself. Both the questions and the appropriate answers might be quite different if they were raised or answered for the market or individual consumers.

To a practicing engineer, formulation of the question includes both a review of the basic information with appropriate knowledge of the scientific or engineering fundamentals, and a consideration of the audience or persons interested in the solution of the problem. The engineer, trained in the basic concepts of science, utilizes his abilities to sift the basic information, and then skillfully evaluates these data to formulate the interest area. Choosing a trivial or inappropriate aspect of a problem can lead to substantial waste of effort and resources. Careful formulation of the relevant factors will make solution of the fundamental problem both simpler and more meaningful.

> From the pertinent facts and his knowledge of engineering, Joe Padget (with the motivation to market his own product) could ask many questions. Some obvious questions might be, "How much profit can I make?" "How should the fuelmiser be packaged?" "How many can be made per week?" "How many should be delivered to the market each time?" "Can I afford to sell on consignment?" One of the most basic questions of immediate concern would be, "How should the fuelmiser design be modified to provide optimum use of material without changing its performance characteristics?" This is the question that Joe chooses to consider first.

3.2 Method of solution

Once the problem has been ascertained within the constraints of the available information (both general and scientific), the next step is to establish a model of the problem under consideration. Some problems may be sufficiently simple or straightforward as to permit a solution directly. Other problems, however, may be multifaceted and require complex and involved models and submodels in order to permit solution. A schematic of guidelines for formulating a problem solution is given in Figure 3-3.

Models. Many types of models are in use today. Some of them are tangible. Scale models of airplanes, boats, and cars serve as miniature replicas of the real things. There are models for clothes, houses, and buildings, models of new electronic components and so on. Most large

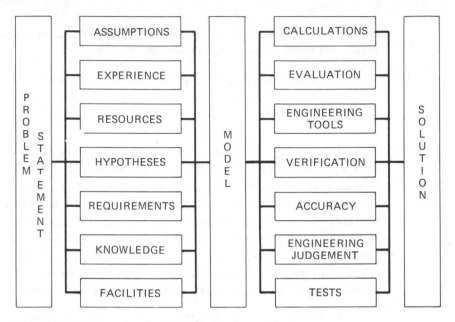

Figure 3-3 Schematic of guidelines for formulating a problem solution.

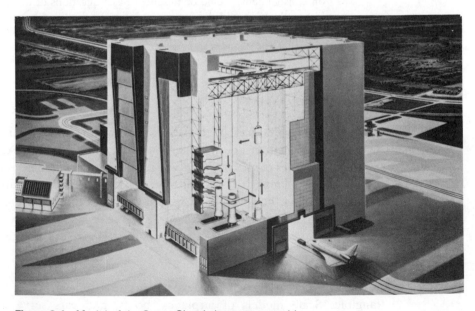

Figure 3-4 Model of the Space Shuttle booster assembly facility at Kennedy Space Center. (*Courtesy* NASA.)

construction operations, as well as industrially-produced products, start with a model, often full scale. Models are common and useful in our everyday lives. They are particularly helpful in the world of science and engineering (Figure 3-4).

Mechanical models aid analysis. For example, the simple classical model of the atom was devised to assist scientists in understanding its real characteristics. Astronomers have modeled the solar system with spheres and concentric circular orbits to aid in the study of the planets. Models for engineering applications require substantial precision where specific components or scale models are concerned. There are models of flight vehicles for wind tunnel testing, models of new electrical circuits, models of bridges, and scale models of propulsion systems. In these cases it is essential that care be taken in the preparation of the models so that test results may be extrapolated to full-size conditions.

Models may also be intangible. They may be "word pictures" of a process, or mathematical simulations, or equations. A model for problem-solving purposes is a graphical, written, or mathematical description of a real process, a real object, or an idea, in terms of easily used, simplified parameters or representations. The formulation of an engineering model requires substantial creativity and insight in order to consider the "big picture," which also includes the scientific or engineering details. Since most problems are complex with many variables, it is easier to model the complex problem with a simplified system rather than to attempt to design a model to fit the complete problem.

The use of a model permits better understanding of the problem through simplification or reduction in size and points the direction toward the solution. The use of modeling, then, is of great importance in the solution of engineering problems. Every attempt should be made to formulate a model that is simple, straightforward, and easily understood, as well as an accurate representation of the area needing engineering investigation.

In the garage of Padget's Gadjets, Inc., Joe Padget makes a preliminary model to guide him in the manufacture of fuelmisers. He surveys the 69 irregular sheets of carbosteeloy and finds that it is possible to divide them into blocks of 1 square meter and have no wastage. Instead of figuring out the number of fuelmisers that can be made out of the 69 sheets, he may simplify the process and determine the number for 1 square meter. He may modify the design of the fuelmiser to best fit the material by changing the angle and length of the brackets, and the location of the guzzlegas atomiser and depleter. These changes, of course, change the strength and resulting reliability of the fuelmiser, requiring an optimization of the fuelmiser characteristics.

Joe Padget is thus modeling the manufacturing process by choosing a layout of fuelmiser components on 1 square meter of material to permit optimum production. He will later use this model in producing the parts for fuelmisers from all 69 sheets of material.

Many questions are raised during the formulation of an engineering model: How should the problem be solved? How should the solution be presented? What are the major parameters involved? What type of solution is advisable? What cost, equipment, time, and so on are involved? The various influences on the problem should be considered so that their effects on the model may be determined. This is an important consideration in the model formulation, since a model may be simplified to the point where it no longer represents the project under consideration. The engineering model then, is based on knowledge of the factual data surrounding the problem, knowledge of engineering and scientific fundamentals, and the skill of the individual or team performing the analysis. Both knowledge and ability are amplified by the experience and perspective which one gains from solving many problems. The formulation of the simplified model, then, permits constructive analysis of the problem.

Assumptions. In the process of developing the model for the problem, or the simplification process, a number of assumptions must be made and considered very carefully. It is easy to develop a hypothesis based on original information; however, its plausibility must be considered. The testing of each of the assumptions employed must be conducted in such a manner as to keep the thrust of the problem in mind. Does the assumption have a major or minor effect on the problem? Would this specific assumption cause a substantial change in the problem if it were incorrect?

When different assumptions lead to the same solution and one is more general, resulting in a simpler model, the assumption leading to the simpler model is generally accepted until further evidence causes a re-evaluation of the factors used in the resolution of the problem. In many fields, the assumptions made and hypotheses proposed often are accepted as valid without adequate tests. In engineering, however, verification of the validity of the assumptions made should be an important aspect of the solution.

> Joe Padget has made a number of assumptions in the fuelmiser manufacturing operation. These assumptions include: the fuelmisers will have the same strength and reliability if they are manufactured in the same manner; the material properties of the 69 different sheets will be the same; the machines and processes that will be used to produce the fuelmisers will operate uniformly as needed, and so on. Joe also believes that the design modifications of the new fuelmiser will work as well as the patented version, and that the performance characteristics will not change. Because he is a qualified and

responsible engineer, Padget checks his assumptions by conducting tests on random samples of the carbosteeloy to assure that his product meets the advertised specifications.

Often, problems are generalized on the basis of a few observations or bits of data. This is true not only in scientific endeavors, but also in our actions in our daily lives. When such generalizations are associated with engineering endeavors, we must make a greater effort to assure ourselves that the assumptions have been proven to be correct for the particular application. Is it safe to say that the chemical analysis of a sample of ocean water off the Virginia coast would be appropriate for use in India? Could the chemical analysis and heating value of a fuel sample obtained from one supplier be considered the same as that of a fuel sample obtained from a different supplier? It is important for the professional engineer to ascertain that generalizations and assumptions made in the formulation of the problem and its model are accurate and valid.

Method of attack.   Once the model has been formulated and the assumptions tested for validity, the next step in the problem solutions is the development of a plan of attack. Again, questions should be raised: What type of answers are required? In what form should the answers be presented? What engineering tools are available to assist in the solution of the problem? What is the magnitude of the problem to be solved? How accurate should the answer be? These and many other questions arise as the problem solver begins to attack his problem in earnest.

The basic data associated with the formulation of the problem must be reviewed. It was important to decide which data were necessary for formulation of the problem and model. Now we need to know which data are necessary for the final solution and which data are peripheral. The characteristic units of these data also should be considered. Information often is supplied in different ways, for different reasons, and the problem solution can only be effected by use of a consistent set of units.

> Padget's method of attack is to sit down at his drawing board and consolidate his information in order to come up with the solution, i.e., the final design of the fuelmiser to produce the optimum number of good, reliable fuelmisers out of each square meter of material. He is careful to put away his yardstick and use his new precision meterstick.
>
> Joe makes isometric or three-dimensional sketches of the fuelmiser, and after two or three designs, develops a set of final working drawings. He determines the strengths of the parts, the fittings that must be purchased, and the sequence for manufacturing the fuelmiser in his garage. He also checks to be sure that the final configuration of the fuelmiser is covered by his original patent.

A skillful review of the necessary information combined with the problem statement and model, sets the path for solution.

Engineering tools. What engineering tools are needed? Which engineering tools should be used? Is the problem to be solved graphically? Should we use a tee square and triangles or a computer graphics terminal? Is the problem to be solved numerically (Figure 3-5)? Should we use an abacus, a slide rule, a hand held calculator, a desk calculator, an analog computer, a digital computer, or other computational device? Should the hand-held calculator be four function, multifunction, or programmable?

The choice of the engineering tool is governed partially by the form in which the answer is to be presented. The overall economic considerations also influence the choice of tools. Should the volume of a cone be determined by slide rule, hand calculator, or digital computer? Use of the digital computer for such a problem would be like cracking a peanut with a sledge

Figure 3-5 Should the problem be solved numerically? (*Courtesy* Hewlett Packard.)

hammer. It would not be worth the cost in machine time, paper, and programming effort.

Joe Padget has determined his problems, devised a model, and now prepares for the modification of the fuelmiser design. Should the modifications be generated graphically, by calculator, or by computer? What method would yield results which are of adequate accuracy at minimum cost? After reviewing the design, he decides to make the modifications graphically and then check the dimensions by calculator.

Padget also must compute performance specifications for his fuelmisers using the material property characteristics which he has test-checked. Preliminary performance tests of the newly produced fuelmisers are conducted to verify the performance specifications. The results of these tests are then computed by calculator, since the complexity and accuracy of the performance specifications do not require the use of more precision computational equipment.

It is necessary to consider the selection of the engineering tool in terms of the value of the answer. If the answer were needed to the twentieth decimal point, the use of more precision equipment may be warranted. In general, however, calculators provide sufficient flexibility and accuracy for most of the problems encountered in normal engineering work. Techniques for computation using the more common engineering tools are covered in later sections.

Accuracy. How accurately should results be reported? The answer might be: As accurate as the data from which the solution was derived. Such a response requires the review of the information used in formulating the problem and the model. How accurate was the original data? How was it obtained? Was it measured with precision equipment? Answers to these questions will provide guidance for determining the degree of accuracy required in an answer.

Obtaining an accurate answer also requires common sense. The problem solver should be able to estimate a "ball-park," reasonable solution, and should compare the calculated answer with that estimate. Just as the radio weatherman would be well advised to look out of his window before forecasting "no chance of rain," so the engineer should ascertain that his solution is indeed within the realm of reasonable possibility. As problems become more complex, however, the correct value may become more difficult to estimate, and it will be necessary to rely on the calculated value and the confidence that one may have in his own calculations.

Joe Padget must be concerned with the accuracy of the fabrication of the fuelmisers. He plans to measure all parts of the fuelmiser with calibrated equipment. In laying out the number of fuelmisers on a square meter block of material, however, he finds that it is not necessary to figure the number of fuelmisers to the sixth decimal place. For manufacturing purposes, 7.132 866 fuelmisers per square meter would be no better than 7.

With the various characteristics of materials, machine processes, and fabrication in mind, Joe recalls his engineering studies of such areas as plant layout, automatic controls, jigs and fixtures, quality control, and materials routing. Padget combines his engineering know-how and judgment with his ability to perform precision machine work, in order to fabricate his own product.

Engineering judgment is vital to the accurate solution of engineering problems. Engineering, like all professions, has a code of ethics and a sense of responsibility. Engineers must make decisions on many things which relate to our public safety: the design of buildings that will not collapse in a storm, bridges that do not fall when loaded with cars, electronic units that do not electrocute, engines that do not explode. In fact, almost all sectors of technology rely on some aspect of engineering judgment along with the accuracy and reliability of results. In later sections of this book, various means of evaluating and determining accuracy and error will be discussed.

3.3 Final solution—results

Once a problem has been analyzed and a successful solution to the problem obtained, the procedure, design, tests, and results should be presented in as complete a form as possible to permit a thorough understanding of the answer and methods used. In other words, the complete project, from start to finish, should be presented. The accuracy of the results also should be specified in order to qualify the answer.

Final answers and resulting recommendations normally are presented in written documents. Results may be presented as a single answer, in tabular form, or in graphical form. The results of a problem solved by engineering techniques are generally some form of numerical value with units. The clarity with which the answers are presented will enhance the understanding and value of the work.

Graphical presentation of the solutions to problems helps demonstrate trends as well as ranges of variables. In engineering, graphical results convey a good deal of information that would be difficult to obtain from tables or single numerical values. Ranges of error or accuracy also may be presented graphically to give a degree of reliability to the results.

Whether the solution is reported by means of an exhaustive treatise, graphs, a single value, or a tabulated result, it should be presented in a form that will be easy to understand and interpret. Assumptions used in carrying out the solution should be stated, and special conditions, ranges, sizes, and other factors that limit the resulting answers should be mentioned.

> Joe Padget was careful in the development of his fuelmisers, followed engineering principles carefully, made accurate calculations, and produced an innovative, reliable product. Joe has developed other engineering products using the same sound engineering procedures that he used with the fuelmisers. Today he is the president of a multimillion dollar corporation.

3.4 Objectives—engineering problem solving

The engineer depends upon his own ingenuity and creativity in the formulation and solution of problems—specifically, his ability to evolve new ideas, new components, new techniques, new materials, or new processes. Such exercises of creativity stimulate the engineer's imagination, challenging him to try other and more complicated technical projects. The development of a firm foundation in scientific investigation and problem solving techniques will contribute to his skill and professional growth.

The purpose of this book is to develop a successful engineering problem-solving technique, to provide information on logical approach methods and an opportunity for exercising these methods, and to develop some ability in selecting and using the various engineering tools for computational analysis.

REFERENCES

BEAKLEY, GEORGE C. and H. W. LEACH. *Engineering: An Introduction to a Creative Profession*, Second Edition. New York: The Macmillan Company, 1972.

GRAHAM, A. RICHARD. *An Introduction to Engineering Measurements*. Englewood Cliffs, N.J.: Prentice-Hall, Inc., 1975.

HOLMAN, J. P. *Experimental Methods for Engineers*, Second Edition. New York: McGraw-Hill Book Company, Inc., 1971.

KRICK, EDWARD V. *An Introduction to Engineering and Engineering Design*. New York: John Wiley & Son, Inc., 1965.

RUBINSTEIN, MOSHE F. *Patterns of Problem Solving*. Englewood Cliffs, N.J.: Prentice-Hall, Inc., 1975.

SMITH, RALPH J. *Engineering as a Career*, Third Edition. New York: McGraw-Hill Book Company, Inc., 1969.

WILSON, E. BRIGHT, Jr. *An Introduction to Scientific Research*. New York: McGraw-Hill Book Company, Inc., 1952.

Electric taxi. (*Courtesy* Lucas Industries, London.)

Dimensions and unit systems

4

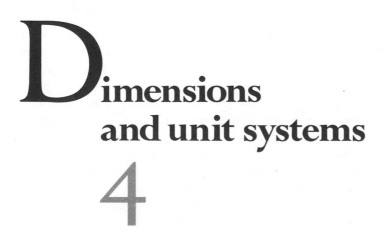

Engineering computation involves much more than the mere manipulation of numbers. The proper use of models and formulated equations, the units of measurement of the physical quantities used in problems, the precision of the data and numbers used, the degree of accuracy of the answers—all these are intimately involved in the solution of problems.

Most engineering calculations involve information obtained from measurements of some form. These data are used in equations that are composed of symbols representing unknown values as well as numerical coefficients. The basic dimensions and appropriate units of the equation must be consistent in order to permit the correct calculation of a solution. The basic set of dimensions most often used in engineering are length, mass, and time. These dimensions may be reported in a number of different units, depending upon the magnitude of the dimension involved.

The two major systems of units which have been used in recent times are the English system and the metric system. The English system of units, developed in England in the thirteenth century, has been used primarily by British Commonwealth countries and the United States. The remainder of the world has long used the metric system. In 1972, the metric system was designated the Système International d'Unités (SI) by a worldwide federation of national standards institutes including the National Bureau of Standards of the United States. This unit system, then, is to be the universal unit system for all measurements and calculations.

The English system of units, with a few modifications, has been used extensively by American engineers. The primary modification for engineering applications was the inclusion of force units, which were based on the gravitational system, i.e., the force due to gravity. Many engineering constants and characteristics were developed using this modified English system of units. Many practicing engineers have memorized a great many material properties in English units and have come to think in these terms. Conversion to SI units, then, poses some conceptualization difficulties. Since scientists and engineers in nearly all other countries now work in SI units, however, a change to this system of units by American engineers is long overdue.

As early as 1790, Thomas Jefferson recommended that the United States convert to the decimal measurement system, a system of units based on multiples of 10. His recommendation was rejected, however, because of congressional fear that such a conversion would interfere with U.S. trade, which was primarily with the British Commonwealth at that time. Today, however, the worldwide exchange of technical information and products that are specified in the metric system of weights and measures has led the United States to adopt the International System of Units.

4.1 The decimal system

The monetary system in the United States is set up on the basis of multiples of 10. For example, 10 mils are one penny, 10 pennies are one dime, 10 dimes are one dollar, and so on. The system involving multiples of 10, then, is not strange to Americans, but rather, is a part of everyday life.

The metric system of weights and measures is a decimal system comparable to the U.S. monetary system. A unit is 10 times larger or smaller than the next smaller or larger unit. Each of these divisions is designated by a prefix which specifies its relationship to the basic unit. These prefixes, which are listed in Table 4-1, remain the same regardless of the units involved, and permit the reporting of measurements over a wide range.

Table 4-1 Metric Prefixes

SI Prefix	Symbol	Numerical Size
tera	T	1 000 000 000 000 (10^{12})
giga	G	1 000 000 000 (10^{9})
mega	M	1 000 000 (10^{6})
kilo	k	1 000 (10^{3})
hecto	h	100 (10^{2})
deka	da	10 (10^{1})
deci	d	0.1 (10^{-1})
centi	c	0.01 (10^{-2})
milli	m	0.001 (10^{-3})
micro	μ	0.000001 (10^{-6})
nano	n	0.000000001 (10^{-9})
pico	p	0.000000000001 (10^{-12})
femto	f	0.000000000000001 (10^{-15})
atto	a	0.000000000000000001 (10^{-18})

4.2 Fundamental dimensions

In the International System of Units (SI), there are seven primary or fundamental dimensions of physical quantities from which other units are derived. These fundamental quantities and recommended symbols are given in Table 4-2. These basic quantities are defined in terms of the standards (criteria established by authority or agreement as the measure of a quantity) used to establish the primary units.

Table 4-2   Fundamental Units—International System of Units (SI)

Primary Units	Symbol	Unit of Measure	Abbreviation
Length or distance	l	meter	m
Mass	m	kilogram	kg
Time	t	second	s
Thermodynamic temperature	T	kelvin	K
Electric current	I	ampere	A
Amount of substance	n	mole	mol
Light or luminous intensity	l_v	candela	cd
Supplementary Units			
Plane angle	$\alpha, \beta, \gamma, \theta, \phi$	radian	rad
Solid angle	ω	steradian	sr

Length or distance.   The measurement of the length or distance of an object, such as the length or diameter of a piece of steel rod, is reported in terms of *meters*. The meter is defined as being exactly "the length equal to 1 650 763.73 wavelengths in vacuum of the radiation corresponding to the transition between the levels $2p_{10}$ and $5d_5$ of the krypton-86 atom"* (see Figure 4-1).

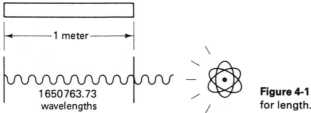

Figure 4-1   Schematic of the standard for length.

Normal distances or measurements of length may be reported in terms ranging from micrometers (10^{-6} meters) to kilometers (10^3 meters) and beyond. Conversion between these units is easily accomplished since they are related by factors of 10. Manipulation of areas (square meters) or volumes (cubic meters) in terms of SI units minimizes the number of steps in computations involving these units.

* National Bureau of Standards, SP 330, p. 3.

Mass. It should be clearly understood that the measurement of the mass of an object, such as a brick, is not the same as the measurement of weight. The mass of the brick will remain constant, whereas the weight is dependent upon gravitational forces which vary with such conditions as altitude and location. The weight of the brick, then, is the force with which the brick is pulled downward.

The *kilogram* is the unit used to describe mass (not weight or force). In common parlance, however, the word "weight" is often used to refer to what is actually the "mass" of an object. These two values are identical, however, only at standard sea level conditions. The standard for the kilogram is a cylinder of platinum-iridium alloy maintained under vacuum conditions by the International Bureau of Weights and Measures in Paris (Figure 4-2). An exact duplicate of this cylinder of platinum-iridium alloy is

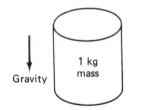

Figure 4-2 Schematic of the standard for mass.

kept by the National Bureau of Standards in Washington, D.C. Mass is the only primary unit for which a tangible object is maintained as a standard.

The relationship between force and mass is defined by means of Newton's second principle:

$$Force = (mass)(acceleration)$$

The force unit is defined in terms of the units of mass, length, and time. The absolute force unit in the International System is the *newton*, designated by the symbol N, and is the force required to accelerate one kilogram of mass one meter per second per second, as shown in Figure 4-3, that is:

$$1\,N = 1\,kg\,m/s^2$$

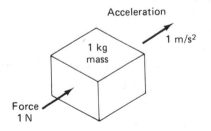

Figure 4-3 Schematic of the relationship between force and mass.

Time. Time is the duration between two distinct events, or the elapsed period since an event has occurred. The basic unit of time is the *second* which is defined as exactly "the duration of 9 192 631 770 periods of the radiation corresponding to the transition between the two hyperfine levels of the ground state of the cesium-113 atom."* The second is determined by tuning an oscillator to the resonant frequency of cesium-113 atoms passing through a magnetic field in a resonant cavity, sometimes referred to as the cesium clock.

There are secondary time standards, in addition to the cesium clock, which may be used for defining the second. Among these are the hydrogen maser, rubidium clock, and quartz frequency standards and clocks.

Time is measured in terms of seconds, minutes, hours, days, weeks, months, and years. For periods of time of one second or less, the decimal system is used, e.g., milliseconds or microseconds. (Five milliseconds may be written 0.005 seconds; 27 microseconds may be written 0.000 027 seconds.) For periods of time from one second to years, individual increments are involved and do not follow the decimal system. There are 60 seconds in a minute (rather than 100), 60 minutes in an hour, 24 hours in a day, 7 days in a week, and so on. For periods greater than one year, the decimal system is again used, i.e., 10 years in a decade, 10 decades in a century, and 10 centuries in a millenium.

Electric current.   The measure of electric current is the measure of the rate of flow of electric charge through electrically conducting material. The unit of electric charge is the coulomb. The charge on an electron has been observed in measurements on the hydrogen atom. This charge, designated by the symbol e, is $1.602\ 1 \times 10^{-19}$ coulombs.

The flow of electric charge through an electrically conducting material, such as a length of wire, produces a force field. If an electric current is passed through two long parallel wires separated by one meter of free space, a magnetic field would be produced between the wires. The *ampere* is defined as "that constant current which, if maintained in two straight parallel conductors of infinite length, of negligible circular cross section, and placed one meter apart in a vacuum, would produce between these conductors a force equal to 2×10^{-7} newtons per meter of length"† (see Figure 4-4). The ampere is a measure of the rate of flow of charge and is one coulomb per second. It should be noted that the flow of electrons through a conducting media is opposite to the direction of current.

* NBS SP 330, p. 3.
† NBS SP 330, p. 4.

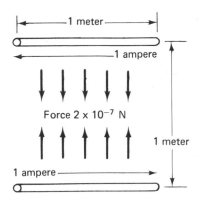

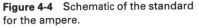

Figure 4-4 Schematic of the standard for the ampere.

Temperature. The measure of temperature is a measure of relative "hotness" or "coldness." In 1854 Lord Kelvin proposed a thermodynamic temperature scale based on six fixed temperature points including the freezing and boiling points of water. In 1968 the International Practical Temperature Scale was adopted by an international conference concerned with the establishment of temperature standards. This International Temperature Scale is based on a number of fixed points, as noted in Table 4-3.

Several different instruments are used to measure temperatures for use in standard temperature measurements. Among these instruments are the platinum resistance thermometer, the platinum-platinum/10% rhodium thermocouple, and the monochromatic optical pyrometer. These instruments are calibrated in terms of the reproducible temperature points, or fixed points, some of which are listed in Table 4-3.

The *kelvin* is used as a measure of temperature in the International System of units, and has been defined as "the fraction 1/273.16 of the thermodynamic temperature of the triple point of water,"* that is, the point at which water exists in all three phases—solid, liquid, and vapor. A special calibration cell has been constructed, which will permit the calibration of temperature measuring devices at the triple point. The kelvin scale, generally referred to as the *absolute temperature scale*, is frequently used by scientists and engineers.

The Celsius scale, usually referred to as the Centigrade scale (i.e., 100 graduations between freezing and boiling of water) also is used in the International System of Units. Although the increment of one degree Celsius is equal to the increment of one degree kelvin, the magnitude of a given temperature in degrees Celsius is different from the magnitude in degrees kelvin, as noted in Table 4-3. Absolute zero is 0 K and −273.15°C, and

* NBS SP 330, p. 4.

Table 4-3 Temperature Scales

International System		Standard	English System*	
Kelvin	Celsius		Rankine	Fahrenheit
K	°C		°R	°F
0.0	−273.15	Absolute zero	0.0	−459.69
20.28	−252.87	Hydrogen liquid-vapor equilibrium	36.51	−423.19
90.188	−182.962	Oxygen liquid-vapor equilibrium	162.344	−297.346
273.15	0.00	Water solid-liquid equilibrium	491.69	32.00
273.16	0.010	Water triple point	491.71	32.018
373.15	100.0	Water liquid-vapor equilibrium	671.68	212.00
692.73	419.58	Zinc solid-liquid equilibrium	1 246.93	787.24
717.82	444.67	Sulfur liquid-vapor equilibrium	1 291.97	832.28
1 235.08	961.93	Silver solid-liquid equilibrium	2 221.09	1 761.4
1 337.58	1 064.43	Gold solid-liquid equilibrium	2 405.09	1 945.4
1 827	1 554	Palladium solid-liquid equilibrium	3 288	2 829
2 044.8	1 771.7	Platinum solid-liquid equilibrium	3 680.8	3 221.1

(Left axis scale marks: 0, 100, 200, 300, 400, 500, 600, 700, 800, 1200, 1300, 1800, 1900, 2000, 2100)

* Defined in Appendix A.

273.15 K equals 0°C. Therefore °C = K − 273.15. The kelvin scale and the Celsius scale, then, are closely related and are both a part of the International System of Units.

Amount of substance. In many analyses, there is a need to refer to quantities of substance or amount of constituent particles. In the past, terms involving the number of atoms or molecules were used to specify amounts of chemical elements or chemical compounds. These terms were directly related to the molecular or atomic weights of the substance. Isotopes of oxygen were used as a standard for a period of time. In 1960, an agreement was reached to establish a unified scale of relative atomic mass with the isotope Carbon 12 as the base.

The unit of amount of a substance was established as the *mole*, and has been fixed as "the amount of a substance which contains as many elementary entities as there are atoms in 0.012 kilograms of Carbon 12."[*] These elementary entities may be atoms, molecules, ions, electrons, or other particles or groups of particles.

Consider a pure substance (chemical symbol A) composed of atoms. By definition, a mole of atoms of A contains as many atoms as there are Carbon 12 atoms in 0.012 kilograms of Carbon 12. Since the masses of these atoms in both substance A and Carbon 12 cannot readily be measured, a ratio of the masses can be determined, such that

$$M(A) = \left(\frac{m(A)}{m(^{12}C)} \right) \times 0.012 \text{ kg/mol}$$

where M is the mass of a mole of substance A. The ratio may be determined by mass spectrograph. It is possible, then, to calculate the molar mass of any substance by utilizing the ratio of the mass of any substance to the mass of Carbon 12.

A mole of particles of any perfect gas at a given temperature and pressure occupies the same volume. Therefore, it is possible to determine the ratio of amounts of substance for gases. For electrolytic solutions (i.e., solutions in which the conduction of electricity is accompanied by chemical decomposition), the ratio of amounts of substance is proportional to the electrical output. Other techniques may be used to establish a ratio of the amounts of substance for extremely dilute solutions.

[*] NBS SP 330, p. 5.

Light or luminous intensity. Virtually all bodies emit or absorb radiant energy. If the temperature of a body is sufficiently high, the emitted radiation will be in the visible spectrum. Thermal radiation is not the only form of light emission. Other forms include fluorescence, chemiluminescence, electrical excitation, and electroluminescence. In order to classify the degree of visible light emitted, a unit of measure has been adopted in the International System. This unit of measure of luminous intensity is the *candela*, and is defined as "the luminous intensity, in the perpendicular direction, of a surface of 1/600 000 square meters of a blackbody at the temperature of freezing platinum under a pressure of 101 325 newtons per square meter"* (see Figure 4-5).

Blackbody

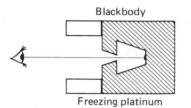

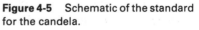

Figure 4-5 Schematic of the standard for the candela.

Freezing platinum

There are, in addition, secondary standards that may be used for measurement of luminous intensity. Among these are specially manufactured incandescent lamps with d.c. power supplies. These lamps are calibrated to provide definite luminous intensities at given voltage settings.

Plane angle. One of the more commonly used supplementary units of angular measure is the plane angle. This angle is designated as the *radian* and is defined as "the plane angle between two radii of a circle which cut off on the circumference an arc equal in length to the radius"† (see Figure 4-6).

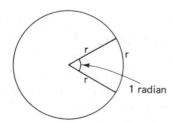

Figure 4-6 Schematic of the radian.

* NBS SP 330, p. 5.
† NBS SP 330, p. 11.

There are 2π radians in a circle, and therefore in 360°. As a result, one radian is 57.295 779 5°. In addition,

$$1 \min (1') = (1/60)° = \pi/10\ 800\ \text{rad}$$

$$1 \sec (1'') = (1/60)' = \pi/648\ 800\ \text{rad}$$

Solid angle. The solid angle is used in several types of engineering calculations and is one of the supplementary units of the International System. The measure of solid angle is the *steradian* (sr) and is defined as "the solid angle which, having its vertex in the center of a sphere, cuts off an area of the surface of sphere equal to that of a square with sides of length equal to the radius of the sphere"* (see Figure 4-7).

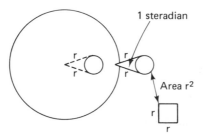

Figure 4-7 Schematic of the steradian.

4.3 Derived units

The previously described primary units may be used to formulate more complex units for specific situations. These additional units, or derived units, are formed algebraically by multiplication or division. Some of these derived units have been given special names and symbols. A number of these units are listed in Table 4-4.

The engineer often is called upon to work with both the International System of Units and the English system of units. To assist in this process, the primary units in the English system are described in Appendix A, and a detailed table of conversion factors is given in Appendix B.

* NBS SP 330, p. 11.

4.4 Checking units

Once the parameters for a problem have been established, it is necessary to check all of the units involved in order to be sure that they are specified in the same unit system (i.e., that they are homogeneous), and that the units of the answer will be in the desired form. If data with different units are multiplied or added together, erroneous answers will result which may become the basis for erroneous judgments. The combination of apples and oranges to obtain an orple would hardly be a fruitful exercise.

In preparing a problem solution, the fundamental equations used also must be dimensionally correct. Since an equation may involve several variables, the test of dimensional homogeneity can be made by substituting the appropriate units for each variable in the equation (without numbers). The units on the left side of the equation should be equal to those on the right side.

EXAMPLE 4-1   Kinetic energy is defined as

$$KE = \frac{1}{2}MV^2$$

Using appropriate units from Table 4-4:
   Energy is measured in terms of joules
   Mass . . . . kg
   Velocity . . . . m/s

Then substituting in the kinetic energy equation,

$$joule = kg\,\frac{m^2}{s^2}$$

From Table 4-4, the joule is defined as

$$joule = kg\,m^2\,s^{-2}$$

The equation, therefore, is dimensionally correct.

Table 4-4 SI Basic and Derived Units*

Quantity	Symbol	Unit of Measure	Abbreviation
Basic			
length	l	meter	m
mass	m	kilogram	kg
time	t	second	s
thermodynamic temperature	T	kelvin	K
electric current	I	ampere	A
amount of substance	n	mole	mol
luminous intensity	l_v	candela	cd
plane angle	$\alpha, \beta, \gamma, \theta, \phi$	radian	rad
solid angle	ω	steradian	sr
Derived			
acceleration		meter/second squared	m/s^2
activity (of radioactive source)		disintegration/second	s^{-1}
angular acceleration		radian/second squared	rad/s^2
angular velocity		radian/second	rad/s
area		square meter	m^2
concentration		mole/cubic meter	mol/m^3
current density		ampere/square meter	A/m^2
density (mass)		kilogram/cubic meter	kg/m^3
electric capacitance		farad (F)	$A \cdot s/V$
electric conductance		siemens (S)	A/V
electric charge		coulomb (C)	$A \cdot s$
electric field strength		volt/meter	V/m
electric inductance		henry (H)	$V \cdot s/A$
electric potential difference		volt (V)	W/A
electric resistance		ohm (Ω)	V/A
electromotive force		volt (V)	W/A
energy		joule (J)	$N \cdot m$
energy density		joule/cubic meter	J/m^3
entropy		joule/kelvin	J/K
force		newton (N)	$kg \cdot m/s^2$
frequency		hertz (Hz)	cycle/s
heat		joule (J)	$N \cdot m$
heat capacity		joule/kelvin	J/K
heat flux density		watt/square meter	W/m^2
illuminance		lux (lx)	lm/m^2
luminance		candela/square meter	cd/m^2
luminous flux		lumen (lm)	$cd \cdot sr$
magnetic field strength		ampere/meter	A/m
magnetic flux		weber (Wb)	$V \cdot s$

(continued)

Table 4-4 SI Basic and Derived Units* (continued)

Quantity	Unit of Measure	Abbreviation
magnetic flux density	tesla (T)	Wb/m^2
magnetomotive force	ampere (A)	C/s
permeability	henry/meter	H/m
permittivity	farad/meter	F/m
power	watt (W)	J/s
pressure	pascal (Pa)	N/m^2
quantity of electricity	coulomb (C)	$A \cdot s$
quantity of heat	joule (J)	$N \cdot m$
radiance	watt/square meter steradian	$W/m^2 \cdot sr$
radiant intensity	watt/steradian	W/sr
radiant flux	watt (W)	J/s
specific energy	joule/kilogram	J/kg
specific heat	joule/kilogram · kelvin	$J/kg \cdot K$
specific volume	cubic meter/kilogram	m^3/kg
speed	meter/second	m/s
stress	pascal (Pa)	N/m^2
surface tension	newton/meter	N/m
thermal conductivity	watt/meter · kelvin	$W/m \cdot K$
thermal conductance	watt/square meter kelvin	$W/m^2 \cdot K$
velocity	meter/second	m/s
viscosity, dynamic	pascal · second	$Pa \cdot s$
viscosity, kinematic	square meter/second	m^2/s
voltage	volt (V)	W/A
volume	cubic meter	m^3
wave number	reciprocal meter	m^{-1}
work	joule (J)	$N \cdot m$

* NBS SP 330.

There are occasions when the problem solver would like to reduce the calculation time for a specific problem by rearranging the problem into groups of dimensionless quantities. One of the more frequently used procedures in engineering is the dimensional analysis technique. This technique permits the combination of several variables into one dimensionless quantity for easier calculation. Basically, these dimensionless quantities are the result of multiplication or division of terms involving the basic units. In checking the units of such dimensionless numbers, the individual units of the numerator and denominator should be equal.

EXAMPLE 4-2   The drag coefficient used in aerodynamics is defined as

$$C_d = \frac{D/A}{\rho(v^2/2)}$$

where D = drag force
A = area over which drag force acts
ρ = density
v = velocity
In order to demonstrate that C_d is a dimensionless number, from Table 4-4 we find
    Drag force is measured in terms of newtons
    Area . . . . m²
    Density . . . . kg/m³
    Velocity . . . . m/s
Substitution of these values into the drag coefficient equation yields:

$$C_d = \frac{N/m^2}{(kg/m^3)(m^2/s^2)} = \frac{N}{N} = 1$$

Thus C_d is dimensionless.

There are numerous references at the end of this chapter describing dimensional analysis techniques, including the Buckingham theorem (a technique for the selection of dimensionless groups of variables), for use by the reader interested in the reduction of variables.

Unit checking of equations not only clarifies the information needed to solve the problem, but also assures that the correct units and conversion factors are involved. It is an essential part of engineering computations.

4.5 Summary

A substantial effort has been made in recent years to standardize the various units and dimensions used in science and engineering. The adoption of the International System of Units simplifies the international exchange of information and products, and provides new opportunities for collaboration on scientific problems of worldwide scope.

Once the engineer has developed an understanding of the basic SI units and has used them repeatedly in problem solving, he will develop a perception of the appropriate magnitudes of various parameters and their use in engineering computations. Knowledge of SI units and their use, then, will facilitate the solution of engineering problems.

PROBLEMS **4.1** Energy is generated when a current is passed through a resistance. Show that the equation

$$P = I^2 R$$

is dimensionally homogeneous if

$$P = \text{power}$$

$$I = \text{current}$$

$$R = \text{electric resistance}$$

4.2 The speed of sound in an enclosure filled with gas may be calculated as

$$C = (kRT/M)^{1/2}$$

where C = speed

R = universal gas constant

T = thermodynamic temperature

k = ratio of the specific heat at constant pressure to the specific heat at constant volume

M = molecular mass of the gas

What should the units of R be in order for the equation to be dimensionally homogeneous?

4.3 When a conductor moves through a magnetic field, the voltage generated may be determined by the expression

$$V = BLv$$

where $\quad B$ = magnetic flux density

$\quad L$ = length of the conductor

$\quad v$ = velocity of the conductor through the field

Show that the equation is dimensionally homogeneous.

4.4 The normal modes of vibration in a string fixed at each end result in frequencies expressed by the equation

$$f_n = \frac{n(F/m)^{1/2}}{2L}$$

where $\quad f$ = frequency (f_n = frequency of specific mode n)

$\quad F$ = tension

$\quad m$ = mass/unit length

$\quad L$ = length of string

$\quad n$ = mode of vibration

Show that the equation is dimensionally homogeneous.

4.5 When a current carrying conductor is placed in a magnetic field, a force is generated according to the equation

$$F = BLI$$

where $\quad B$ = magnetic flux density

$\quad L$ = length of the conductor

$\quad I$ = current

Show that the equation is dimensionally homogeneous.

4.6 In the field of optics, the equation for a double convex lens may be written as

$$\frac{1}{\ell_1} + \frac{1}{\ell_2} = (\mu - 1)\left(\frac{1}{R_1} + \frac{1}{R_2}\right)$$

where ℓ_1 = object distance

ℓ_2 = image distance

R = radius of curvature of lens surfaces

μ = index of refraction of lens material

What are the units of μ?

4.7 Determine the units for the variable K in the Euler formula

$$\frac{P}{A} = \frac{K\pi^2 E}{(L/R)^2}$$

where A = area

E = modulus of elasticity

R = radius of gyration

L = column length

P = force

4.8 If an electron of mass m is permitted to fall through a voltage, V, the velocity, v, reached by the electron may be determined through use of the equation

$$v = (2eV/m)^{1/2}$$

where e = electric charge

V = voltage

m = mass

v = velocity

Show that the equation is dimensionally homogeneous.

4.9 The Bernoulli equation may be used for nonviscous, incompressible steady flow through a pipe of variable cross section. The equation between points 1 and 2 may be written as

$$p_1 + \tfrac{1}{2}\rho v_1^2 + \rho g z_1 = p_2 + \tfrac{1}{2}\rho v_2^2 + \rho g z_2$$

where
p = pressure

ρ = density

v = velocity

g = gravitational acceleration

z = distance

Show that the equation is dimensionally homogeneous.

4.10 Determine the units for dimensional homogeneity in the equation for the Stormer type rotating viscometer.

$$\mu = \frac{\Delta\Theta(r_2^2 - r_1^2)r_3^2 g\, \Delta m}{4\pi r_1^2 r_2^2 z(h + \delta)}$$

where
$r_1, r_2, r_3, z, h, \delta$ = units of length

g = acceleration due to gravity

Θ = time $\Delta\Theta$ = increment of time

m = mass Δm = increment of mass

4.11 Demonstrate that the following dimensionless parameters are without units. (Use the information given in Table 4-4.)

(a) Reynolds Number, Re = $\rho V d/\mu$

ρ = density

V = velocity

d = diameter

μ = viscosity

(b) Nusselt Number, $Nu = hD/k$

h = convective conductance

D = length

k = thermal conductivity

(c) Prandtl Number, $Pr = \mu c_p/k$

μ = viscosity

c_p = specific heat

k = thermal conductivity

(d) Biot Number, $Bi = hr/k$

h = convective conductance

r = radius

k = thermal conductivity

(e) Froude Number, $Fr = V^2/Lg$

V = velocity

L = length

g = acceleration due to gravity

4.12 A monkey has a mass of 10 kg. What is the force exerted by the monkey (in newtons) at standard sea level conditions near the equator where g is 9.82 m/s^2, and in a satellite orbiting 400 kilometers from earth where g = 9.0 m/s^2? What would the weight of the monkey be at the same conditions?

4.13 Calculate the mass of an inverted conical container filled with water if the altitude of the conical section is 43 cm and the radius of the base is 8 ins. (Assume standard conditions.)

4.14 The total distance traveled by an automobile at constant acceleration is

$$s = v_0 t + \tfrac{1}{2}at^2$$

and the final velocity reached is

$$v_f = (v_0^2 + 2as)^{1/2}$$

Calculate the distance, s (in km), traveled and final velocity, v_f (in km/hr) if

$$v_0 = 10 \text{ mph}$$

$$t = 60 \text{ sec}$$

$$a = 4 \text{ ft/sec/sec}$$

4.15 With what force (in newtons) will a balloon filled with water hit a designated target when it is dropped from a third story window 10 m above the given target. Assume that the balloon is a rigid sphere 12 in. in diameter. (Use standard conditions.)

4.16 Calculate the heat loss through a brick furnace wall (in joules per second) using the Fourier conduction equation

$$q = \frac{kA(T_2 - T_1)}{L}$$

where $T_2 = 2000°F$ (inside temperature)

$T_1 = 100°C$ (outside temperature)

$k = 0.25$ Btu/hr/ft^2/°F/ft (thermal conductivity)

$L = 23$ cm (furnace wall thickness)

$A = 1$ m^2 (surface area)

4.17 Calculate the kinetic energy (in newton-meters) for a bowling ball rolling down a lane in a bowling alley if the ball weighs 5 lb and the average velocity is 700 cm/s. (Assume standard conditions.)

4.18 The fire hydrants in a city water system are being tested. Calculate the velocity, v, of the water (in m/s) flowing out of the hydrant if the center of the outlet is 75 cm above the ground and the issuing jet of water strikes the ground 9 ft from the outlet. The velocity may be calculated from

$$v = \sqrt{\frac{x^2 g}{2y}}$$

(Assume standard conditions.)

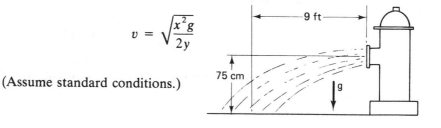

4.19 The deflection, δ, of a cantilevered flat parallel spring is given by the expression

$$\delta = \frac{2}{3} \frac{sL^2}{Et}$$

where the safe tensile stress, s, is 50,000 psi, the modulus of elasticity, E, is 30×10^6 psi for steel springs, the length L is 0.75 m, and the thickness, t, is 0.5 cm. Calculate the permissible deflection of the spring in centimeters.

4.20 The general equation for pressure loss due to pipe friction is

$$\Delta p = f\rho \frac{L}{D} \frac{v^2}{2}$$

where Δp = pressure loss, N/m^2

f = friction factor, dimensionless

ρ = density of fluid flowing in pipe, kg/m^3

L = pipe length, m

D = pipe diameter, m

v = velocity, m/s

Water is flowing through a 2-in. diameter pipe, 20 ft long, at 200 ft/min. Calculate the pressure loss if the friction factor is 0.02.

4.21 A new internal combustion engine is installed on a dynamometer to measure the engine's performance. The power, P, is determined by the relationship

$$P = \frac{2\pi nFL}{C}$$

where the constant, C, is 33 000 ft lb/hp min. The force, F, exerted on the 40 cm moment arm, L, is 25 N when n is 3 000 revolutions per minute. Calculate the power in watts.

4.22 Calculate the Reynolds number for air at atmospheric pressure flowing in a pipe with an inside diameter of 2 in., if the viscosity of the air is 0.021 centipoise, the density is 0.075 lb/ft^3, and the velocity is 1 300 cm/s. Reynolds number is defined as

$$\text{Reynolds Number} = \text{Re} = \frac{\rho D v}{\mu}$$

where

ρ = density

D = pipe diameter

v = velocity

μ = viscosity

4.23 Einstein's theory of relativity may be expressed as

$$E = mc^2$$

where E is energy, m is mass, and c is the speed of light. One of the consequences of this theory is that mass may be converted to energy. Calculate the energy equivalent of one kilogram of mass.

4.24 Newton's law of gravitation may be expressed as

$$F = G\frac{m_1 m_2}{r^2}$$

where F is the force of attraction between two bodies of masses m_1 and m_2 separated by a distance r, and G is the gravitational constant.

If m_1 is 50 gm, m_2 is 125 gm, and r is 2.73 m, calculate the force between the two masses.

4.25 Einstein's theory of relativity demonstrates that mass increases with speed, that is

$$m = m_0/[1 - (v/c)^2]^{1/2}$$

where m_0 is the rest mass or mass with respect to the observer, v is the velocity, and c is the speed of light. If a neutron is traveling at .85 c and the rest mass is $1.674\ 74 \times 10^{-24}$ gm, what is the mass of the particle?

REFERENCES

ACKLEY, ROBERT A. *Physical Measurements and the International (SI) System of Units*, Third Edition. San Diego: Technical Publications, 1970.

"AISI Metric Practice Guide: SI Units and Conversion Factors for the Steel Industry." Washington, D.C.: American Iron and Steel Institute, 1975.

BURTON, WILLIAM K., Ed. "Measuring Systems and Standards Organizations." New York: American National Standards Institute, Inc., 1970.

CHISWELL, B., and E. C. M. GRIGGS. *SI Units*. Sydney: John Wiley & Sons, Inc., 1971.

"Conversion to the Metric System of Weights and Measures," Hearings before the Subcommittee on Science, Research, and Technology of the Committee on Science and Technology, U.S. House of Representatives. Washington: U.S. Government Printing Office, 1975.

DE SIMONE, DANIEL V., Ed. *A Metric America: A Decision Whose Time Has Come.* National Bureau of Standards Special Publication 345, July 1971.

MECHTLY, E. A. "The International System of Units: Physical Constants and Conversion Factors," Second Revision. NASA SP-7012, 1973.

"Metric Practice Guide," E 380-72, American Society for Testing and Materials, 1972. (ANSI Z210.1-1973).

PAGE, CHESTER H., and PAUL VIGOUREX, Eds. "The International System of Units (SI)," National Bureau of Standards Special Publication 330, July 1974.

"SI Units and Recommendations for the Use of Their Multiples and of Certain Other Units," International Organization for Standardization, ISO 100, 1973.

STIMSON, H. F. "The International Temperature Scale of 1948," *NBS J. Research*, Vol. 42, March 1949.

Analysis of solar collectors.
(*Courtesy* Copper Development Association, Inc.)

Engineering analysis

All of the finest computational techniques are of little value in solving problems unless the data used in the calculations are reliable.

A small aluminum slug, nominally 2.54 cm in length, was measured by each member of a class of engineering students with the same micrometer. The resulting frequency distribution of measured values is shown by means of a histogram in Figure 5-1. Note that for 25 measurements, there was a wide range of values for length of the aluminum slug.

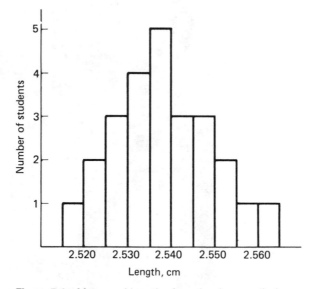

Figure 5-1   Measured length of an aluminum cylinder.

This example demonstrates two points. First, in obtaining data some errors often occur, particularly as a result of the human involvement. There may be incorrect readings, improper use of measuring devices, or perhaps errors in the measuring devices themselves. Second, the range of data shown indicates that there is a need for some means of dealing with data or numerical information if more than a single value is involved.

In order to use measured or computed data in engineering calculations, it is necessary to establish appropriate means both for presenting and for employing these data.

5.1   Notation

When dealing with data, the number of accurate figures or digits, the way in which the data are rounded, and the way in which numbers are written all must be considered.

Significant figures. A significant figure or significant digit is an accurate digit in a numerical value. The number of significant figures in a numerical value (excluding zeros used in locating the decimal point) is the number of digits which may be used with confidence in an engineering computation. Numerical values resulting from precision experimental measurements generally have several significant figures. General measurements, however, such as the distance to town or the area of a room, usually have few significant figures.

EXAMPLE 5-1   The number of significant digits in 0.000 482 is 3 (since the first accurate digit is 4 and there is a total of 3 digits given). The number of significant figures in 6.760 0 is 5 (since the first accurate digit is 6 and the number is specified with 4 decimal places). The number of significant figures in 437 000 may be 3 or more, depending upon the preciseness of the number reported. If the number 437 000 is an exact count, there are 6 significant figures. If, however, the number is approximate, the number of significant figures would be less.

The question arises as to how many significant figures are appropriate for a particular use. For example, when a measurement of $\frac{1}{3}$ meter is made, would 0.33 m be sufficient, or should the decimal equivalent be 0.333 333 333 3 m? When multiplying 2.2 by π (3.141 59), would the answer be 6.911 503 8 or 6.9? The choice of significant figures is important in almost every engineering computation. Generally the number of significant figures used in a calculation or reported in a result should be no more than the minimum number of significant figures in the other numerical values involved in the calculation. That is, when performing a calculation involving three values such as 3.717 4, 97.119 257 3, and 0.918, one would use three significant figures both in the calculation and in reporting the result since one of the numbers has only three significant figures.

EXAMPLE 5-2   In a road test, an automobile travels 222.0 kilometers on 16.137 liters of gasoline. What is the performance of the automobile in terms of km/ℓ? The answer is 222.0 ÷ 16.1, and is approximately 13.8 km/ℓ.

Rounding numbers. The manner in which calculated numbers are rounded contributes to the overall accuracy of the solution. Significant figures may be truncated or rounded up. A number is generally rounded up if the digit following the cut is 5 or greater, and left the same if the digit following the cut is 0 to 4.

EXAMPLE 5-3 The following numbers are to be rounded to two significant figures to the right of the decimal.

438.569 is rounded to 438.57
52.694 3 is rounded to 52.69
919.365 is rounded to 919.37
27.195 is rounded to 27.20

Scientific notation. Calculations involving very large or very small numbers may easily be performed by using scientific notation. For such notation, the significant digits (excluding zeros immediately preceding or following the decimal) are retained, and the numerical value is reported as a number between 1 and 10 multiplied by 10 to a power. Scientific notation may be written as $C \times 10^n$ or C E n.

EXAMPLE 5-4 Rewrite the following numbers in scientific notation:

36 720 000.   may be written as 3.672×10^7
              (3.672 E07)
79 010.   may be written as 7.901×10^4
              (7.901 E04)
0.000 004 728   may be written as 4.728×10^{-6}
              (4.728 E-06)

The use of powers of 10 simplifies many computations, since multiplication of numbers with powers of 10 is performed by adding the exponents, and division of numbers with powers of 10 is performed by subtracting the exponents. Scientific notation, then, facilitates the solution of many engineering problems.

Logarithms. Two types of logarithms are used in engineering operations: the common logarithm (log to the base 10), and the natural or Naperian logarithm (log to the base e, where the value of e is approximately 2.718). The common logarithm (abbreviated $\log_{10}$, or more commonly, log) is a number composed of a characteristic, placed on the left of the decimal, and a mantissa on the right. The characteristic portion of the logarithm ($\log_{10}$) for a number greater than 1.0 is positive and one less than the number of digits to the left of the decimal (e.g., the characteristic of 376 is 2). The characteristic portion of a logarithm ($\log_{10}$) of a number less than 1.0 is negative and is equal to the number of zeros to the right of the decimal (e.g., the characteristic of 0.000 274 is -3). The mantissa portion of the logarithm ($\log_{10}$) is the fractional part of the logarithm representing the specific number for which the $\log_{10}$ is obtained.

Natural logarithms, or logarithms to the base e (abbreviated $\log_e$, or more commonly, ln), are used in many engineering computations. These natural logarithms are related to logarithms to the base 10 as follows:

$$\log_{10} x = \log_e x / \log_e 10 = \ln x / \ln 10$$

Thus

$$\ln x = \ln 10 \cdot \log x$$

$$\ln x = 2.302\ 585 \log x$$

Logarithms often are used in engineering analyses and frequently are an integral part of problem solutions.

5.2 Errors and uncertainty

Most engineering problems involve the use of experimental data or measurements of some form. Several types of errors may be associated with the accumulation or collection of these data. A careful problem solver may find that most of the error involved in a problem's solution will result not from computational error, but from errors in the experimental or computed values used in the calculation.

The error in an experimental measurement is defined as the true value of the quantity minus the measured value of the quantity, that is

$$\text{Error} = \text{True value} - \text{Measured value}$$

The error has units and can have either a positive or negative sign, depending upon the magnitude of the measured value. The fractional error is the error divided by the true value, that is

$$\text{Fractional Error} = \frac{\text{Error}}{\text{True value}}$$

The percent error is the error divided by the true value multiplied by 100%, or the fractional error multiplied by 100%.

$$\text{Percent Error} = \frac{\text{Error}}{\text{True value}}(100\%)$$

The determination of errors requires that all quantities be in the same units. A two centimeter error in a measurement of one meter is really a 0.02 meter error or a 2 percent error.

EXAMPLE 5-5   A football coach is concerned that a recently finished football field is too long and asks an assistant to measure the length of the field. The assistant reports that the measured length is 91 meters exactly.

The true length of the field should be 91.44 meters, thus the field is 44 centimeters too short. What is the percent error?

$$\text{Error} = 91.44 \text{ meters} - 91.00 \text{ meters} = 0.44 \text{ meters}$$

$$\text{Fractional Error} = \frac{0.44}{91.44} = 0.004 \ 8 \text{ or } \frac{1}{208}$$

$$\text{Percent Error} = (0.004 \ 8)(100\%) = 0.48\%$$

The football field is too short by about $\frac{1}{2}\%$.

An error in a measurement may be determined when the true value of the measurement is known. There are many occasions in engineering, however, when the true value of a measurement is unknown or not available, and only measured values are known. In this situation, a value for the error is estimated, and this estimated error is termed the *uncertainty*. The uncertainty in a measurement, then, represents what the error might be if a true value were known. The uncertainty generally is determined by statistical means and is written in the form

(measured value) ± (uncertainty)

If experimental or computed data are provided for use in a calculation, the problem solver can do little but assume that the data are valid and proceed to use them for computation. If, however, the error or uncertainty is available or can be determined, the problem solver should ascertain what effect this uncertainty will have on the calculated results.

For example, if a numerical value such as 2.5 is provided for a calculation, the number should be used directly. If, however, the data are reported as 2.5 with an uncertainty of ±0.5 (i.e., 2.5 ± 0.5), the calculation should be performed with the upper limit (3.0) and the lower limit (2.0), as well as the base value (2.5). The problem solver can then see what effect the uncertainty will have on the results.

EXAMPLE 5-6 Suppose a problem involved the calculation of kinetic energy, i.e.,

$$KE = 1/2\, m\, v^2$$

where $m = 2$ kg and $v = 2.5 \pm 0.5$ m/s. The resulting calculations would be:

for $v = 2.0$ m/s $KE = 4.0$ kg m^2/s^2 (36% error)

for $v = 2.5$ m/s $KE = 6.3$ kg m^2/s^2

for $v = 3.0$ m/s $KE = 9.0$ kg m^2/s^2 (−43% error)

In this case, the percent error in kinetic energy, resulting from the uncertainty, is determined by treating the base value (2.5 m/s) as the true value and the values calculated for the upper and lower limits (2.5 + 0.5 m/s and 2.5 − 0.5 m/s) as the measured values. The answer calculated with the base value is subtracted from the other answers, and these results are divided by the base value answer and multiplied by 100%. Clearly the result of the uncertainty here is substantial and greatly affects the overall solution.

The effect of uncertainties or errors in data used in problems requiring computation can be substantial. The problem solver should try to assess the reliability of data used in order to assure himself of the validity of the answers calculated.

There are more refined techniques for evaluating and dealing with uncertainties, and references which describe these techniques are listed at the end of the chapter.

5.3 Statistical analysis of data

When problems involve a set of data, one must learn how to analyze these data mathematically for use in engineering calculations. Suppose, as in the example at the beginning of the chapter, that a number of measurements of the same variable have been made at the same test conditions, and a range of values results. The problem solver must then determine which value should be chosen for use in the calculation and what error should be assigned to the selected value. In order to analyze such data, we must understand statistical concepts such as the average or mean, median, deviation, mean deviation, standard deviation, and variance. Knowledge of these terms will assist the problem solver in selecting which data to use in engineering problems.

Mean or average. The mean, sometimes referred to as the arithmetic average, is the summation of the experimentally measured or computed values divided by the number of measured or computed values. In equation form

$$\text{arithmetic mean or average} = \bar{x} = \frac{1}{n}(x_1 + x_2 + x_3 + \cdots + x_n)$$

$$= \frac{1}{n}\sum_{i=1}^{n} x_i$$

The arithmetic mean or average is the value which most closely represents the true value and is generally used in engineering calculations.

The more data that are used in calculating the mean, the more representative the mean value becomes. The number of significant digits in the mean value, however, stays the same regardless of the number of data points used.

EXAMPLE 5-7 An experimental test of the energy dissipation by fuel rods in nuclear reactors is to be conducted using a single element of a fuel rod under controlled test conditions. This element is fabricated from a zircalloy tube loaded with 20 uranium oxide fuel pellets. In order to ascertain the energy dissipation per gram of uranium oxide, the mass of each pellet was determined in grams as

25.1	25.3	24.9	24.8	24.6
25.0	25.4	25.0	25.2	24.8
24.8	24.7	24.9	25.2	25.1
25.1	25.0	24.9	25.0	24.9

These data are presented in a distribution curve in Figure 5-2.

Instead of arbitrarily selecting one of these values for use in the computations, the problem solver should determine and use the mean value, i.e.,

$$\bar{x} = \tfrac{1}{20}(25.1 + 25.0 + 24.8 + \cdots + 24.9) = 24.985 \text{ gm}$$

Since the data are reported to one significant digit to the right of the decimal, the mean should be rounded to reflect the same accuracy, therefore

$$\bar{x} = 25.0 \text{ gm}$$

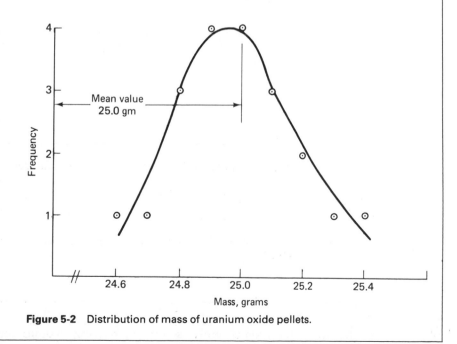

Figure 5-2 Distribution of mass of uranium oxide pellets.

Deviation.   The deviation in a data point is the difference between the value of the individual data point and the mean, or

$$\text{deviation} \quad d_1 = x_1 - \bar{x}$$
$$d_2 = x_2 - \bar{x}$$
$$\begin{matrix} \cdot & \cdot & \cdot \\ \cdot & \cdot & \cdot \\ \cdot & \cdot & \cdot \end{matrix}$$
$$d_n = x_n - \bar{x}$$

In the previous example (5-7), the deviation for the first data point would be $25.1 - 25.0 = 0.1$ gm; for the second, $25.0 - 25.0 = 0.0$ gm, etc.

The deviation, then, varies for each data point.

Mean Deviation.   The mean deviation is the arithmetic average of the absolute values of the deviations of each data point, divided by the number of data points, i.e.,

$$\text{mean deviation} = \bar{d} = \frac{|d_1| + |d_2| + |d_3| + \cdots + |d_n|}{n}$$

$$= \frac{1}{n} \sum_{i=1}^{n} |x_i - \bar{x}|$$

For the uranium fuel pellet example (5-7), the mean deviation is

$$\bar{d} = \tfrac{1}{20}(|0.1| + |0.0| + |-0.2| + \cdots + |-0.1|)$$

$$= 0.155$$

This answer also should be rounded to one significant digit to the right of the decimal, therefore

$$\bar{d} = 0.2$$

The mean deviation is rarely used in engineering computations.

Standard Deviation. The standard deviation, like the mean deviation, is a method of determining probable error. The standard deviation, or root mean square deviation, is defined as

$$\text{standard deviation} = \sigma = \left(\frac{(d_1)^2 + (d_2)^2 + (d_3)^2 + \cdots + (d_n)^2}{n} \right)^{1/2}$$

$$= \left(\frac{1}{n} \sum_{i=1}^{n} (x_i - \bar{x})^2 \right)^{1/2}$$

Again, for the case of the uranium pellet example (5-7), the standard deviation for the mass of the uranium pellets becomes

$$\sigma = \left(\frac{(0.1)^2 + (0.0)^2 + (-0.2)^2 + \cdots + (-0.1)^2}{20} \right)^{1/2}$$

$\sigma = 0.196$ gm and is rounded to 0.2 gm.

The standard deviation is, in this case, equal to the mean deviation.

In engineering calculations, the standard deviation is the value most often used as the uncertainty.

Variance. The variance of a data set is the measure of the degree of change in the data, or the spread of the data. The variance is calculated as the square of the standard deviation, i.e.,

$$\text{variance} = \sigma^2 = \frac{1}{n} \sum_{i=1}^{n} (x_i - \bar{x})^2$$

In the case of the set of uranium pellet data,

$$\sigma^2 = (0.2)^2 = 0.04$$

Median. The median is the value of the data point in the middle of a data set, halfway between the highest and lowest value.

> In the case of the uranium pellet example (5-7), the median is 25.0 gm. The median serves as an estimate of the pellet mass, and usually is close in value to the average or mean value.

The median is frequently used in reporting a variety of data. Information on salaries, for example, often is given in terms of the median, the upper and lower quartiles (25%), and the upper and lower deciles (10%).

Mode. The mode is the value of the data point which appears most frequently in the set of data. The mode of the data may be determined by counting the number of times each data point of given magnitude occurs.

> In the case of the uranium pellet example (5-7), the values of 24.9 gm and 25.0 gm both occur an equal number of times. This data set, therefore, has two modes and may be called bimodal.
>
> To summarize example (5-7), the uranium oxide fuel pellets exhibit the following characteristics:
>
> $$\text{Mean or average} \quad \bar{x} = 24.985 \simeq 25.0 \text{ gm}$$
>
> $$\text{Mean deviation} \quad \bar{d} = 0.155 \simeq 0.2 \text{ gm}$$
>
> $$\text{Standard deviation } \sigma = 0.196 \simeq 0.2 \text{ gm}$$
>
> $$\text{Variance} \quad \sigma^2 = 0.2^2 = 0.04 \text{ gm}$$
>
> $$\text{Median} \quad = 25.0 \text{ gm}$$
>
> $$\text{Mode (bimodal)} \quad = 24.9 \text{ and } 25.0 \text{ gm}$$
>
> These characteristics may be shown more clearly on a plot of the data, as shown in Figure 5-3. It is interesting to note that all of the data occur within two standard deviations of the mean, and that the mean and median are essentially the same.

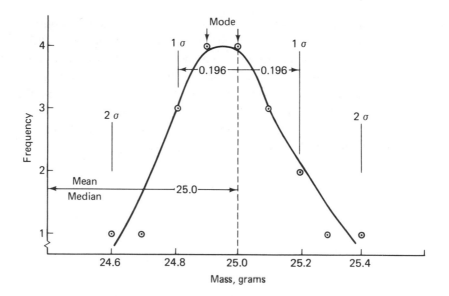

Figure 5-3 Graphical representation of the statistical characteristics of Example 5-7.

Other computational tools for the statistical treatment of data (such as the harmonic mean, root mean square, and so on) also may be used in engineering computations. The use of these statistical methods of treating data will permit a more thorough evaluation of information for accurate problem solving.

5.4 Probability

The concept of probability is not new, but has been used for assessing the odds in games of chance (such as cards, dice, and roulette) for several centuries. In 1654 Pascal developed the foundation for the theory of probability as we know it today.

In mathematics, probability is a precisely defined value indicating the chance or odds of the occurrence of a specific answer or event. It may also be defined as a ratio of the number of ways an event or answer can occur to the total number of ways that it can or cannot occur.

Consider an event z which may or may not occur within a certain number of trials. The probability, $P(z)$, that event z will occur has the limits of 0 to 1; that is, the event may not occur at all, it may possibly occur, or it may occur with certainty. These limits may be written more formally

$$0 \leq P(z) \leq 1$$

When the event definitely will not occur, then the probability $P(z)$ is 0, and when the event definitely will occur, then the probability $P(z)$ is 1.

There are occasions when more than one event may occur during a certain number of trials. These events may be mutually exclusive, i.e., they cannot occur at the same time, or they may not be mutually exclusive and may occur simultaneously. For situations where there are two mutually exclusive events, event X and event Y, the probability that either event X or event Y will occur may be written as

$$P(X \text{ or } Y) = P(X) + P(Y) \qquad (X \text{ and } Y \text{ mutually exclusive})$$

For those situations in which events are not mutually exclusive, the probability that either event X or event Y (but not both) will occur may be written as

$$P(X \text{ or } Y) = P(X) + P(Y) - P(X \text{ and } Y) \qquad (X \text{ and } Y \text{ not mutually exclusive})$$

These expressions are forms of the *addition rule*.

When event X and event Y are independent (that is, in situations where the occurrence of one event does not influence the likelihood of the occurrence of the other), the probability of both events occurring simultaneously is expressed as

$$P(X \text{ and } Y) = P(X)P(Y) \qquad (X \text{ and } Y \text{ independent})$$

This is termed the *multiplication rule*. When events X and Y are not independent (that is, when the occurrence of one event influences the likelihood of the occurrence of the other), the probability that both X and Y will occur is the probability of X times the probability of Y when X has occurred, or

$$P(X \text{ and } Y) = P(X)P(Y/X)$$

This expression defines the conditional probability $P(Y/X)$ and is another form of the multiplication rule.

EXAMPLE 5-8   In order to know how to wager in a game of dice, one would be wise to determine the probabilities that certain combinations of numbers will occur when the dice are rolled. (Let us assume that the dice are not loaded and have not been modified in any way.)

Suppose one is interested in rolling one or more 6's with a pair of dice. Let X represent a 6 on one die and Y a 6 on the other die. The probability $P(X)$ or $P(6)$ is $\frac{1}{6}$ for one die (since there are six sides, each with one of the numbers 1 through 6). There is, then, one chance in 6 that a 6 will occur. The same explanation applies to the second die, i.e., $P(Y) = P(6) = \frac{1}{6}$.

The chance that at least one 6 will occur when two dice are thrown follows the addition rule:

$$P(X \text{ or } Y) = \frac{1}{6} + \frac{1}{6} = \frac{1}{3}$$

The chance of rolling at least one 6 is one in three. The probability of rolling one and only one 6 in a single roll of two dice would be figured thus:

$$P(X \text{ or } Y) = \frac{1}{6} + \frac{1}{6} - \frac{1}{36} = \frac{11}{36}$$

The chance of rolling only one 6, then, is slightly less than one in three.

Since each die is independent, the probability of rolling a double six follows the multiplication rule

$$P(X \text{ and } Y) = P(6 \text{ and } 6) = \left(\frac{1}{6}\right)\left(\frac{1}{6}\right) = \frac{1}{36}$$

That is, there is one chance in 36 of obtaining a double six in a single roll of two dice.

There are, of course, other probabilities which may be calculated. The reader is referred to the references at the end of the chapter for a more detailed analysis of probabilities.

5.5   Normal distribution

In engineering, as we have noted, a set of data obtained at similar test conditions may result in a range of answers. These answers or measured values may be analyzed in terms of the number of answers that are the same, that is, the frequency with which similar measured values are obtained. These measured values may be plotted in terms of a histogram (see Figure 5-1) or a frequency distribution curve (see Figure 5-2). As the number of measurements approaches infinity, the frequency distribution of the data will usually approach a symmetrical bell-shaped curve about the mean, as shown in Figure 5-4. This bell-shaped curve generally is called the normal distribution curve or the Gaussian distribution curve.

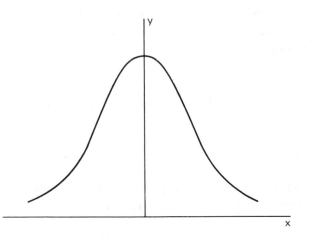

Figure 5-4   Normal distribution curve.

The normal distribution curve is an idealized frequency distribution curve in which the mean, mode, and median coincide. This curve may be represented mathematically as

$$y(x) = \frac{1}{\sigma\sqrt{2\pi}}\, e^{-(x-\bar{x})^2/2\sigma^2}$$

where σ is the standard deviation and $\bar{x}$ is the mean. The curve is more peaked for small standard deviations, and becomes rather flat as the value for σ becomes large.

The normal distribution curve is particularly useful in determining the proportion of data which fall within a given distance of the mean. No matter how peaked or flat the curve, regardless of the magnitude of the mean or standard deviation involved, a given proportion of the data will fall within a given interval in terms of standard deviations from the mean. For example, 68.26% of the data will occur within one standard deviation on either side of the mean (Figure 5-5). More than 95% of the data will be included within

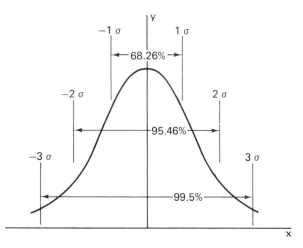

Figure 5-5 Normal distribution curve with standard deviation increments.

two standard deviations on either side of the mean, and more than 99% of the data will be included within three standard deviations.

As previously noted, the mean is the value which is generally used in engineering calculations to approximate the true value, and the standard deviation is the value which is generally used to approximate the uncertainty. The normal distribution curve demonstrates the propriety of these approximations.

5.6 Graphical analysis

Mathematical determination of the statistical characteristics of a set of data does not always provide sufficient insight. For this reason, there is frequently a need to present numerical data in other forms for easier interpretation and/or for nontechnical audiences. Graphical presentation of data, or use of the line graph, simplifies the determination of trends and characteristics of the data set.

Several coordinate systems may be used in the graphical presentation of data. Among these are Cartesian or rectangular coordinate system, semilogarithmic, and logarithmic coordinate systems. Cartesian coordinates, frequently called x-y coordinates, are formed by two intersecting perpendicular straight lines (x and y) with equidistant divisions in both directions. The independent variable generally is plotted on the horizontal (x) axis or abscissa, and the dependent variable is plotted along the vertical (y) axis or ordinate. Logarithmic graphs also are formed by intersecting perpendicular straight lines, however the divisions are in terms of logarithmic distances. Again, the axes are referred to as the abscissa and the ordinate. The log-log coordinate system is composed of logarithmic intervals in both the x and y directions. The semilog coordinate system has logarithmic intervals in one direction and rectangular intervals in the other. Other coordinate systems such as polar and hyperbolic are used occasionally in engineering graphical analysis.

Thorough graphical analysis of engineering data requires the development of techniques for fitting straight or curved lines through these data, as well as for interpolating (estimating values between consecutive terms in a series of data) and extrapolating (estimating values beyond the range of the data) values.

Curve fitting.   For some analyses, data points are plotted on Cartesian coordinates. For engineering data, x (the abscissa) is plotted horizontally and is generally the independent variable, and y (the ordinate) is plotted vertically and is the dependent variable.

In order to analyze the trends of the data, it may be necessary to represent the data by a single line. In some cases an approximation to the data, or a "best fit" straight line, may be drawn through the data by hand. This best fit line generally is sufficiently accurate to permit estimation of trends and prediction of performance, unless the data are widely scattered. There are times, however, when it is necessary to develop an equation for use in calculations. The equation for a straight line, shown in Figure 5-6, is

$$y = mx + b$$

where m is the slope of the line and b is the y intercept. The expression for

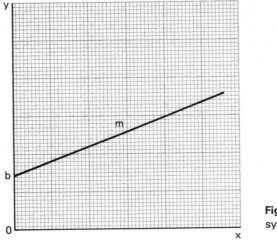

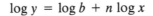

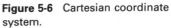

Figure 5-6 Cartesian coordinate system.

the straight line may be obtained from the best fit line by determining values for m and b from the graph.

Data often are plotted on logarithmic coordinate systems to facilitate analysis. Log-log coordinates are particularly useful for those data sets which exhibit some scatter and curvature on rectangular coordinates. Data exhibiting a straight line when plotted on log-log coordinates (Figure 5-7) may be represented by an equation of the form

$$\log y = \log b + n \log x$$

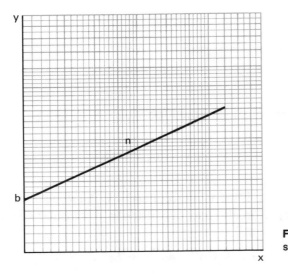

Figure 5-7 Log-log coordinate system.

The slope of the line through the data is represented by n, and b is the intercept on the y axis. These values may be determined directly from the graph. This equation for the line through the data also may be written in rectangular coordinates as

$$y = bx^n$$

Occasionally there are sets of data which exhibit a straight line when plotted on semilogarithmic coordinates (Figure 5-8). These data may be

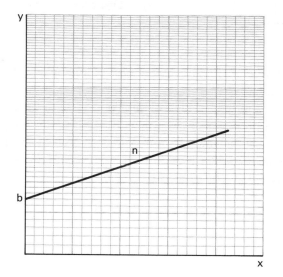

Figure 5-8 Semilog coordinate system.

represented by an equation of the form

$$\log y = \log b + nx$$

For this expression, b is the y intercept and n is the slope of the line through the data. This equation also may be written in rectangular coordinates as

$$y = b(10)^{nx} \quad \text{or} \quad y = be^{2.302\ 585nx}$$

EXAMPLE 5-9   The performance of a centrifugal fan may be analyzed in the following manner, assuming that a fixed wheel diameter and orifice are used. As the fan speed increases, the volume of air handled varies directly with the speed; the delivery pressure varies as the square of the speed; and the power required for the fan motor varies as the cube of the speed, that is

$$\text{Volume capacity, m}^3/\text{min} = f_1 \, (\text{rpm})^1$$

$$\text{Delivery pressure, N/m}^2 = f_2 \, (\text{rpm})^2$$

$$\text{Power required, watts} = f_3 \, (\text{rpm})^3$$

where f_1, f_2, f_3 represent functions.

The speed or rpm of the fan, then, is an independent variable which is an important factor in the overall performance of the fan. When data for fan performance tests are obtained (such as volume flow rate, pressure, and power), these data may be plotted on Cartesian coordinates as shown in Figure 5-9. The determination of an equation for a curve through these data, for use in analysis, would be difficult.

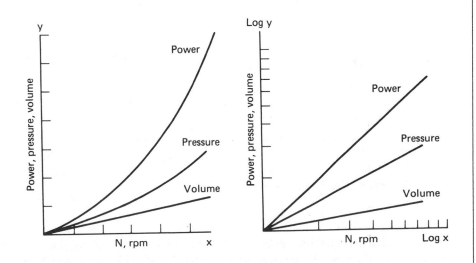

Figure 5-9 Schematic of Cartesian and log-log plots of fan performance.

When these performance data are plotted on log-log coordinates, however, it is easy to ascertain the slope of the line through the data. The resulting values for the slopes may then be compared with the expected performance, as shown in Figure 5-9. Generally, the exponent or slope of the pressure curve is slightly greater than 2, and the exponent or slope of the horsepower curve may be substantially less than 3 if the drive belt and bearing losses are included in the overall power requirements. Analysis of these data, then, is simplified through the use of log-log coordinates.

Interpolation.   The determination of values for data between data points is termed *interpolation.* For example, if two data points ($x_1 = 1$, $y_1 = 30$; $x_2 = 2$, $y_2 = 12$) are given, how would one determine a value for y when $x = 1.5$? A straight line or linear interpolation would involve construction

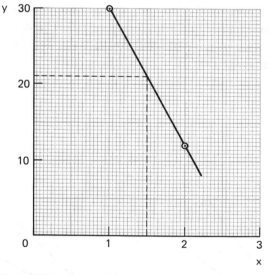

Figure 5-10   Interpolation.

of a straight line between the data points and noting the value of y when $x = 1.5$ on the straight line (Figure 5-10). This result also may be obtained by ratio without graphical construction. The procedure for determining the ratio is

$$
\begin{array}{cc}
x & y \\
1.0\begin{pmatrix}1.0 \\ 1.5 \\ 2.0\end{pmatrix}.5 & \Delta y\begin{pmatrix}30 \\ ? \\ 12\end{pmatrix}18
\end{array}
$$

$$\frac{.5}{1} = \frac{\Delta y}{18}; \qquad \Delta y = 9; \qquad y = 12 + 9 = 21$$

Thus when x is 1.5, the value of y is 21.

Interpolation is frequently used to obtain data from engineering tables for use in the solution of problems. There may be occasions when data are such that linear interpolation is not possible and graphical means, using curves, would be helpful. There are also analytical techniques for nonlinear interpolation.

Extrapolation. Determining values for data that lie outside the range of the set of data is termed *extrapolation*. For example, the performance characteristics of an engine from 0 to 3 000 rpm may be known, and an estimate of performance at 3 500 rpm may be desired. Extension of the data will permit a reasonable estimate of performance at the higher rpm.

Graphical straight line extrapolation involves the same procedure as interpolation (Figure 5-11). If two data points ($x_1 = 1$, $y_1 = 10$; $x_2 = 2$,

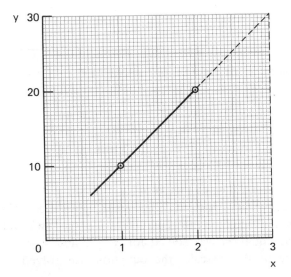

Figure 5-11 Extrapolation.

$y_2 = 20$) are given, a value for y when $x = 3$ may be determined by developing a straight line through the data points and noting the value of y at the point $x = 3$.

A word of caution: extrapolation should be handled with care. Without using common sense, it would be easy to extrapolate values beyond the range of physical reality.

Nomographs.   In some analyses of data, there is a need to evaluate several equations involving different variables. Although such an evaluation may be done numerically, there is a graphical technique that readily provides the answer. The nomograph is a series of scales of dependent functions which are related to an independent scale such that line interpolations may be made. A nomograph may be a simple comparison between two different parallel scales, such as the Celsius and Fahrenheit scales shown in Table 4.3. A horizontal line drawn from 100° on the vertical Celsius scale would intersect the vertical Fahrenheit scale at 212°. The nomograph may be more complex, to permit the determination of such variables as the property values of material alloys at varying conditions.

The parallel scale nomograph, or alignment chart, may be used quite easily for three variables by means of three parallel vertical scales. The scale divisions are established in terms of the given equations and/or independent variables. The desired quantity or result is determined from the third scale by drawing a straight line between the two independent variables and reading the result on the dependent variable scale.

EXAMPLE 5-10 A nomograph for the solution of the equation

$$3x + 2y = z, \quad \begin{cases} 1 \le x \le 4 \\ 10 \le y \le 20 \end{cases}$$

is constructed as shown in Figure 5-12.

In order to construct the nomograph, several combinations of variables were calculated mathematically. For the lower value of the z scale, the equation was solved for $x = 1$ and $y = 10$. For the upper value of the z scale, the equation was solved for $x = 4$,

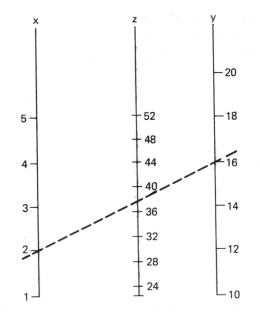

Figure 5-12 Nomograph for the solution of the equation $3x + 2y = z$.

$y = 20$. A z scale was then located so that a straight line drawn from 1 on the x scale to 10 on the y scale intersects the z scale at some point which was designated 23. Similarly, a straight line between $x = 4$ and $y = 20$ intersects the z scale at a point designated 52. The z scale was then calibrated in appropriate increments between the upper limit of 52 and the lower limit of 23. Once the z scale has been established, the value of z may be obtained for any values of x and y within the limits given simply by drawing a straight line between x and y and noting the z intercept. For example, when $x = 2$ and $y = 16$, the straight line will intersect the z scale at 38.

5.7 Numerical analysis

Often there are many scattered data points within a data set, making graphical analysis of the trends complicated. In these instances, numerical techniques such as a least-squares analysis will permit the accurate determination of an equation of a curve to represent the data. A least-squares analysis minimizes the sum of the squares of the difference between the data points and the calculated curve through the data, as shown in Figure 5-13.

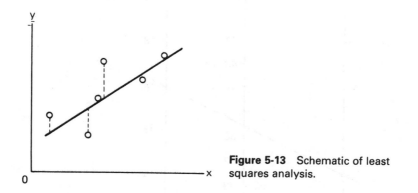

Figure 5-13 Schematic of least squares analysis.

Least-squares analyses may be performed for large quantities of data. This technique of data analysis results in a polynomial equation which is the most representative curve through the data. The general form of the equation is

$$y = A_0 + A_1x + A_2x^2 + A_3x^3 + \cdots + A_nx^n$$

The values for A_0, A_1, $\cdots$ are determined by simultaneous solution of the equations

$$\Sigma y = A_0m + A_1\Sigma x + A_2\Sigma x^2 \cdots$$

$$\Sigma xy = A_0\Sigma x + A_1\Sigma x^2 + A_2\Sigma x^3 \cdots$$

$$\Sigma x^2y = A_0\Sigma x^2 + A_1\Sigma x^3 + A_2\Sigma x^4 \cdots$$
$$\vdots \qquad \vdots \qquad \vdots \qquad \vdots$$

when n represents the order of the desired curve fit equation. The total number of data points, m, involved in the analysis must be at least one greater than the order of the desired curve fit.

For a first-order or straight-line analysis of a data set, the polynomial equation becomes

$$y = A_0 + A_1x$$

and the simultaneous equations are

$$\Sigma y = A_0 m + A_1 \Sigma x$$

$$\Sigma xy = A_0 \Sigma x + A_1 \Sigma x^2$$

In order to minimize the sum of the differences between the data points and the calculated polynomial curve, it is necessary to take the derivative of the sum and set it equal to zero. Therefore, to determine A_1, the sum is differentiated with respect to A_1 and set equal to zero. In the same manner the derivative of the sum is taken with respect to A_0 and set equal to zero. The resulting values for A_1 and A_0 permit the determination of a best fit line. For m data points, each with coordinates x and y,

$$A_1 = \frac{m\Sigma xy - \Sigma x \Sigma y}{m\Sigma x^2 - (\Sigma x)^2}$$

$$A_0 = \frac{\Sigma x^2 \Sigma y - \Sigma x \Sigma xy}{m\Sigma x^2 - (\Sigma x)^2}$$

The resulting equation for the straight line may be written using the calculated values of A_1 and A_0. The first order least squares analysis, then, is relatively straightforward and may be performed easily.

EXAMPLE 5-11 For the following set of data, use the least squares method to determine the first order equation that will represent the data

x	y
1.0	1.5
2.0	3.0
3.0	3.5
4.0	4.5
5.0	7.0
6.0	7.5

The equation for the line is

$$y = A_0 + A_1 x$$

(The constants A_0 and A_1 are defined above.)

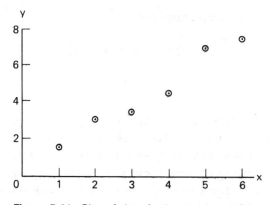

Figure 5-14 Plot of data for least squares fit.

A calculation table would simplify the problem solution:

x	y	xy	x^2
1	1.5	1.5	1
2	3.0	6.0	4
3	3.5	10.5	9
4	4.5	18.0	16
5	7.0	35.0	25
6	7.5	45.0	36
$\Sigma x = 21$	$\Sigma y = 27$	$\Sigma xy = 116$	$\Sigma x^2 = 91$

Then

$$A_0 = \frac{(91)(27) - (21)(116)}{(6)(91) - (21)^2} = 0.2$$

$$A_1 = \frac{(6)(116) - (21)(27)}{(6)(91) - (21)^2} = 1.229$$

Then

$$y = A_0 + A_1 x = 0.2 + 1.2\,x$$

This equation is useful for the range $1 \le x \le 6$ and may be extrapolated further.

There are occasions when a set of data is not conducive to a straight line analysis. Higher-order least-squares analyses may be used for these cases in order to establish an equation for a curve which will best fit the data. Solution to the simultaneous equations for higher-order polynomials is complicated, but there are numerous techniques for performing such analyses on digital computers.

5.8 Summary

When engineering calculations involve the use of data consisting of more than a single data point, statistical treatment of those data is necessary. The problem solver must be able to deal with uncertainties and errors, and to determine representative quantities for use in calculations. The development of statistical and graphical techniques for analysis of these data is essential to the accurate solution of problems and meaningful presentation of results.

PROBLEMS **5.1** Determine the number of significant figures for the following values:

(a) 728.4

(b) 0.002 40

(c) 12.617

(d) 0.090 04

(e) 59 000 000

(f) 27.3×10^{-2}

(g) 9.106×10^{6}

(h) $3.141\ 57 \times 10^{-3}$

(i) $1.100\ 0 \times 10^{12}$

(j) 8.5×10^{4}

5.2 Rewrite the following numbers in scientific notation.

(a) 347 500

(b) 0.000 179

(c) 94 000 000

(d) 275.281

(e) 41 500

(f) 0.000 000 002 97

(g) 794 250 000 000 0

(h) 1.478 000 0

(i) 0.008 800 0

(j) 0.060

5.3 Calculate the following and round the results to the appropriate number of significant figures.

(a) $(3.7 \times 10^{-4})(5\ 970)$

(b) $(0.017\ 06)(42.3)$

(c) $(22.7)/(12)$

(d) $(0.000\ 62)/(3.7 \times 10^{-4})$

(e) $(2)(3.141\ 57)$

(f) $(47.36)(0.054)$

(g) $(73.247)(1.577 \times 10^{-2})$

(h) $(0.000\ 059)/(2.3)$

(i) $(1.92 \times 10^{-7})/(1.176\ 9)$

(j) $(2.708)/(1.4 \times 10^{-1})$

5.4 Perform the following operations, round the answers, and present the results in scientific notation:

(a) $(54\ 914)(0.781)$ (f) $(2.58 \times 10^{-2})(0.000\ 398)$

(b) $(2.73)(6.91 \times 10^{-3})$ (g) $(22.2)(1.728 \times 10^{2})(31)$

(c) $(0.009\ 17)(0.0025)$ (h) $(0.000\ 006\ 4)(14 \times 10^{-6})$

(d) $(6.527 \times 10^{6})(3\ 195 \times 10^{6})$ (i) $(927\ 520\ 5)(246\ 151\ 0)$

(e) $(327\ 842)(14.1 \times 10^{-2})$ (j) $(2 \times 10^{-3})(7.28 \times 10^{4})$

5.5 Newton's second law states that the force exerted by an object is equal to the mass of the object multiplied by its acceleration, or

$$F = ma$$

If the acceleration of an object is reported to be 3.3 ± 0.2 meters/s^2, and the mass is 50 kilograms, what are the fractional error and the percent error in the force?

5.6 The distance traveled by an automobile moving at constant velocity during an increment of time is

$$s = vt$$

where s is distance, v is velocity, and t is time. If the velocity is 80 ± 2 km/hr and the time is 30 min, what are the fractional error and percent error in the distance traveled?

5.7 Calculate the arithmetic mean and standard deviation for the following set of numbers

$$4\quad 2\quad 4\quad 7\quad 5\quad 6\quad 5\quad 8\quad 6\quad 9$$
$$8\quad 5\quad 7\quad 3\quad 6\quad 2\quad 5\quad 1\quad 4\quad 5$$

5.8 For the following set of numbers,

$$21\quad 25\quad 30\quad 20\quad 24\quad 19\quad 23\quad 18$$
$$29\quad 31\quad 26\quad 32\quad 27\quad 22\quad 28\quad 25$$

determine the arithmetic mean, mean deviation, standard deviation, variance, median, and mode.

5.9 The grades on a recent final examination were reported as follows:

$$80\quad 89\quad 82\quad 87\quad 75$$
$$52\quad 71\quad 71\quad 92\quad 79$$
$$77\quad 80\quad 64\quad 96\quad 91$$
$$67\quad 81\quad 85\quad 73\quad 84$$

Calculate the arithmetic mean, the median, and the standard deviation.

5.10 For the following set of numbers

$$1.321\quad 1.56\quad 1.493\quad\quad 1.9\quad 1.25\quad\quad 1.68$$
$$1.13\quad\quad 1.1\quad\quad 1.897\ 4\quad 2.1\quad 2.176\quad 1.25$$

determine the arithmetic mean, mean deviation, standard deviation, variance, median, and mode. (Remember to consider significant figures and rounding.)

5.11 A machine shop has been fabricating pistons for the manufacturer of small engines. A recent quality control check of 20 pistons resulted in the following measurements (in centimeters).

6.301	6.289	6.285	6.291	6.290
6.291	6.279	6.277	6.282	6.272
6.269	6.289	2.296	6.286	6.296
6.268	6.278	6.279	6.300	6.288

Calculate the arithmetic mean, the mean deviation, the standard deviation, the variance, and the median. Do you think the machine shop maintains good quality control over its product?

5.12 In order to determine the density of a teflon sample nominally 1 in. in diameter and 1 in. in length, the sample was measured 15 times. The resulting data are

Trial	*Mass, gm*	*Length, in.*	*Diameter, in.*
1	27.65	0.996 6	1.001 4
2	27.64	1.000 0	1.002 0
3	27.65	0.999 9	1.000 3
4	27.63	0.999 6	1.000 7
5	27.645	0.999 5	1.000 6
6	27.64	0.998 4	1.001 6
7	27.635	0.996 7	1.002 5
8	27.645	0.996 9	1.001 9
9	27.642	0.997 0	1.001 7
10	27.64	0.997 5	1.002 0
11	27.64	0.998 6	1.002 9
12	27.633	0.998 1	1.001 5
13	27,645	0.998 9	1.002 5
14	27.633	0.998 5	1.002 0
15	27.65	0.997 0	1.002 0

Calculate the mean density in g/cm^3 and the standard deviation.

5.13 What would be the probability of rolling a total of 7 with a single roll of a pair of dice?

5.14 You, your friend, and 430 others have applied for sophomore dormitory housing. This housing consists of three dormitories, each four stories high, with 12 rooms on each floor and two students to each room. Applicants are selected at random to fill the dorms. What is the probability that
(a) You will be successful in securing sophomore dormitory housing?

(b) Both you and your friend will secure such housing?

(c) You and your friend will be assigned to the same dorm?

(d) You and your friend will be assigned to the same floor of the same dorm?

(e) You and your friend will be assigned to the same room of the same dorm.

5.15 The following set of density data was obtained by a class of engineering students as part of their laboratory exercises:

> 35.22 35.18 35.18 34.62 35.18 35.04
> 33.79 33.18 35.04 34.91 36.18 37.84
> 37.01 35.22 35.64 35.22

Calculate the mean and standard deviation, and plot the normal distribution curve for these data on rectangular coordinates.

5.16 Plot the following data set on rectangular coordinates

x	y
1.13	1.31
1.25	2.24
1.32	3.11
1.49	4.42
1.56	5.81
1.68	6.24
1.89	7.99
1.95	8.52

Draw a straight line through these data and formulate an equation for the line.

5.17 For the data set given in problem 5.16, calculate values for y when x is 2.5, 5.0, 7.5, and 10.0. Can these values be determined accurately by interpolation and extrapolation?

5.18 Plot the following set of data on semilog coordinates, with x on the rectangular scale and y on the log scale.

x	y
1.9	3.7
2.4	6.1
3.1	9.2
4.1	14.7
4.9	21.0
5.3	25.9
6.4	39.5
6.9	47.1
7.1	55.0

Draw a straight line through these data and formulate an equation for the line.

5.19 For the data given in problem 5.18, determine values for y when x is 2.0, 5.7, 7.5, and 20.0. Can these values be determined accurately by interpolation and extrapolation?

5.20 For the following data set

x	y
0.32	1.38
0.70	2.01
1.50	4.48
2.22	9.21
2.60	13.46
3.05	21.12
3.82	45.60
4.33	75.94
4.60	99.48

plot the data on log-log coordinates. Ascertain an equation for a curve through the data by the technique of your choice.

5.21 The following data were obtained during an experimental test:

x	y
0.01	−4.61
0.05	−3.00
0.09	−2.41
0.18	−1.71
0.35	−1.05
0.60	−0.51
0.93	−0.07
1.63	0.49
3.84	1.35
7.33	1.99
9.99	2.30

Plot these data on an appropriate coordinate system and ascertain an equation which most accurately represents the data.

5.22 Plot the following set of data on an appropriate coordinate system and develop an equation for the curve.

x	y
0.19	.003 3
0.57	.009 9
3.75	.065 4
16.52	.284 4

x	y	
39.98	.642	5
63.27	.893	1
88.88	.999	8
113.39	.917	8
134.63	.711	7
157.45	.383	5
177.18	.049	2
179.52	.008	4

5.23 For the plot of the data set given in problem 5.18, determine the equation for the first-order least-squares fit of the data. Indicate the region over which the equation may be used.

5.24 For the plot of the data set in problem 5.20, determine the equation for the data curve by means of the first-order least-squares technique. Once the equation has been established, calculate values for y when x is 5.0 and 7.0.

REFERENCES

BEAKLEY, GEORGE C., and H. W. LEACH. *Engineering: An Introduction to a Creative Profession*, Second Edition. New York: The Macmillan Company, 1972.

BECKWITH, T. G., and N. LEWIS BUCK. *Mechanical Measurements*. Reading, Mass.: Addison-Wesley Publishing Company, 1969.

BLALOCK, HUBERT M. *Social Statistics*. New York: McGraw-Hill Book Company, Inc., 1960.

BRAGG, GORDON M. *Principles of Experimentation and Measurement*. Englewood Cliffs, N.J.: Prentice-Hall, Inc., 1974.

GIBSON, JOHN E. *Introduction to Engineering Design*. New York: Holt, Rinehart and Winston, Inc., 1968.

GRAHAM, A. RICHARD. *An Introduction to Engineering Measurements*. Englewood Cliffs, N.J.: Prentice-Hall, Inc., 1975.

RUBENSTEIN, MOSHE F. *Patterns of Problem Solving*. Englewood Cliffs, N.J.: Prentice-Hall, Inc., 1975.

SCHENCK, HILBERT, Jr. *Theories of Engineering Experimentation*. New York: McGraw-Hill Book Company, Inc., 1961.

SMITH, JON, M. *Scientific Analysis on the Pocket Calculator.* New York: John Wiley & Sons, Inc., 1975.

SPIEGEL, M. R. *Theory and Problems of Statistics.* New York: Schaum Publishing Company, 1961.

Seventeenth century Leibnitz's calculator.
(*Courtesy* Monroe.)

Calculators

Hand-held calculating devices have been in use for centuries. The abacus was developed in China around the twelfth to fourteenth centuries and has been used by Chinese scholars and tradesmen ever since (Figure 6-1). The abacus, with its rows of sliding beads, was found to be useful not only for simple addition and subtraction, but also for multiplication and division.

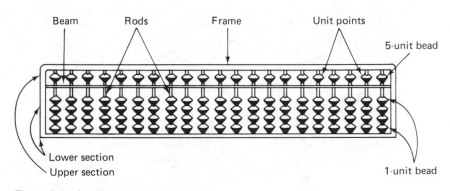

Figure 6-1 A typical abacus.

In about 1600, Napier developed logarithms, and the formulation of logarithmic scales soon followed. In 1622, another hand calculating device, the first slide rule, was developed to perform basic multiplication. A more modern version of the slide rule appeared about 1850. After that time, the slide rule was revised and improved until it became a versatile, widely used computational device, which was indispensable to engineering problem solvers for generations.

A standard slide rule for engineering use may have twenty or more scales. These scales were designed to enable calculations involving most of the mathematical functions commonly required for engineering problem solving. A typical slide rule is shown in Figure 6-2.

Early mechanical calculators, like today's electronic calculators, were the fruit of creative engineering. A photographic history of calculator development is shown in Figure 6-3. Perhaps the first mechanical adding machine was the one devised by Pascal in 1642, while he was still in his teens. This device used geared wheels to perform the addition process, necessary for computations in his father's tax office. About 30 years later, von Leibniz modified this concept to produce an adding device with stepped wheels, a device which could also multiply by means of the repeated addition process. The first commercial calculating device was developed by Thomas in 1820. This calculator utilized a stepped drum mechanism and

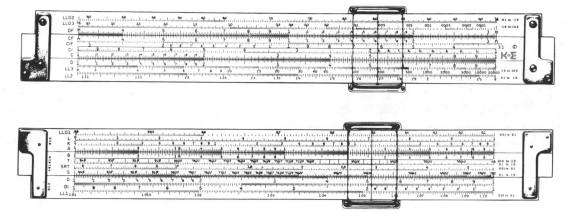

Figure 6-2 A typical slide rule. (*Courtesy* of the K & E Company.)

could be used for addition, subtraction, multiplication, and division. W. J. R. Monroe refined the calculator through continued modifications and finally patented a key-operated calculator in 1850. Nearly 40 years later, W. S. Burroughs developed a key-operated adding machine which was activated by means of a crank.

In the early 1900s, the modification of calculators continued. Between 1930 and 1942 a number of calculators, both mechanical and electrical, were developed. In addition, a simple electronic computer, styled like a telephone switch board, was developed for governmental use.

In the period of rapid technological growth which followed, more varied and versatile calculators and computers were developed. Calculators became advanced electromechanical systems which could perform not only the four basic functions of addition, subtraction, multiplication, and division, but also many different mathematical operations. The rapid growth of the electronics industry and its continuing efforts to miniaturize systems resulted in the development of desk calculators/computers which are extremely useful in computational problem solving, especially for scientists and engineers.

In the late 1960s, electronic desk calculators/computers were commercially available, and many of these systems incorporated multifunction operation with programmable capabilities. In 1971–72, the first hand-held portable electronic scientific calculators, or pocket calculators, became available. These calculators are small, battery operated, and extremely versatile. These minicalculators have revolutionized engineering computational techniques and have virtually replaced the slide rule in daily engineering

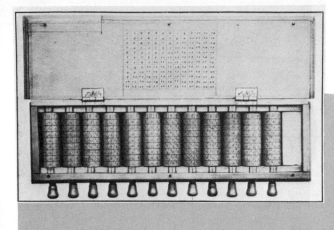

Napier's Rods—Early 1600's

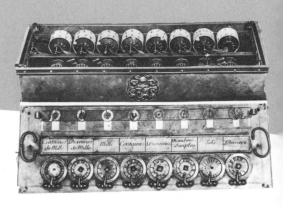

Pascal's Calculator—1642

1976

1975

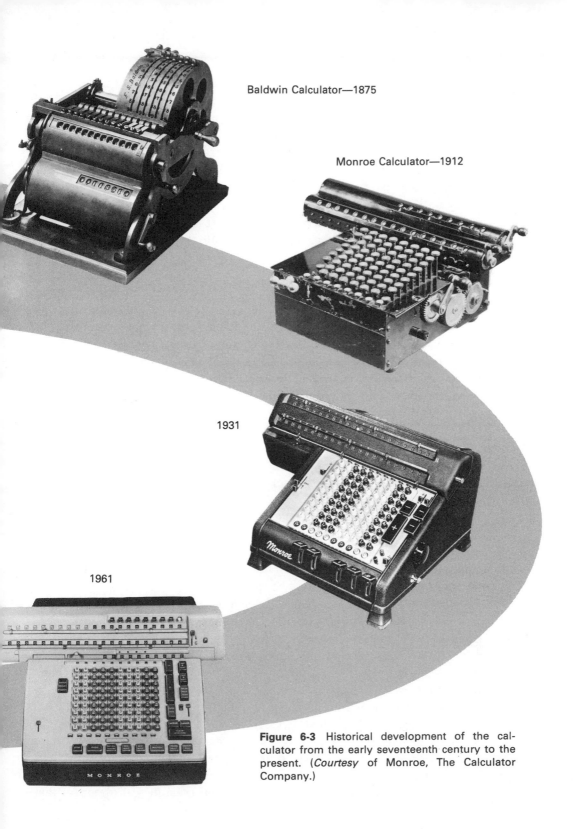

Baldwin Calculator—1875

Monroe Calculator—1912

1931

1961

Figure 6-3 Historical development of the calculator from the early seventeenth century to the present. (*Courtesy* of Monroe, The Calculator Company.)

practice. They not only simplify engineering problem solving, but they also provide greater accuracy than former techniques and minimize laborious numerical calculations. Recent advances in calculator design and increases in sales volume have made them generally affordable, as well.

There are currently more than 500 different calculators available with various functional capabilities. Because of the number of calculators currently on the market and the rapidity with which new models appear, it is impossible to discuss all the types of calculators and techniques for their use. It is possible, however, to classify these calculators and to discuss the general characteristics of the various types, and their application to engineering computational methods.

In this chapter, primary emphasis will be placed on the common, versatile, mini or pocket calculators. Most of the techniques and descriptive material presented, however, are also applicable to comparable desk calculators. It is important that the engineer be familiar with and be able to skillfully use all of the basic types of calculators. He or she will then be able to use whatever tool is at hand to assist him in the computational process necessary for engineering problem solving.

6.1   General characteristics

Calculators, both desk and pocket, generally fall into one of three categories, as shown in Figure 6-4.

(a) Four-function calculators: those with the capability only for the basic mathematical functions, i.e., addition, subtraction, multiplication, and division. These calculators find wide use in the home as well as in the general business world, and may be used in conjunction with tables of functions to perform engineering calculations.

(b) Multifunction or scientific calculators: those with basic function as well as special purpose function capabilities. These calculators were designed with the scientist and engineer in mind and are hard wired to perform the mathematical operations most commonly used in engineering (trigonometric functions, logarithms, square roots, and so on). Special purpose multifunction calculators also have been designed specifically for use in other fields such as business, finance, and statistics.

(c) Programmable scientific calculators: those with the capability for preprogrammed and/or self-programmed mathematical operations. These calculators permit an individual to use preprogrammed software (programs for specific applications, provided by the calculator manufacturer) or to develop an analysis for a special purpose and program the calculator for that

(a)

(b)

(c)

Figure 6-4 Typical calculators; (a) Four-Function (*Courtesy* of Casio, Inc.), (b) Multifunction (*Courtesy* of Hewlett-Packard Co.), and (c) Programmable (*Courtesy* of Texas Instruments, Inc.).

analysis. Programmable calculators are particularly useful in engineering because of their applications in data analysis.

The size of calculators has been reduced over the years through the miniaturization of electronic circuits and the development of smaller batteries. Present scientific mini or pocket calculators are of similar size and operate on either replaceable or rechargeable batteries.

The keyboard on the minicalculators may be classified in terms of data entry, basic functions, and special functions. The data entry keys are for numerical data input, i.e., keys 0 through 9 and the decimal · . The basic function keys include addition + , subtraction − , multiplication × , division ÷ , and in some cases an equals key = . The keyboard also may include special function keys such as trigonometric functions, logarithmic functions, statistical functions, and exponential functions. Other special function keys facilitate computational operations. These may include a clear C or all clear AC key and a clear entry CE key, register exchange xy , sign change +/− , and others. The more sophisticated (and expensive) the calculator, the more special functions the keyboard will contain.

Most calculators have a display which results from light-emitting diodes (LED). These LEDs form numbers through a series of small red line segments. A few calculators use a gas discharge or fluorescent light source for their display, with readouts in orange and green or blue, respectively. The output or number of digits of display capacity may vary from a low of 6 to a high of 16.

Calculators are available with both fixed and/or floating decimal systems. Some of the four-function calculators have a fixed decimal system which limits their accuracy and flexibility by displaying only a fixed number of digits (usually two) to the right of the decimal. As a result, many smaller answers will not appear unless the expression for the calculation is rewritten. The calculation of $0.03 \div 7.0$, for example, should yield 0.004 285 7. On a two-digit display calculator, however, 0.00 will appear as the solution.

Other calculators have a floating decimal system which automatically keeps track of the decimal at all times. Some calculators have a choice of floating or fixed decimal systems. One important feature, scientific notation, is extremely useful in engineering calculations because of the magnitude of numbers which may be handled, i.e., $9.999\ 9 \times 10^{99}$ to $1.000\ 0 \times 10^{-99}$.

The range of accuracy involved in the use of calculators depends not only upon the system of decimals employed by the particular calculator, but also upon the various rounding errors (especially for fixed decimal calculators), overflow, underflow, and the internal accuracy of the individual calculator used.

Each calculator performs its rounding in a set manner. The calculator may chop a calculated number at a specific point past the decimal regardless of the number following the cutoff point. Other calculators chop off a number at a particular point when the digit following the chop point is less than 4, and round it up when the following digit is 5 or higher. There are also a few calculators which round the number up if the digit following the chop point is greater than zero.

Rounding errors can be important, especially if numbers of similar size are subtracted. For example $\pi = 3.141\ 592\ 654$. A calculator with four decimals may indicate either 3.141 5 (if it simply chops off excess digits) or 3.141 6 (if it rounds up). If the number 3.141 7 is to be subtracted from π, the answer could be in error by a factor of two, depending upon the rounding characteristics of the calculator. This type of situation may also occur in the use of logarithms when the mantissas are of similar size.

Overflow occurs when a calculated quantity becomes too large to be displayed on the calculator. This situation is, of course, far less likely to occur on calculators with scientific notation. The overflow is generally signaled by a blinking display or some other form of notation in the display. Underflow occurs when a calculation results in a number smaller than the smallest readout or display on the calculator. Underflow generally will not be indicated on calculators without scientific notation capabilities. In such cases the display simply will show zero. For calculators using scientific notation, underflow is signaled by a blinking display or some other form of notation in the display. Problems of overflow and underflow sometimes may be avoided by rewriting the expression so as to reduce or increase the magnitude of the number to be keyed into the calculator.

6.2 Calculator logic

In order to use any calculator, one must be familiar with the method of procedure, or logic, appropriate to its operation. There are several different types of logic or languages used with calculators to perform mathematical operations: adding machine logic, algebraic (including elementary algebraic, algebraic with hierarchy, and algebraic operating system), and reverse polish. Each of these languages differs in the manner in which the instructions are keyed into the calculator. A specific calculator is designed to use one and only one of these languages, although some operations may be performed in the same manner in more than one language.

Adding machine logic permits the performance of operations in the same manner as one would perform them on an adding machine. This form of logic is appropriate only for addition and subtraction. Algebraic logic is convenient in that expressions are numerically evaluated in the form in which they are algebraically described. In the type of algebraic logic termed algebraic with hierarchy, multiplication and division operations are completed before addition and subtraction. The algebraic operating system incorporates parentheses as well as mathematical functions and performs operations within each set of parentheses as part of the problem solution. In reverse polish logic, the operand is entered into the calculator first, followed by the operating instruction.

EXAMPLE 6-1   Consider the sum 7 + 3 = ?
  adding machine logic
      touch the 7;
      touch the + key;
      touch the 3;
      touch the + key;
      then touch the total key and get 10.

   | 7 | | + | | 3 | | + | | Total |

  A total of 5 operations.

  algebraic logic (elementary, with hierarchy, and operating system)
      touch the 7;
      touch the + key;
      touch the 3;
      then touch the equals key, and the answer of 10 is displayed.

   | 7 | | + | | 3 | | = |

  A total of 4 operations.

  reverse polish logic
      touch the 7;
      enter the 7;
      touch the 3;
      touch the plus, and the answer of 10 is displayed.

   | 7 | | Enter | | 3 | | + |

  A total of 4 operations.

There are advantages and limitations to each of these logics or languages, and each is appropriate for specific applications. In engineering and science, the two languages most commonly used are the algebraic systems and reverse polish. The algebraic entry process is a straightforward procedure for evaluating algebraic expressions. The reverse polish procedure facilitates information storage and reduces the number of key strokes in some calculations.

EXAMPLE 6-2   Consider the product $3.15 \times 5.72 \div 12.2 = ?$

algebraic logic (elementary, with hierarchy, and operating system)
   touch 3.15;
   touch the multiplication key;
   touch 5.72;
   touch the division key;
   touch 12.2;
   touch the equals key, and the answer is 1.476885.

| 3.15 | | × | | 5.72 | | ÷ | | 12.2 | | = |

reverse polish logic
   touch 3.15;
   touch the enter key;
   touch 5.72;
   touch the multiplication key;
   touch 12.2;
   touch the division key, and the answer is 1.476885.

| 3.15 | | Enter | | 5.72 | | × | | 12.2 | | ÷ |

Most mathematical expressions which are used in engineering computations may be written in a form to facilitate computation (i.e., arranged in a manner to permit the most efficient calculation) for the language of the calculator being used. It should be noted that none of the hand-held calculator languages may be used for direct alphanumeric computation, since the languages were developed for numerical and mathematical operations. It is possible, however, that future calculators might incorporate some form of alphanumeric operation.

6.3 Four-function calculators

Most of the four-function calculators are relatively inexpensive, have replaceable batteries, and have been designed for general arithmetic use (Figure 6-5). The four-function calculator generally operates on the elementary algebraic logic principle. Use of this type of calculator for engineering problem solving usually necessitates the calculation of special functions and/or the use of supplementary materials such as tables of logarithms and trigonometric functions, or series representing these functions.

Figure 6-5 Typical four-function calculator. (*Courtesy* of Casio, Inc.)

The calculation of some "special" functions, such as powers, on a four-function calculator is relatively simple. Other calculations, however, are more complex. Calculation of roots, for example, requires a basic trial-and-error or iterative approach. Computation of needed mathematical functions may involve the solution of power series of various forms. As the number of terms increases, both the accuracy and the chance of human error also increase.

The series expressions for some of the basic functions which may be needed in engineering calculations are listed in Table 6-1. These series expressions may be evaluated with a four-function calculator in order to determine the needed mathematical functions.

Table 6-1 Series Expansions for Some Mathematical Functions

$$\sin x = x - \frac{x^3}{3!} + \frac{x^5}{5!} - \frac{x^7}{7!} + \cdots \qquad\qquad |x| < \infty$$

$$\cos x = 1 - \frac{x^2}{2!} + \frac{x^4}{4!} - \frac{x^6}{6!} + \cdots \qquad\qquad |x| < \infty$$

$$\tan x = x + \frac{x^3}{3} + \frac{2}{15}x^5 + \frac{17}{315}x^7 + \cdots \qquad |x| < \frac{\pi}{2}$$

$$\sec x = 1 + \frac{x^2}{2} + \frac{5}{24}x^4 + \frac{61}{720}x^6 + \cdots \qquad |x| < \frac{\pi}{2}$$

$$\csc x = \frac{1}{x} + \frac{x}{6} + \frac{7}{360}x^3 + \frac{31}{15120}x^5 + \cdots \qquad |x| < \pi$$

$$\cot x = \frac{1}{x} - \frac{x}{3} - \frac{x^3}{45} - \frac{2}{945}x^5 - \cdots \qquad |x| < \pi$$

$$\sinh x = x + \frac{x^3}{3!} + \frac{x^5}{5!} + \frac{x^7}{7!} + \cdots \qquad\qquad |x| < \infty$$

$$\cosh x = 1 + \frac{x^2}{2!} + \frac{x^4}{4!} + \frac{x^6}{6!} + \cdots \qquad\qquad |x| < \infty$$

$$\tanh x = x - \frac{x^3}{3} + \frac{2}{15}x^5 - \frac{17}{315}x^7 + \cdots \qquad |x| < \frac{\pi}{2}$$

$$\operatorname{sech} x = 1 - \frac{x^2}{2} + \frac{5}{24}x^4 - \frac{61}{720}x^6 + \cdots \qquad |x| < \frac{\pi}{2}$$

$$\operatorname{csch} x = \frac{1}{x} - \frac{x}{6} + \frac{7}{360}x^3 - \frac{31}{15120}x^5 + \cdots \qquad |x| < \pi$$

$$\coth x = \frac{1}{x} + \frac{x}{3} - \frac{x^2}{45} + \frac{2}{945}x^5 - \cdots \qquad |x| < \pi$$

$$\sin^{-1} x = x + \frac{x^3}{6} + \frac{3}{40}x^5 + \frac{15}{336}x^7 + \cdots \qquad |x| < 1$$

$$\tan^{-1} x = \begin{cases} x - \dfrac{x^3}{3} + \dfrac{x^5}{5} - \dfrac{x^7}{7} + \cdots & |x| \le 1,\; x^2 \ne -1 \\[2mm] \dfrac{\pi}{2} - \dfrac{1}{x} + \dfrac{1}{3x^3} - \dfrac{1}{5x^5} + \cdots & |x| > 1,\; x^2 \ne -1 \end{cases}$$

$$e = 1 + \frac{1}{1!} + \frac{1}{2!} + \frac{1}{3!} + \frac{1}{4!} + \cdots$$

$$e^x = 1 + x + \frac{x^2}{2!} + \frac{x^3}{3!} + \frac{x^4}{4!} + \cdots$$

$$e^{-x} = 1 - x + \frac{x^2}{2!} - \frac{x^3}{3!} + \frac{x^4}{4!} - \cdots$$

$$a^x = 1 + x \log a + \frac{(x \log a)^2}{2!} + \frac{(x \log a)^3}{3!} + \cdots$$

$$\ln x = 2\left[\frac{x-1}{x+1} + \frac{1}{3}\left(\frac{x-1}{x+1}\right)^3 + \frac{1}{5}\left(\frac{x-1}{x+1}\right)^5 + \cdots\right]$$

$$\log_{10} x = 0.868\,589\left[\frac{x-1}{x+1} + \frac{1}{3}\left(\frac{x-1}{x+1}\right)^3 + \frac{1}{5}\left(\frac{x-1}{x+1}\right)^5 + \cdots\right]$$

[*Note:* The value of x must be in radians for evaluation of all trigonometric functions.]

$$\sin^{-1} x = \theta = x' + 0x^2 + \frac{x^3}{2\cdot3} + 0x^4 + \frac{1\cdot3}{2\cdot4\cdot5}x^5 + 0x^6 + \frac{1\cdot3\cdot5}{2\cdot4\cdot6\cdot7}x^7 \cdots$$

where $|x| < 1$, $\frac{\pi}{2} < \theta < \frac{\pi}{2}$

In radians

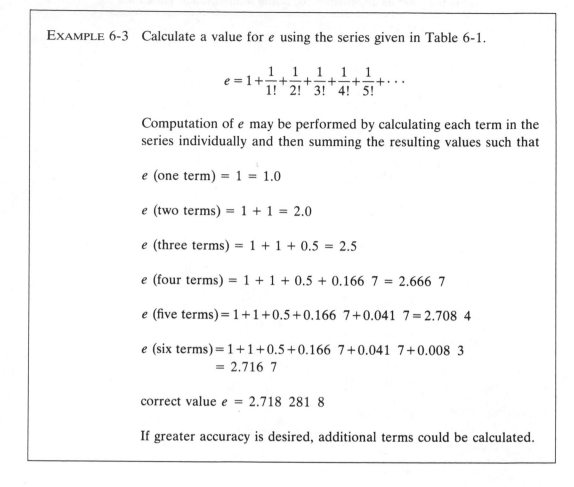

EXAMPLE 6-3   Calculate a value for *e* using the series given in Table 6-1.

$$e = 1 + \frac{1}{1!} + \frac{1}{2!} + \frac{1}{3!} + \frac{1}{4!} + \frac{1}{5!} + \cdots$$

Computation of *e* may be performed by calculating each term in the series individually and then summing the resulting values such that

e (one term) = 1 = 1.0

e (two terms) = 1 + 1 = 2.0

e (three terms) = 1 + 1 + 0.5 = 2.5

e (four terms) = 1 + 1 + 0.5 + 0.166 7 = 2.666 7

e (five terms) = 1 + 1 + 0.5 + 0.166 7 + 0.041 7 = 2.708 4

e (six terms) = 1 + 1 + 0.5 + 0.166 7 + 0.041 7 + 0.008 3
            = 2.716 7

correct value *e* = 2.718 281 8

If greater accuracy is desired, additional terms could be calculated.

EXAMPLE 6-4   Calculate the natural log of 3 using the series expression given in Table 6-1.

$$\log_e x = \ln x = 2\left\{ \left(\frac{x-1}{x+1}\right) + \frac{1}{3}\left(\frac{x-1}{x+1}\right)^3 + \frac{1}{5}\left(\frac{x-1}{x+1}\right)^5 + \cdots \right\}$$

Then

ln 3 (one term) = 2(0.5) = 1.0

ln 3 (two terms) = 2(0.5 + 0.041 7) = 1.083 4

ln 3 (three terms) = 2(0.5 + 0.041 7 + 0.006 3) = 1.096 0

ln 3 (four terms) = 2(0.5 + 0.041 7 + 0.006 3 + 0.001 1)
= 1.098 2

ln 3 (five terms) = 2(0.5 + 0.041 7 + 0.006 3 + 0.001 1 + 0.000 2)
= 1.098 6

correct value ln 3 = 1.098 612

The increase in the number of terms evaluated clearly improves the overall accuracy of the answer.

EXAMPLE 6-5 Calculate a value for the sine of 30°. The series expansion for calculation of the sine may be obtained from Table 6-1 as:

$$\sin x = x - \frac{x^3}{3!} + \frac{x^5}{5!} - \frac{x^7}{7!} + \frac{x^9}{9!} - \cdots$$

The angle of 30° must first be converted to radians by noting that there are 2π radians in 360°, thus

$$30\left(\frac{2}{360}\right) = 0.5236 \text{ radians}$$

Then

sine 30° (one term) = 0.523 6

sine 30° (two terms) = 0.523 6 − 0.023 9 = 0.499 7

sine 30° (three terms) = 0.523 6 − 0.023 9 + 0.000 3
= 0.500 0

correct value sin 30° = 0.5

The functions generated in this manner may be used in normal engineering computations with reasonable confidence. Should special mathematical functions be needed on a regular basis for problem solving, it is recommended that a table of functions be used in conjunction with the four-function calculator in order to minimize the time spent in calculations.

There are both advantages and limitations to the four-function calculator. Low cost, relative accuracy, and ease of operation make the four-function calculator quite useful. In engineering computations, however, its usefulness is limited because of the need for special functions. Although the needed functions may be generated with the calculator, the results are only relatively accurate, and the tedious calculations necessary to obtain these functions and/or the constant reference to tables of functions reduces the overall efficiency of the four-function calculator for engineering purposes.

6.4 Multifunction calculators

The multifunction calculator, or scientific calculator, has been designed to meet the needs of the engineer and the scientist (Figure 6-6). This calculator provides not only the basic functions, but also many special functions and special operational features. The scientific multifunction pocket calculator for engineering applications is extremely versatile and performs all of the

Figure 6-6 Typical multifunction calculator. (*Courtesy* of Texas Instruments, Inc.)

functions of the traditional slide rule, with some additional capabilities as well.

The multifunction calculator is available over a large range of prices, generally has a floating-point decimal system with the capability of scientific notation, and operates in one of the algebraic or reverse polish logic systems. A schematic of a typical multifunction calculator is shown in Figure 6-7.

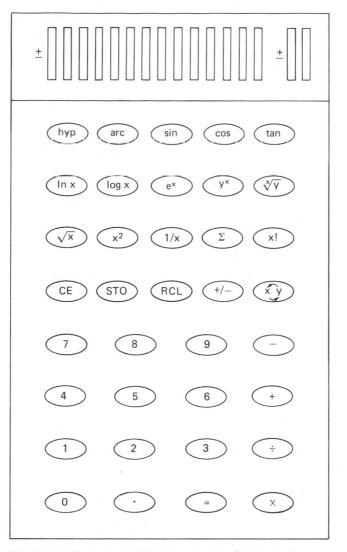

Figure 6-7 Typical multifunction calculator for algebraic logic.

The range of special features or hard-wired functions available determines the range of usefulness of the calculator to the engineer. The special features available on the various multifunction calculators generally fall into one of three categories: (a) mathematical functions, (b) specific constants or conversion factors, and (c) operational keys to facilitate problem solving.

In addition to the basic mathematical functions, scientific calculators have other mathematical operations such as logarithms (both natural and base 10), the basic trigonometric functions (sine, cosine, and tangent) as well as inverse and hyperbolic trigonometric functions, and the exponential functions (both e^x and y^x). In addition, special features such as squares, square roots, summations, factorials, mean and standard deviations, linear regression, and various other statistical functions are available on some calculator models. With these functions available at the touch of a key, most engineering problems may be evaluated without the need to resort to any approximations or external tables of functions.

Many calculators have specific constants and conversion factors which are helpful in engineering problem solving. Such constants as π, conversions from degrees to radians, metric conversions, and polar to rectangular conversions can be extremely useful.

The calculator operations which facilitate easier problem solving include register exchange or exchange of x for y, reciprocals, clear entry, change of sign, and a constant factor for multiplication. Some calculators permit operation or computation of the trigonometric functions in either degrees or radians without conversion.

Multifunction calculators often have one or more memory registers, a feature which is particularly helpful in engineering computations. The number of available registers of memory (usually between 1 and 10) depends upon the brand and style of calculator. This operational feature facilitates lengthy calculations or chain calculations by making it unnecessary to write down the intermediate steps.

EXAMPLE 6-6   Perform the calculation $(3 + 6) \times (4 - 2) = ?$ To accomplish this calculation on a multifunction calculator, one would proceed as follows:

algebraic logic

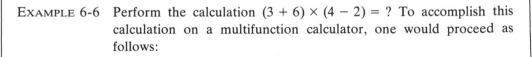

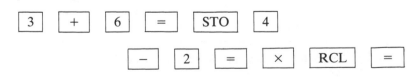

The answer is 18.

algebraic operating system

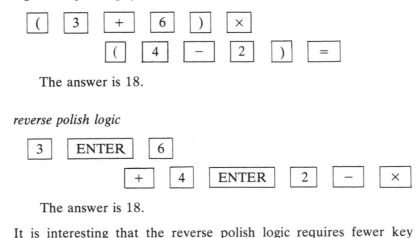

The answer is 18.

reverse polish logic

The answer is 18.

It is interesting that the reverse polish logic requires fewer key strokes to perform this calculation than does the algebraic logic.

On some calculator models it is possible to perform register arithmetic, i.e., numbers stored in the memory registers may be used directly in arithmetic operations. "Stacked" memories enable automatic storage of a number of previous calculations or entries for review or use in subsequent calculations.

Additional special features will continue to appear as new multifunction calculators are introduced. Those mentioned above represent the features most commonly available in current models. Techniques for the use of these special features depend upon the nature of the problem at hand and the particular combination of features available on the calculator to be used. Detailed discussions of operational techniques for particular calculators must be left to owners' handbooks. Some example problems, however, might demonstrate the manner in which basic scientific knowledge can be combined with skillful use of the scientific calculator in order to solve engineering problems.

EXAMPLE 6-7 A highway off-ramp curve has been designed with a 200-meter radius and an angle of bank of 20 degrees (0.349 1 rad). At what speed may an automobile travel this curve without a tendency to skid sideways? ($g = 9.8 \, \text{m/s}^2$). From principles of physics we may evaluate a force balance and find that

$$V = (\text{Tan } \theta)(R)(g)^{0.5}$$

The velocity, then, would be calculated as follows:

algebraic logic

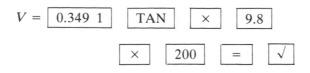

$V = \boxed{0.349\ 1} \quad \boxed{\text{TAN}} \quad \boxed{\times} \quad \boxed{9.8}$

$\boxed{\times} \quad \boxed{200} \quad \boxed{=} \quad \boxed{\sqrt{}}$

$= 26.710\ 6\ \text{m/s}\ (96.158\ 2\ \text{km/hr})$

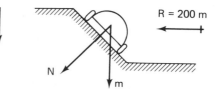

reverse polish logic

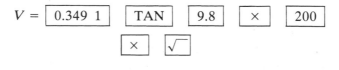

$V = \boxed{0.349\ 1} \quad \boxed{\text{TAN}} \quad \boxed{9.8} \quad \boxed{\times} \quad \boxed{200}$

$\boxed{\times} \quad \boxed{\sqrt{}}$

$= 26.710\ 6\ \text{m/s}\ (96.158\ 2\ \text{km/hr})$

The automobile may travel this curve at speeds up to 96.158 2 km/hr without a tendency to skid sideways.

EXAMPLE 6-8   A cannon fires a cannon ball at 35 degrees (0.610 9 rad) above the horizontal with a muzzle velocity of 250 m/s. What is the ultimate height that the cannon ball will reach if the air resistance is neglected? ($g = 9.8\ \text{m/s}^2$).

The velocity may be calculated from basic principles as

$$v_y = V \sin 35°$$

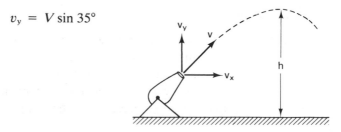

algebraic logic

→ 143.401 2 m/s

reverse polish logic

The maximum height reached by the cannon ball will occur when the velocity in the vertical direction is zero. From basic principles we find that

$$h = v_y^2/2g$$

algebraic logic

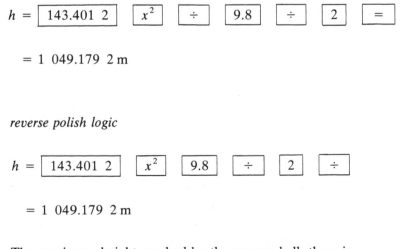

reverse polish logic

The maximum height reached by the cannon ball, then, is 1 049.179 2 m.

EXAMPLE 6-9   A ship at sea sights a lighthouse at an angle of 60 degrees (1.047 2 rad) with the ship's course. The ship then proceeds on course for 20 km until the lighthouse is directly off the left side of the ship. How far away is the ship from the lighthouse?

opposite side of triangle = (Tan θ)(adjacent side)

distance = (Tan 1.047 2)(20 km)

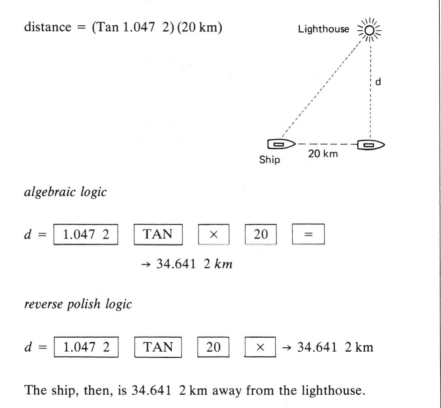

algebraic logic

d = | 1.047 2 | | TAN | | × | | 20 | | = |

→ 34.641 2 *km*

reverse polish logic

d = | 1.047 2 | | TAN | | 20 | | × | → 34.641 2 km

The ship, then, is 34.641 2 km away from the lighthouse.

There are many advantages to the multifunction calculator. Its high degree of accuracy within the range of engineering needs and its ease of operation make the multifunction scientific calculator extremely versatile and useful for engineering computations. Most multifunction calculators perform all of the functions of slide rules and provide additional reliability and accuracy. They minimize the tediousness of complicated engineering

EXAMPLE 6-10 An electric resistance wire heating device has been designed for use in home heating on a 110-volt system. The resistance has been calculated to be 24.2 ohms. How much heat is generated by this device?

From basic electrical engineering, we find that

$$P = V^2/R$$

Heater unit

R = 24.2 Ω

110 volts

Therefore, the energy generated by the heating device may be calculated as follows:

algebraic logic

heat = | 110 | | x^2 | | ÷ | | 24.2 | | = | → 500 watts

reverse polish logic

heat = | 110 | | x^2 | | 24.2 | | ÷ | → 500 watts

calculations and also permit a more thorough analysis of the parameters involved. The main limitation to many multifunction calculators is the shortage of addressable memory registers and the fact that electronically stored information may be lost when the calculator is turned off. These problems have been remedied, to some extent at least, by the programmable calculators.

6.5   Programmable calculators

The scientific programmable pocket calculators have opened a new dimension in computational techniques and permit a wide range of calculations heretofore limited to large computing facilities (Figure 6-8). As programmable calculators are introduced to different disciplines, their applications become more numerous, permitting rapid solution to an ever-increasing range of problems.

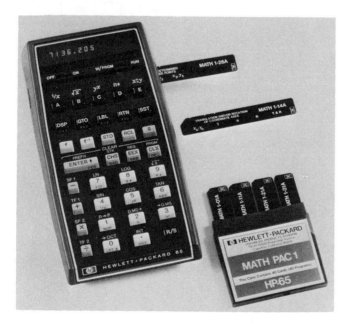

Figure 6-8   Typical programmable calculator. (*Courtesy* of Hewlett-Packard Co.)

There are two general types of scientific programmable calculators: those in which the program is keyed into the calculator and stored electronically, and those that also permit the use of external programs stored on magnetic strips or cards. These programmable calculators are designed to permit full editing of the programs which have been keyed into the calculator. The programs may be reviewed one step at a time, thus permitting the addition of new steps or the correction of existing steps already in the program.

The number of steps of programming capability varies among models but generally is sufficient for most engineering problems. The calculators with programs which are keyed in by the operator and stored electronically may permit 100 or more steps of program length, and the program is generally lost when the calculator is turned off. Those programmable calculators with a software package, i.e., preprogrammed magnetic cards, generally permit programs of 200 steps or more, depending upon the number of magnetic strips used.

Software packages or preprogrammed material for programmable calculators are available in a wide range of subjects and permit specialized calculation in mathematics, statistics, finance, stress analysis, medicine, aviation, and many other fields. The individual software packages include many of the common calculations for the specific discipline.

The programmable scientific calculator generally has, in addition to the capability of short programs, the complete complement of engineering and scientific special functions found on the multifunction calculators. These calculators also have a large number of addressable program registers and addressable memory registers. Most have stacked memories with the capability of retrieving the last calculated number. Some calculators also include special functions which permit branching, i.e., comparing the relationship between two numbers (less than, equal to, greater than) to facilitate iterative solutions. A schematic of a typical programmable calculator is shown in Figure 6-9.

The accuracy of the programmable scientific calculators is comparable to that of the previously described multifunction calculators and is sufficient for most engineering applications. These calculators generally operate in the floating point decimal system with overflow into scientific notation, and some permit shifting between floating-point and fixed-point decimals. Special features include the capability for selection of integers, the fractional parts of a number, or absolute values. In addition, some programmable calculators permit the selection of round-off characteristics, further improving their accuracy on specific problems.

Programmable calculators are useful for a wide range of calculations. When used in conjunction with preprogrammed software, they satisfy the computational needs of most engineering problems. Specific programs for use with individual calculators are unique to the specific calculator and cannot be discussed here. The technique for general programming of a calculator and use of the associated software, however, can be reviewed.

The procedure for programming a programmable calculator may be outlined as follows:

(a) *Formulation of the problem.* In order adequately to formulate the problem to be solved, it is necessary to review the fundamental information

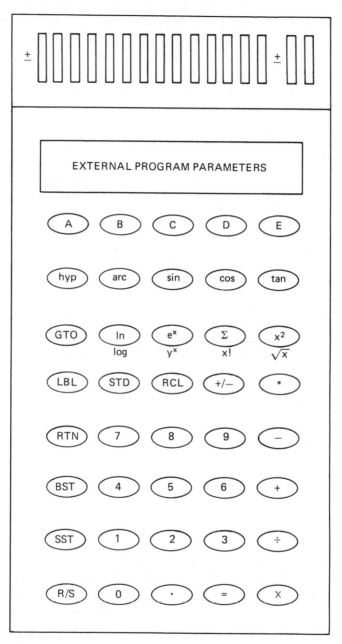

Figure 6-9 Typical programmable calculator.

and equation(s) that will be needed to effect a problem solution. It is desirable to formulate the equation(s) in the form most efficient for calculators in order to minimize the number of program steps (especially if the calculator has a limited capability).

(b) *Program outline.* The succession in which the information is to be keyed into the calculator must be established. Note should be taken of internal functions already available in the calculator, and care should be exercised that the sequence of calculations is consistent with the equation(s) and boundary conditions.

(c) *Programming the calculator.* The predetermined steps of the program must next be keyed into the calculator in the order outlined in the preceding step. The program may then be reviewed one step at a time to check the input information.

(d) *Test program.* In order to check the program, a test case should be run using input variables which will yield known answers. This test case may be hand calculated in order to ascertain that the program as keyed into the calculator will provide a correct result.

(e) *Program operation.* Once the program has been checked with known information, it is ready for use and may be run automatically, i.e., the input data may be keyed into the calculator and the program operated.

(f) *Program retrieval.* The program may be saved for future use either by reviewing the program step by step and noting the step sequence on a scratch pad, or by removing the programmed magnetic strip.

Of all the calculators currently available, the programmable calculators are certainly the most versatile and most useful for engineering calculations. They may be used not only for problem solving, but also for data analysis in the field or in the laboratory. The programmable scientific pocket calculator is the next best thing to having a personal portable computer facility always on call.

6.6 Summary

Hand-held scientific calculators have revolutionized both engineering problem solving and engineering education. Today the pocket calculator is as integral a part of the student and professional engineer as is his textbook, his briefcase, or his engineering handbook. Prices of pocket calculators vary as widely as their capabilities. In selecting a calculator for purchase, the student would be well advised to consider the use to which the calculator will be put and the capabilities most necessary for problem solving in his particular discipline.

In spite of the usefulness of the electronic calculators, many problems still require large-scale analysis which is beyond the scope of these minimiracles. Such analysis can be performed only on digital and analog computers.

PROBLEMS   **6.1**   Perform the following operations:
(a) $(3 \times 6) + (4 \div 2) - (9 \times (4 - 3)) + ((9 \div 3) \times 4) =$
(b) $(4 - 2) \times (6 + 3) \div (4 - 2 \times (3 + 2)) \times (9 - 4 + 7) =$
(c) $(8.53 + 2.54) \div (3.88 - 5.74) \times (9.24 + 6.47 \times (8.21 - 5.68)) =$
(d) $(9.98 \div 5.27 \times 3.39) + (8.72 \times 6.47 \div 5.71)$
$$- (9.16 - 4.27 \times 9.64) =$$
(e) $(8.33 \times 6.48 + 7.46) \div (3.94 + 5.75 \div 6.42)$
$$\times (9.62 \times (7.48 - 3.37)) =$$

6.2   Perform the following operations:
(a) $\sin 0° = \qquad \cos 0° = \qquad \tan 0° = \qquad \cot 0° = \qquad \sec 0° = \qquad \csc 0° =$
(b) $\sin 30° = \qquad \cos 30° = \qquad \tan 30° = \qquad \cot 30° = \qquad \sec 30° = \qquad \csc 30° =$
(c) $\sin 45° = \qquad \cos 45° = \qquad \tan 45° = \qquad \cot 45° = \qquad \sec 45° = \qquad \csc 45° =$
(d) $\sin 60° = \qquad \cos 60° = \qquad \tan 60° = \qquad \cot 60° = \qquad \sec 60° = \qquad \csc 60° =$
(e) $\sin 90° = \qquad \cos 90° = \qquad \tan 90° = \qquad \cot 90° = \qquad \sec 90° = \qquad \csc 90° =$

6.3   Perform the following operations:
(a) $(\cot 79° \div 1.22 \times (\sin 37° \div \sec 53°))$
$$\times (\cos 37° + \tan 51° \times \sec 12°) =$$
(b) $(\sec (21° + \cos^{-1} .88) \times \tan 29° \div \sin (\sin^{-1} .82 + \cos^{-1} .86)) =$
(c) $((\cot (14° + 28 + -\sec^{-1} 2.8) + \tan 84°) \times 48.27 \div \sin 47°) =$
(d) $(\log 0.81 \times 11.11^{2.71} \div \ln 642 - e^{-0.67} + \cos 47° \times \ln 0.31$
$$+ 87.45^{0.2}) =$$
(e) $(e^{.27} \times 81.52 \times \log 8.75 + 89.52^{.37} \times \sin 82° \times \ln 64.52$
$$- \cos^{-1} .13) =$$

6.4   Perform the following calculations:
(a) $((8.75 \times 10^{21})(e^{-3.9})/(\log 14.28)(3.75^{12}))$
$$+ ((\sin 24.21°)(\ln 83.75)/(\tan 0.27°)) =$$
(b) $(\sec (26.45° + \tan^{-1} 29.43)/(\ln 10.45)(e^{-1.81}))$
$$- (87.4^{-0.71})(9.87 \times 10^4)(4.69 \times 10^{-6}) =$$
(c) $(\ln 81495)(\cot 69.47°)(\log 0.00065)$
$$+ (13.9)^{-.18}(\sin 39.21°)(8.71)^2 - (8!)(\csc 81°) =$$
(d) $(3.11^{-.29})(e^{-15})(\cos 12.17°) + (0.000\ 17)^{.52}(\sin 89.5°)$
$$- (\ln 0.000\ 8)(e^{-8.27})(10^{-3}) =$$
(e) $(\tan (\csc^{-1} 6.2 + \cot^{-1} 1.39)(\ln 2.74)(\log 8\ 147))$
$$+ (1.69)^{-.82}(e^{1.5})/(1.73)(8.94 \times 10^{-2}) =$$

6.5   Calculate the sinh of 0.6 to 6 decimal places using 6 terms of the series expansion given in Table 6-1. Compare the answer with the result obtained on your calculator or from tables. What is the percent error?

6.6   Calculate a value for $e^{-.5}$ to 6 decimal places using 6 terms of the series expansion given in Table 6-1. Compare the answer with the result obtained on your calculator or from tables. What is the percent error?

6.7 Calculate the value for $\tan^{-1}(1.700)$ to 6 decimal places using 6 terms of the series expansion given in Table 6-1. Compare this answer with the result obtained on your calculator or from tables. What is the percent error?

6.8 A tensile force is being applied to a steel bar to determine how much it can be stretched for a given force. The elongation is determined by the equation

$$\delta = FL/AE$$

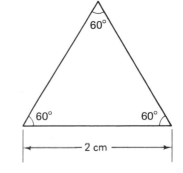

where F = applied force, newtons

L = length of bar, meters

A = cross-sectional area of bar, m^2

E = modulus of elasticity, N/m^2

If the steel bar has the shape shown, is 5 m long, the force is 10 000 N, and the modulus of elasticity for steel is 20.67×10^{10} N/m^2, calculate the elongation of the bar.

6.9 In problem 6.8, the steel bar is placed in a tensile test facility and elongated 0.25 cm. What tensile force was applied to the bar?

6.10 The speed of sound in air can be calculated by means of the following equation:

$$c = \sqrt{kRT}$$

where c = speed of sound (m/s)

k = ratio of specific heats ($= 1.4$ for air)

R = gas constant ($= 287.05$ J/kg K for air)

T = temperature (K)

If the temperature of the air is 30°C, what is the speed of sound, c?

6.11 From thermodynamics it can be shown that the following equation describes the flow of an ideal, compressible gas:

$$\frac{P_0}{P} = \left(1 + \frac{k-1}{2}M^2\right)^{\frac{k}{k-1}}$$

where P_0 = stagnation pressure (N/m² absolute)

   P = test section pressure (N/m² absolute)

   k = ratio of specific heats (= 1.4 for air)

   M = Mach number

For air flowing in a wind tunnel, calculate the Mach number if

$$P_0 = 7.0 \times 10^5 \text{ N/m}^2 \text{ absolute}$$

and $$P = 35.0 \times 10^3 \text{ N/m}^2 \text{ absolute}$$

6.12 The thermal resistance of a conducting material is generally dependent on the temperature of the material. The variation in resistance with temperature may be calculated by the empirical expression

$$R_2 = R_0[1 + \alpha_0(T_2 - T_0)]$$

where R_0 is the resistance of the material at temperature T_0, in °C, and α_0 is the temperature coefficient of resistance of the material at T_0. The resistance of the material also is a function of the resistivity, ρ, the length, l, and the cross-sectional area, A, such that

$$R = \rho\frac{l}{A}$$

For standard annealed copper at 20°C, the resistivity, ρ, is 1.724 1 micro-ohm-cm, and the temperature coefficient, α, is 0.003 93°C^{-1}. Calculate the resistance of a 10 m length of copper wire 20 mm in diameter at 80°C.

6.13 Newton's second law states that the force exerted by an object is equal to the mass of the object multiplied by its acceleration, or

$$F = ma$$

Acceleration is defined as the rate of change of velocity, or the change in velocity per unit of time, and is

$$a = \frac{\Delta v}{t} = \frac{v_f - v_0}{t}$$

where v_f is the final velocity and v_0 is the initial velocity. A 6 000-lb automobile accelerates from 0 to 128 kph in 55 s. At that instant an object moves in front of the path of the automobile. With what force in newtons would the automobile strike the object?

6.14 In problem 6.13, if the automobile struck an object with a force of 2 500 N, what was its acceleration? If the automobile was initially standing still, and attained a final velocity of 95 mph, how long was the automobile moving before it struck the object?

6.15 The equivalent resistance for resistances in parallel may be calculated from the expression

$$\frac{1}{R_{equiv}} = \frac{1}{R_1} + \frac{1}{R_2} + \frac{1}{R_3} + \cdots + \frac{1}{R_n}$$

where R is the resistance and n indicates the number of resistances in parallel. Resistances in series may be calculated from the expression

$$R_{equiv} = R_1 + R_2 + R_3 + \cdots + R_n$$

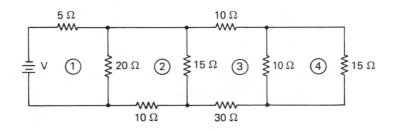

Calculate the equivalent resistance for the circuit shown.

6.16 For the resistance network of problem 6.15, calculate the current (I) in each loop if the voltage supply (V) is 32 volts. (For each loop, $V = IR$.)

6.17 The general gas law relating pressure, volume, and temperature may be written in the form

$$\frac{P_1 V_1}{T_1} = \frac{P_2 V_2}{T_2} = \text{constant}$$

In a thermodynamic process, air is compressed from standard atmospheric conditions to a pressure of 3 atmospheres and one-fourth of the original volume. Calculate the change in temperature. (For thermodynamic processes, absolute temperatures must be used.)

6.18 For a body to be in equilibrium, the resultant of all forces and moments acting on the body must be zero, that is, the sum of all forces and moments must be zero such that

$$\Sigma F_x = 0 \qquad \Sigma F_y = 0 \qquad \Sigma M_0 = 0$$

where F_x and F_y designate forces in the x and y directions, and M_0 refers to the moments. What force F will cause the force system to be in equilibrium, based on the force field shown.

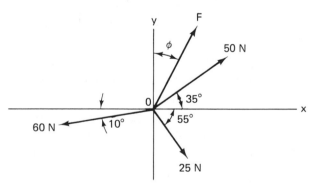

6.19 The moment of inertia for an I-beam may be calculated by means of the following expression:

$$I_z = \frac{1}{12}(BA^3 - ba^3)$$

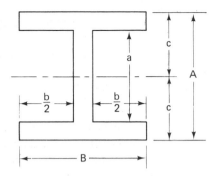

If A = 25 cm, B = 15 cm, a = 15 cm, and b = 10 cm, calculate the moment of inertia. From strength of materials, the flexural stress for a beam is expressed as

$$S = \frac{M\,c}{I_z}$$

where M is the maximum bending moment and c represents the distance from the neutral axis to the outer edge. If the bending moment on the I-beam is 5 758 Nm, calculate the flexural stress for the beam.

6.20 In problem 6.19, if the dimensions of the I-beam were changed to A = 30 cm, B = 20 cm, a = 20 cm, b = 15 cm, and the bending moment remains the same, what is the reduction in the flexural stress of the beam?

6.21 For a single-phase a.c. circuit, the current in a parallel connection may be calculated from the expression

$$I = \left[\left(\frac{E}{R}\right)^2 + \left(\frac{E}{X_L} - \frac{E}{X_C}\right)^2\right]^{1/2}$$

where I = current, amp

E = potential, v

R = resistance, ohms

X_L = inductive reactance, ohms = $2\pi f L$

f = frequency, Hz

$$L = \text{inductance, henrys}$$

$$X_C = \text{capacitive reactance, ohms} = 1/(2\pi f C)$$

$$C = \text{capacitance, farads}$$

If the current is 10 amps, the resistance is 12 ohms, the inductance is 1 000 henrys, and the capacitance is 50 microfarads, calculate the voltage across the circuit (Assume $f = 60$ Hz).

6.22 A moment represents a tendency to turn and occurs when a force is applied to an object at some point other than the axis or the center of forces. The moment of a force about an axis, then, is the product of the force multiplied by the moment arm or perpendicular distance from the axis or center of forces to the line of action of the force, such that

$$M = Fd$$

where F is the force and d is the moment arm. For the moment system shown, determine the force, F, needed to place the moment system in equilibrium.

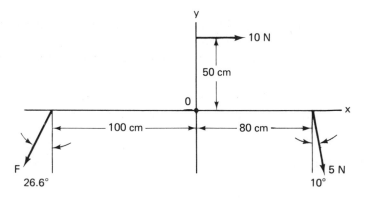

6.23 The torsional shearing stress, s_s, for a circular shaft subject to a torque or twisting moment, T, may be determined from the equation

$$s_s = \frac{Tr}{J}$$

where J is the polar moment of inertia and r is the distance from the center of the shaft to the point at which the torsional shearing stress is desired. The polar moment of inertia for the cross sectional area of a hollow circular shaft may be expressed as

$$J = \frac{\pi}{32}(D_0^4 - D_i^4)$$

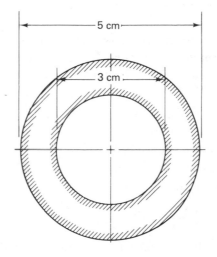

where D_0 is the outer diameter and D_i is the inner diameter. Calculate the shearing stress in a hollow circular shaft at a radius of 2 cm, if the outer diameter is 5 cm, the inner diameter is 3 cm, and the twisting moment is 2 500 newton-meters.

6.24 For a capacitance-inductance circuit, the resonant frequency may be calculated from the equation

$$f = \frac{1}{2\pi\sqrt{LC}}$$

where
f = frequency, Hz

L = inductance, henrys

C = capacitance, farads

If the inductance is 4 microhenrys and the capacitance is 15 microfarads, what is the resonant frequency of the circuit?

6.25 For the resonant frequency equation given in Problem 6.24, plot a series of curves (using log-log paper) for resonant frequency with capacitance as the abscissa and frequency as the ordinate. Plot these curves for inductance values ranging from 1 microhenry to 1 henry and capacitance from 1 microfarad to 1 farad.

REFERENCES

ABRAMOWITZ, MILTON, and IRENE A. STEGUN, Eds. *Handbook of Mathematical Functions with Formulas, Graphs, and Mathematical Tables.* Washington, D.C.: National Bureau of Standards (Applied Mathematics Series 55), 1964.

BEAKLEY, GEORGE C., and H. W. LEACH. *The Slide Rule, Electronic Hand Calculator, and Metrification in Problem Solving,* Third Edition. New York: The Macmillan Publishing Co., Inc., 1975.

HODGMAN, CHARLES D., Ed. *C.R.C. Standard Mathematical Tables,* Eleventh Edition. Cleveland: Chemical Rubber Publishing Co., 1957.

KAPLAN, WILFRED. *Advanced Calculus.* Reading, Mass.: Addison-Wesley Publishing Co., Inc., 1952.

SMITH, JON M. *Scientific Analysis on the Pocket Calculator.* New York: John Wiley & Sons, Inc., 1975.

"Texas Instruments Slide Rule Calculator, SR-50," Texas Instruments, Inc., 1974.

Hydrofoil with analog computer control.
(*Courtesy* The Boeing Company.)

Overview
of the computer

Perhaps no single invention in the history of modern man has contributed more to the enhancement of technological knowledge than the invention of the computer. Because of its speed, versatility, and accuracy, the computer can bring solutions to extremely complex problems within the grasp of every engineer. Because it is such a powerful tool for engineering analysis and synthesis, accreditation standards for every engineering discipline now suggest that engineering students be provided with the opportunity to use this computational tool. It is the purpose of this chapter to provide an initial overview of the form and function of the digital computer and the analog computer. This overview will focus on the basic components of these devices as well as on the rationale that forms the basis for their principles of operation. Since it is used more often, the digital computer will be considered first.

7.1 Digital computer hardware

An engineering college can be described either in terms of the tangible buildings and laboratory equipment it utilizes in its operation, or in terms of the curriculum, information, and academic rules essential to the intangible education process. Needless to say, both elements are essential in a complete description. In like manner, a digital computer system possesses two complementing elements. These elements are called the hardware and the software. Hardware is the term used to describe the tangible electronic components and other physical equipment of a computer. Software is the term used to describe the intangible programs and systematic rules used by the computer in processing information. Digital computer hardware will be discussed in this section, and the various aspects of digital computer software will be discussed in later sections.

Digital computers are found in many different sizes ranging from versions as small as a file cabinet up to systems large enough to completely fill several floors of a large industrial building. Typical digital computers used to solve engineering problems are shown in Figures 7-1 and 7-2. Although digital computers may differ in size, their basic form and function remain quite similar. As a general rule, digital computers are classified and categorized according to such things as:

1. Physical size
2. Memory storage size
3. Type of application
4. Speed of operation

Figure 7-1 The operations room of a large-scale digital computer. (*Courtesy* of IBM.)

Small, special-purpose computers are referred to as *minicomputers*. These machines are usually dedicated to a specific task such as on-line data reduction, analog to digital conversion, or process control. They provide considerable "hands-on" operation for the engineer who uses them. The

Figure 7-2 A minicomputer system. (*Courtesy* of Interdata, Inc.)

large-scale computer, on the other hand, is generally used for a variety of different data-processing tasks and usually has its own operational staff. Consequently, the engineering programmer may never see the machine he is using. Input and output operations may be handled over a counter in much the same way as one deals with a dry-cleaning establishment where one never sees the machines that do the dry cleaning.

Minicomputers have a memory capacity of 4 000 to 256 000 words* of storage while large computer complexes may have memory sizes of 30 000 to 556 000 words. The speed of a computer is expressed in terms of the time required to access data from its memory. These times vary from 3 to 0.5 nanoseconds (10^{-9} sec). Other standard measures of computer speed include add time or multiply time. These rapid access times are somewhat misleading since the system is only as fast as its slowest element. Since input and output devices (card readers, line printers, etc.) depend on mechanical parts, they may limit the overall processing speed of a digital computer.

Most contemporary digital computers have no single element that can be isolated and identified as being "the computer." Rather, each element works in harmony with many other components to produce what is called a *computer system*. An example diagram of one such computer system is shown in Figure 7-3.

Central processing unit.   The *nerve center* of the computer system is the central processing unit usually referred to as the CPU. This unit contains three important functional parts:

1. internal memory (main storage)
2. the arithmetic and logic unit
3. a control section.

The arithmetic and logic unit contains special work spaces called *registers* in which the computation and arithmetic manipulation take place. The control section of the CPU regulates the computational process by providing sequence instructions to the arithmetic/logic unit, by recalling and storing information from main storage, and by initiating communication between storage and input/output (I/O) devices.

The internal memory section consists of a matrix of specially prepared magnetic *cores* which are organized and arranged so as to hold data or

* The concept of a "word" is defined in Section 7.2.

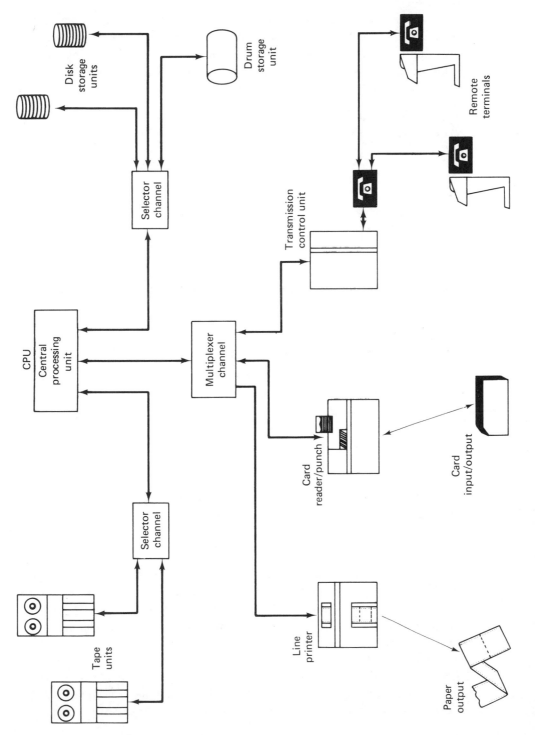

Figure 7-3 An example of a large-scale computer system.

Disk storage units

Drum storage unit

Selector channel

Remote terminals

Transmission control unit

CPU Central processing unit

Multiplexer channel

Selector channel

Card reader/punch

Card input/output

Tape units

Line printer

Paper output

159

program instructions. The cores are actually tiny rings of a ferrous material and are 0.02 to 0.08 inches in diameter. These cores surround one or more wires that pass through their centers and hold them in position in the matrix, as shown in Figure 7-4. If an electric current is passed through the proper

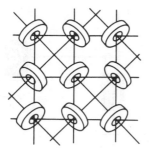

Figure 7-4 A small portion of main storage showing the magnetic cores.

pair of wires, the core will become magnetized. The polarity of the resulting magnetic field will depend on the direction of the current flow, as shown in Figure 7-5. In this way the core stores information in one of two possible magnetic states. This method of storage is called *binary storage* or *base two storage*. Since the magnetic field remains after the current flow has ceased, the core can be "read" at a later time to determine which of the two binary states it contains.

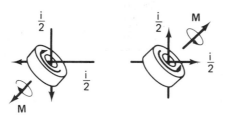

Figure 7-5 The two possible magnetic states of a memory core.

In the memory storage section of the CPU, groups of these cores form words or characters that are identified by a unique "address." This address is used to locate their position in the memory matrix. The memory of the computer can be visualized as a large room full of mailboxes, each having an identifying address and each serving as a storage location into which information can be placed and out of which this information can later be retrieved. Access to data from such internal storage takes place very rapidly and is faster than any other storage device in the computer system. For this reason, internal storage is often referred to as *immediate access* storage.

Internal memory in the CPU is quite expensive to manufacture, and, therefore, every effort is used to insure that this valuable storage space is used as efficiently as possible. In many large computers the internal memory may actually reside in separate cabinets located adjacent to the other sections of the central processor. To supplement the limited capability of internal storage, peripheral units such as magnetic disk packs, magnetic drums, or magnetic tape units may be used; however, the data retrieval times from these devices may be slower by several orders of magnitude.

Magnetic tape unit. The magnetic tape unit is a data storage device that utilizes spools of magnetic recording tape similar to that used for audio recording. A photograph of a typical magnetic tape unit is shown in Figure 7-6.

Figure 7-6 The magnetic tape unit. (*Courtesy* of IBM.)

Magnetic disk packs. The magnetic disk pack is a data storage device that utilizes from one to eleven rotating disks mounted on a common spindle. These disks look very much like oversized stereo phonograph records except that they have a coating of iron oxide which can be magnetized or demagnetized in a manner similar to magnetic recording tape. The data records on a disk pack are accessed by means of read/write heads that move radially from the center of the records to the outer edge. At least one read/write head is used for each disk surface. The heads are externally supported by a comb-like assembly. For a typical 11-disk pack, the comb has twenty read/write heads that can move to as many as 200 discrete radial positions on command. As the disks rotate, the head traces concentric circles, known as *tracks*, at each radial position. The disks rotate at a constant rate of 2 400 rpm, and the heads can record up to 7 000 bytes* of data per track. The average access time for this device is 75 milliseconds.

The prime advantage of the disk pack, when compared with magnetic tape, is that it allows information to be randomly accessed. For example, the first and last data records in a sequential set could be read without the need to pass over every intermediate value. This, of course, is not the case for magnetic tape, which is said to be *serial*. Another advantage of the disk pack is its transportability. Since the disk is moderately sized and can hold an enormous amount of data (equivalent to 70 000 punched cards) it is often used to ship large quantities of data/information from one computer center to another. A photograph of a computer disk drive is presented in Figure 7-7.

Figure 7-7   Magnetic disk pack drive. (*Courtesy* of IBM.)

Magnetic drum storage.   The magnetic drum storage device is a cyclic store device that is based on the same theory of operation as the disk pack. The

* The term *byte* is defined in Section 7.2.

drum cylinder is revolved at a constant speed and the data are stored upon tracks around the circumference. Unlike the disk pack, each track has a single read/write head. Since there is no movement of the read/write head, this device has a faster average data acquisition rate of 8.6 milliseconds. Unfortunately, it does not have the enormous data storage capacity of the disk pack.

Multiplexor. Whenever input/output (I/O) information flows to or from the CPU it is controlled by a piece of equipment called a *channel*. The channel is a device that relieves the CPU of the burden of communicating directly with I/O devices, thus allowing the data processing to proceed concurrently with I/O operations. In this way, valuable CPU time is not wasted in waiting for I/O information to be transmitted.

Two types of channels can be used. These are the multiplexor channel and the selector channel. The selector channel may communicate with only one "selected" I/O device at a time even though it may physically be connected to several different I/O devices. The actual "selection" of a particular subchannel for communication is done by the selector channel in response to commands from the CPU. An example of this type of connection is shown in Figure 7-3 for the tape drives. The multiplexor channel is a communications control device that allows the interleaving or meshing of many simultaneous transmissions in both directions. The multiplexor channel is able to service a large number of different subchannels because I/O devices operate at slow data speed when compared with the CPU operation speed.

I/O Equipment. The most common type of input to a computer is accomplished through the medium of punched cards. Decks of prepunched cards are read using a card reader, as depicted in Figure 7-8. Some of these devices are capable of read speeds of 1 000 cards/minute. Frequently, card readers are also equipped to punch cards as output from the computer if the programmer selects this option. Unfortunately, punch speeds in excess of 300 cards/minute are beyond the current state of design technology. A faster, more commonly used method for hard copy output to the programmer is available through the high-speed line printer (Figure 7-9). These machines are capable of printing 1 100 lines/minute onto special "fan fold" paper using up to 132 print positions per line.

The transmission control unit pictured in Figure 7-3 may be used to allow low-speed transmission of I/O information over regular telephone

Figure 7-8 High-speed card reader. (*Courtesy* of IBM.)

lines from remote locations. Because of their low speed, such configurations are poorly suited for handling large volumes of I/O data.

Magnetic tapes are also used as an I/O medium. Magnetic tape drives allow transmission rates of up to 150 000 bytes/second for serial data.

Figure 7-9. High-speed line printer. (*Courtesy* of IBM.)

Punched paper tape I/O is available at most large computer installations and is a less often used option.

Other special purpose I/O devices include cathode ray screens and drum or flat bed plotters used for output of graphical information. Light pens and sketch pads are sometimes available for input of graphic information (Figure 7-10).

Figure 7-10 A cathode ray output device. (*Courtesy* of NASA.)

7.2 Digital computer number systems

With few exceptions, digital computers are binary devices. This means that they store and manipulate data using the base two number system. This number system greatly simplifies the computation and storage process since it has only two operands, 0 and 1, rather than the ten that are found in the familiar base ten system. The term "binary digit" is often abbreviated to the single word *bit*. In the digital computer the smallest directly addressable unit is called a *byte*, which is formed from a group of adjacent bits. For example, a byte may be eight bits in length. The exact size of a byte will depend on the particular machine. Consecutive bytes in storage are grouped together to form *words*. For example, four bytes may form a single word of storage. Thus, if the bytes consist of eight bits each, the single word may consist of thirty-two total bits.

Although the digital computer relies on the base two number system for all computation and storage, the programmer does not need to use this system for input/output value since the computer is equipped to convert to and from the more familiar base ten system. Occasionally, however, it becomes necessary for the programmer to look at a printout of data/information exactly as it appears in storage. Under these circumstances it will be necessary for the user to understand how to convert to and from various number systems.

Since the base two number system has two operands rather than ten, the binary printout of a given numerical value will require the use of considerably more digits and thus will require more paper. In order to save paper and to make the numbers more manageable for this type of printout, the computer will usually convert to octal (base eight) or hexadecimal (base sixteen.) The reader may be wondering why it is more convenient to convert to such unusual base systems rather than to the more familiar base ten system. The answer lies in the fact that octal and hexadecimal values are easily converted from binary forms whereas decimal values are not so easily convertible; eight and sixteen are exact integer powers of two, and ten is not. It requires exactly three bits to represent a single octal digit and exactly four bits to represent a single hexadecimal digit. A decimal, hexadecimal, octal, binary table is given in Table 7-1. For a more thorough discussion of the conversion between different base systems the reader should consult Appendix C.

Table 7-1 Decimal-Hexadecimal-Octal-Binary Conversion Table

Decimal	Hexadecimal	Octal	Binary
0	0	0	0000
1	1	1	0001
2	2	2	0010
3	3	3	0011
4	4	4	0100
5	5	5	0101
6	6	6	0110
7	7	7	0111
8	8	10	1000
9	9	11	1001
10	A	12	1010
11	B	13	1011
12	C	14	1100
13	D	15	1101
14	E	16	1110
15	F	17	1111

Internal storage formats.   Although the actual form of internal storage for most digital computers will vary from machine to machine, certain characteristics are common to all devices.

Integer numbers are often referred to as *fixed-point* numbers and are represented by a half-word or a full word of binary digits in storage. The left-most binary digit is understood to be the sign where 0 represents "+" and 1 represents "−." Thus a 32-bit word would allow 31 bits to be used to represent an integer. In most cases the selection of half-word or whole word form for an integer is at the option of the programmer. The longer word permits storage of larger numbers but consumes twice as much of the premium storage space.

Real numbers (i.e., numbers having the potential for fractional parts) are referred to as *floating point* numbers. In order to save space and allow the largest number of significant digits, these numbers are stored in the form of scientific notation such as $3A1_{16} \times 16^5$. The left-most bit in a floating point storage space is used to store the sign ($0 = +$, $1 = -$.) The remaining bits of this left-most byte are devoted to storing the exponent (e.g., 5.) The remaining bytes are used to store the significant digits of the mantissa (e.g., $3A1_{16}$.)

To avoid the need for a sign digit on the exponent, most computers utilize an *excess notation* scheme, which means that every exponent is increased by some preselected value to insure that a negative value will never be used. In this way the exponent is stored as a value that is always a fixed amount greater than the power it actually represents. The mantissa of a floating point number is usually normalized before it is stored. This means that the exponent is adjusted so that the most significant digit is nonzero.

Floating point data can be represented in a single word (short form) or double word (long form). The longer form requires more storage space and allows more accuracy in the form of more significant digits. Unlike the long form integer storage mode, the long form floating point storage mode does not allow larger numbers to be stored since it does not modify the allowable size of the largest exponent.

Information in the form of alphabetic and special characters may be stored by means of a multiple-bit code where a unique pattern is used for each character. One standard code that often is used is the Extended Binary Coded Decimal Interchange Code, referred to as EBCDIC. Table 7-2 shows some valid EBCDIC characters and their corresponding 8-bit codes. Another standard code is the American Standard Code for Information Interchange, referred to as ASCII. Table 7-2a shows some valid ASCII characters and their corresponding 7-bit codes.

Table 7-2   EBCDIC Character Conversion Table

EBCDIC	Hex	Binary		EBCDIC	Hex	Binary	
a	81	1000	0001	A	C1	1100	0001
b	82	1000	0010	B	C2	1100	0010
c	83	1000	0011	C	C3	1100	0011
d	84	1000	0100	D	C4	1100	0100
e	85	1000	0101	E	C5	1100	0101
f	86	1000	0110	F	C6	1100	0110
g	87	1000	0111	G	C7	1100	0111
h	88	1000	1000	H	C8	1100	1000
i	89	1000	1001	I	C9	1100	1001
j	91	1001	0001	J	D1	1101	0001
k	92	1001	0010	K	D2	1101	0010
l	93	1001	0011	L	D3	1101	0011
m	94	1001	0100	M	D4	1101	0100
n	95	1001	0101	N	D5	1101	0101
o	96	1001	0110	O	D6	1101	0110
p	97	1001	0111	P	D7	1101	0111
q	98	1001	1000	Q	D8	1101	1000
r	99	1001	1001	R	D9	1101	1001
s	A2	1010	1010	S	E2	1110	0010
t	A3	1010	0011	T	E3	1110	0011
u	A4	1010	0100	U	E4	1110	0100
v	A5	1010	0101	V	E5	1110	0101
w	A6	1010	0110	W	E6	1110	0110
x	A7	1010	0111	X	E7	1110	0111
y	A8	1010	1000	Y	E8	1110	1000
z	A9	1010	1001	Z	E9	1110	1001
space	40	0100	0000	0	F0	1111	0000
+	8E	1000	1110	1	F1	1111	0001
−	BF	1011	1111	2	F2	1111	0010
*	5C	0101	1100	3	F3	1111	0011
/	61	0110	0001	4	F4	1111	0100
.	4B	0100	1011	5	F5	1111	0101
,	6B	0110	1011	6	F6	1111	0110
(	4D	0100	1101	7	F7	1111	0111
)	5D	0101	1101	8	F8	1111	1000
'	7D	0111	1101	9	F9	1111	1001

7.3   Programming languages

When the digital computer was first developed, the only programming languages available were "machine" languages. These languages consisted of strings of binary numbers that served to instruct the computer as to what

Table 7-2a   ASCII Character Conversion Table

ASCII	Binary	ASCII	Binary
a	1100001	A	1000001
b	1100010	B	1000010
c	1100011	C	1000011
d	1100100	D	1000100
e	1100101	E	1000101
f	1100110	F	1000110
g	1100111	G	1000111
h	1101000	H	1001000
i	1101001	I	1001001
j	1101010	J	1001010
k	1101011	K	1001011
l	1101100	L	1001100
m	1101101	M	1001101
n	1101110	N	1001110
o	1101111	O	1001111
p	1110000	P	1010000
q	1110001	Q	1010001
r	1110010	R	1010010
s	1110011	S	1010011
t	1110100	T	1010100
u	1110101	U	1010101
v	1110110	V	1010110
w	1110111	W	1010111
x	1111000	X	1011000
y	1111001	Y	1011001
z	1111010	Z	1011010
space	0100000	0	0110000
+	0101011	1	0110001
−	0101101	2	0110010
*	0101010	3	0110011
/	0101111	4	0110100
.	0101110	5	0110101
,	0101100	6	0110110
(	0101000	7	0110111
)	0101001	8	0111000
'	0100111	9	0111001

fundamental operations were to be executed in the performance of a given computational task. These machine languages were cumbersome and unpleasant to use. In addition, since each computer had its own unique machine language, the programmer was required to learn a new language for every different machine he used. It soon became obvious that, if the computer was to gain widespread use, it would be necessary to make substantial changes in the standardization of programming languages. The result has been the successive development of several generations of sophisticated computer languages to overcome many of these early shortcomings.

Computing languages fall into three general categories: machine languages, symbolic languages, and problem-oriented languages. The machine language is still the language with which the computer works and is unique to a given machine. Machine languages are referred to as *low-level* languages since they require that each instruction be written out one at a time. The problem-oriented languages are usually not machine dependent and can be used on any digital computer. Because they require fewer actual instructions to be written, problem-oriented languages are termed *higher-level* languages. These problem-oriented languages do not require programming by numbers but instead provide instructions through "statements" resembling combinations of mathematical formulas, English words, and English sentences. These statements must adhere to certain specific rules known as *syntax*. Most higher-level languages are specifically oriented toward a particular category of problems or toward a specific discipline. For example, FORTRAN and other languages have been developed for scientific programming while other special languages have been designed for general business and accounting procedures.

Programs written in higher-level languages must be translated into machine language equivalents before they can be executed. The translation process is accomplished by a specific program known as a *compiler*. Compilers read the user-written program and check for syntax errors before completing the final conversion to machine language. As part of this checking procedure the compilers usually print diagnostic messages to help the programmer correct syntax errors that have been discovered. After the program has successfully compiled, it will be stored in the computer memory to await execution. Perhaps the one disadvantage of these convenient, problem-oriented languages is that the compilation process consumes valuable processing time.

Symbolic languages are neither high level nor low level but combine some of the characteristics of each. Their primary purpose is to make the process of machine-level programming an easier task. They make use of *mnemonic* symbols rather than numbers to represent computer instructions. Symbolic languages are also called *assembly* languages and are used whenever one desires to program the computer to perform a certain specific task in the most efficient way. In this sense, symbolic languages allow the programmer more control over how the computer operates than would a higher level language. In order to translate from assembly language into machine language a special translation program known as an *assembler* is used. The actual translation process is performed by the computer before the computational process begins.

Many programming languages are in use today. Some of these languages are but slight variations on other commonly used languages. Others are the result of improvements on earlier, higher languages. Thus, for example, the FORTRAN language has progressed through FORTRAN, to FORTRAN II and on to its most recent version FORTRAN IV. Some of the most commonly used higher-level languages are:

ALGOL. The word ALGOL is an acronym for ALGOrithmic Language. This language was designed by an international committee of persons representing several different disciplines. ALGOL is intended to be a language for scientific problems.

APL. The term APL is an acronym for A Programming Language. APL could be described as a highly refined notation scheme combined with a special purpose computer language. APL was developed in 1962 by K. E. Iverson of Harvard. Because of its large character set and its unusual symbols, APL is used primarily through specially prepared time-sharing terminals having the special APL typeset.

BASIC. The BASIC language was developed at Dartmouth College in 1965 under the sponsorship of the National Science Foundation. The word BASIC is an acronym for Beginners All-purpose Symbolic Instruction Code. Its prime feature is that it is easy to learn and easy to use. Knowledge of BASIC provides an excellent stepping stone to other scientific languages such as ALGOL or FORTRAN.

COBOL. The COBOL language is designed primarily for business data processing. COBOL is an acronym for COmmon Business Oriented Language. It was first used in December 1959 and has since been implemented by every major computer manufacturer.

FORTRAN. The word FORTRAN is an acronym for FORmula TRANslation. It was first used by IBM in 1954. FORTRAN is specifically designed for scientific/engineering programming. It is the most widely used higher-level language in the world for scientific problem solving. A large majority of all engineering programs are written in FORTRAN. For this reason it is the most important language for the engineering student to learn.

PL/I. The PL/I language was developed in 1956 and is termed a *wide scope* language since it can be used for both scientific and business applications. Its notation is symbolic rather than English-like.

7.4 Operating systems

Simply stated, an operating system is the software which manages and regulates the flow of data and programs in and out of the digital computer. Operating systems are classified according to the degree of relative human involvement in the overall information management process. Operating system software has progressed through three generations. Most large-scale computer systems are now operating in the third generation mode to insure maximum efficiency in CPU utilization.

Basic programming support.   The operating system for early computers was implemented manually. Thus the sequence of operations required to execute a program was performed by the user himself. The procedure is illustrated in Figure 7-11. The compiler deck was first read into the computer followed by the user's program. At the completion of the compilation process, the computer would produce a punched card version of a machine language program called an *object* program. This object program deck was then read into the computer followed by any required data cards. The computer would then produce the computed results. This process was repeated for each program run. Such a mode of operation is cumbersome at best and is certainly an inefficient scheme from the aspect of computer utilization.

Batch processing.   In the *batch processing* operating system shown in Figure 7-12, a collection of jobs is submitted on magnetic tape or other mass storage device to a main computer from a peripheral computer. The various higher-level language compilers reside in storage within the main computer and are automatically loaded on request from the user's program. In order

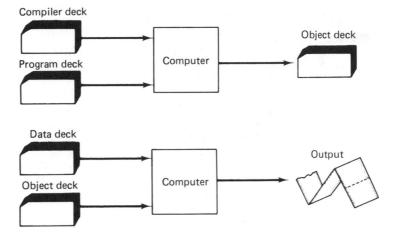

Figure 7-11 The Basic Programming Support Operating System.

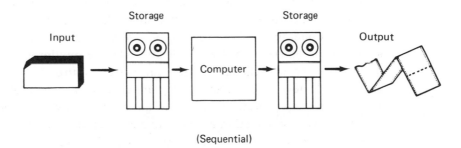

(Sequential)

Figure 7-12 The Batch Processing Operating System.

to allow the programmer to converse with the operating system, a special job control language (JCL) is used. This second generation operating system overcomes many of the difficulties associated with the basic programming support system. For example, it eliminates the need for human intervention in the compiler loading step. It should be noted, however, that this batch system accepts and executes programs in the same sequential order in which they are received. This characteristic can lead to inefficiency of CPU time utilization since, in spite of the automatic job-to-job transition, the input/output requests still cause the CPU to wait.

Multiprogramming. The third generation of computer operating systems utilizes a technique known as multiprogramming. This system was intro-

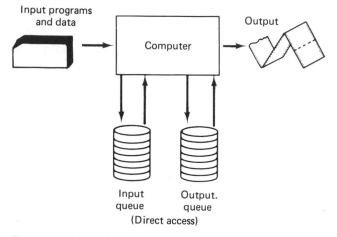

Input programs
and data

Output

Computer

Input
queue

Output.
queue

(Direct access)

Figure 7-13   The Multiprogramming Operating System.

duced in the mid 1960s and is illustrated in Figure 7-13. The unique virtue
of this system is its ability to maintain more than one job in some state of
activity at one time. This concept of *interleaving* of multiple programs
increases the efficiency of CPU utilization. In the multiprogramming environment a special scheduling program passes control from program to
program whenever the executing program encounters a natural wait due to
an input/output request. Input/output information as well as jobs awaiting
execution are maintained in an input queue or an output queue on a direct
access storage device such as a disk pack. The jobs are sequenced from the
queue by the operating system according to set priorities depending on
estimated execution time, estimated memory size required, special features
requested, and so on.

7.5   The analog computer

The words *analog, analogy,* and *analogous* all come from the same base
word formed from a combination of the Greek *ana* meaning "according to"
and *logos* meaning "ratio." Thus, the word analog is used to describe
something that is similar to something else, where the similarity is governed
by a specific ratio or relationship. The analog computer, sometimes referred
to as the differential analyzer, is a device for simulating the behavior of
many different physical systems. The tie that links all physical systems
together is the mathematics of differential equations. Thus, an analog
computer produces an output that changes with time in a manner identical

to the time variation of some physical variable in an engineering problem. Examples of such analog quantities might include the temperature variations in a mechanical system or the chemical composition variations in a chemical system.

Analog integrators using a mechanical, ball-and-disk principle were used as early as 1825. In the years that followed, these devices were developed and improved. In 1876 Lord Kelvin presented a description of a mechanical process for solving an ordinary differential equation. This information and the mechanical integrator provided a basis for the construction of the first large-scale general purpose mechanical differential analyzer in 1930. This machine was developed at the Massachusetts Institute of Technology under the direction of Vannevar Bush. The electronic version of the differential analyzer had its beginning during World War II and has since developed into the sophisticated device that we presently know as the electronic analog computer.

Analog computers come in various sizes ranging from table-top versions (see Figure 7-14) to devices large enough to fill one or more rooms. Most of these devices make use of prepatched panels that allow the programming to be done apart from the computer. In this way, the computer is not tied up for lengthy periods while program construction and program debugging takes place. The actual process of programming consists

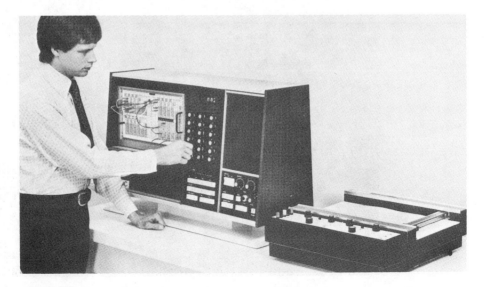

Figure 7-14 A table-top analog computer showing the removable patchboard. (*Courtesy* of Electronic Associates, Inc.)

of connecting various basic functional elements by means of wires so that the proper sequence of mathematical operations is satisfied.

The ability of the analog computer to model so many different types of physical systems makes it an extremely useful tool for the solution of engineering problems. For example, as a design tool, the analog computer allows the engineer to simulate proposed design changes on a system simply by changing a wire or by adjusting a variable resistor. The complete redesign takes only a few seconds and costs no more than the electricity required to operate the computer. In an actual design situation utilizing real hardware, a redesign requires hardware modifications and/or replacement. This procedure can take considerable time and can be quite expensive. The analog computer, then, can be used to save both design time and development costs (Figure 7-15).

A second advantage of the analog computer is its ability to simulate the behavior of a very slow process in a rapid fashion. An example of such

Figure 7-15   Computer simulation of processes aids in the development of complex systems such as petroleum refineries. (*Courtesy* of Foster Wheeler Energy Corporation.)

an application might be found in the electric power industry where a plant engineer wishes to observe the long-range effects of a proposed modification to the power distribution system. Since electric power demands are cyclic within a period of twenty-four hours, it would take several days before the effect of the proposed modification could be assessed. By using the analog computer, the behavior for several days can be compressed into the span of a few seconds. Thus, valuable time can be saved.

Conversely, the analog computer can produce a simulation which will slow down a process that otherwise occurs too fast to be observed. For example, if an engineer wishes to observe the closing of an electronic relay as a function of time, he would be unable to determine much about the motion from a real experiment since the closing process takes far less than one second. In this situation the analog computer could be programmed to simulate the relay closing displacement over a time period of up to a minute or more in order to allow the process to be examined fully. Such detailed "slow-motion" information can be highly valuable in the study of many types of engineering devices and processes.

7.6 A comparison of the analog and digital computers

Because of the flexibility of programming the patchboard, the analog computer can generally be programmed faster than the digital computer. On the other hand, the variables in an analog computer are continuous quantities rather than discrete values. This means that the solutions generated on the analog computer are accurate to within 2%. This accuracy is sufficient for most engineering problems, even though it is far less than that possible with the digital computer. The hybrid computer attempts to circumvent the problem of analog accuracy by utilizing a combination of the analog and digital computers (see Figure 7-16). In this way the hybrid computer combines the programming advantages of the analog computer with the high-precision arithmetic capability of the digital computer.

7.7 Summary

Since an understanding of the mathematics of differential equations is a prerequisite to a study of analog programming, this text will not attempt an in-depth treatment of the use of the analog computer. The interested reader may obtain further information about this and advanced analog topics from the analog references listed at the end of this chapter. In the chapters that

Figure 7-16 A large-scale analog/hybrid computer.
(*Courtesy* of Electronic Associates, Inc.)

follow, the fundamentals of digital computer programming will be presented. The engineering student who is learning about the digital computer for the first time will likely find this study a fascinating and rewarding experience if he or she is willing to invest the time and effort. The sense of satisfaction associated with the successful programming and execution of an engineering problem is in many ways similar to the feelings associated with the first solo landing of an airplane, the successful ski down a challenging slope, or the perfect instrumental performance of a difficult musical score.

PROBLEMS* **7.1**   Convert the following numbers into their decimal equivalents.

(a) 231.6_8 (d) $12C. \times 16^2$

(b) $AC4.B_{16}$ (e) $.007\ 21_8$

(c) $1\ 101.10_2$ (f) $.001\ 10_2$

* Procedures discussed in Appendix C are necessary to the solution of some of these problems.

7.2 Convert the following binary numbers into base 8 and base 16.
(a) 110 110.1 (d) 111.000 1
(b) 101 000.1 (e) 1.010 101
(c) 10.100 100 (f) 0 101.01

7.3 Convert the following decimal numbers into binary equivalents.
(a) 100.46 (d) 1/64
(b) 294. (e) −24.9
(c) .005 (f) 73.

7.4 Convert the following decimal numbers into hexadecimal equivalents.
(a) 1/16 (d) 76.
(b) −29.46 (e) .000 01
(c) 3.2×10^{-4} (f) $\pi/2$

7.5 If interpreted as an EBCDIC character string, what do the following represent?
(a) 1000 1000 1000 0001 1010 0101 1000 0101
(b) 87 89 A5 85

7.6 How would the word "WRITE" be coded in EBCDIC?

REFERENCES (Digital Computer)

ARDEN, BRUCE W. *An Introduction to Digital Computing.* Reading, Massachusetts: Addison-Wesley Publishing Co., Inc., 1963.

CHANDOR, ANTHONY, JOHN GRAHAM, and ROBIN WILLIAMSON. *A Dictionary of Computers.* Harmondsworth, Middlesex, England: Penguin Books, Ltd., 1970

Comtre Corporation, *Operating Systems Survey.* Princeton, N.J.: Auerbach Publishers, 1971.

KATZAN, HARRY, Jr. *Introduction to Programming Languages.* Philadelphia, Pa.: Auerbach Publishers, Inc., 1973.

LEHMAN, RICHARD S., and DANIEL E. BAILEY. *Digital Computing, Fortran IV and its Applications in Behavioral Science.* New York: John Wiley & Sons, Inc., 1968.

RUSHFORTH, J. M., and J. L. MORRIS. *Computers and Computing.* London: John Wiley & Sons, Inc., 1973.

Rutgers—The State University. Center for Computer and Information Services, "Users Manual." Version 1, March 1972.

SAMMET, JEAN E. *Programming Languages: History and Fundamentals.* Englewood Cliffs, N.J.: Prentice-Hall, Inc., 1969.

SCHUR, LEE DAVID. *Time-Shared Computer Languages*: *An Introduction to Conversational Computing.* Reading, Massachusetts: Addison-Wesley Publishing Company, 1973.

REFERENCES (Analog Computer)

BEKEY, GEORGE A., and WALTER J. KARPLUS. *Hybrid Computation.* New York: John Wiley & Sons, Inc., 1968.

1130 Computing System—Applications Program CSMP—Continuous System Modeling Program—Program Description and Operations Manual GH20-0282-2, 1968, IBM Corp.

JOHNSON, CLARENCE L. *Analog Computer Techniques.* New York: McGraw-Hill Book Company, Inc., 1963.

KORN, GRANINO, and THERESA M. KORN. *Electronic Analog and Hybrid Computers.* New York: McGraw-Hill Book Company, Inc., 1964.

PETERSON, GERALD R. *Basic Analog Computation.* New York: The Macmillan Company, 1967.

REKOFF, MICHAEL G., Jr. *Analog Computer Programming.* Columbus, Ohio: Charles E. Merrill Books, Inc., 1967.

Computer disk storage.
(*Courtesy* Copper Development Association, Inc.)

Fundamentals
of FORTRAN programming

8

A fundamental consideration in preparing a problem for digital computer processing should be the question "Is this problem suitable for the digital computer?" Far too frequently the computer is regarded as a magic genie that can solve any problem if only one knows how to ask the appropriate question. This is, of course, far from true. The digital computer is well suited for the solution of problems involving large numbers of repetitive calculations. It is not well suited for the manipulation of abstract ideas or for creative suggestions. These are tasks that at present are best left to the God-given talents of the human mind. Once this distinction is clearly understood, the engineer can utilize the digital computer in an efficient manner to enhance his ability to perform scientific calculations.

The purpose of this chapter is to present the fundamental concepts necessary for the FORTRAN language. Since FORTRAN is a computer language that consists of a set of rules, we will begin our study with a discussion of coding procedures, an explanation of FORTRAN variables, and a description of the procedure for writing FORTRAN expressions using these variables.

8.1 FORTRAN coding

Punched cards are the principal input mode for most computer systems. An example of a standard punched computer card is shown in Figure 8-1. The card is divided into 80 vertical columns numbered from 1 on the left to 80

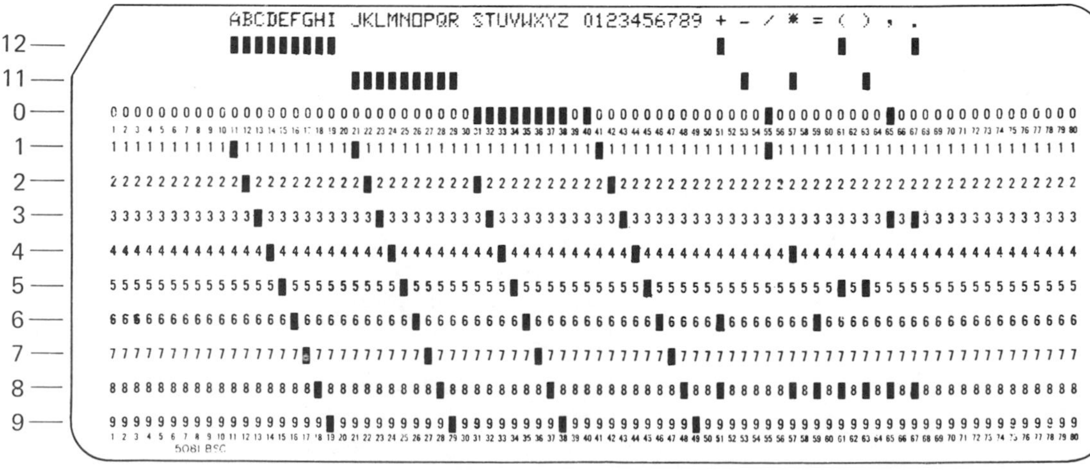

Figure 8-1 A standard computer card.

on the right. There are 12 possible punch positions per column. These punch positions are labeled, from top to bottom, 12, 11, and then 0 through 9. Thus, the top edge of a card is sometimes referred to as the "12 edge" and the bottom edge is sometimes referred to as the "9 edge."

A keypunch machine is used to punch the necessary combination of holes per column to represent the appropriate alphabetic, numeric, or symbolic character. Most keypunch machines also have provisions for printing the characters at the top of the card. In this way the cards may be visually checked for errors. The keypunch may be thought of as a special type of electric typewriter; however, unlike a typewriter, the keypunch has

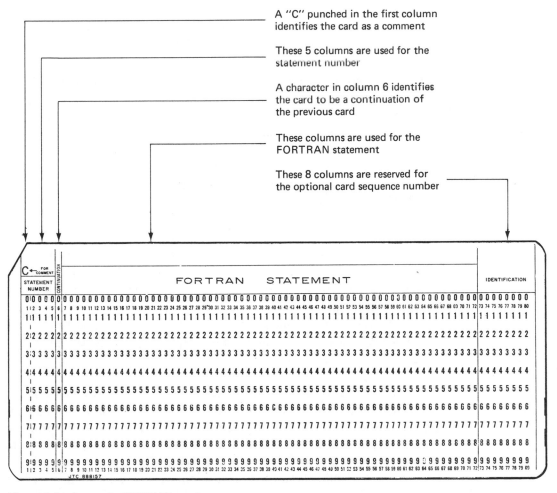

Figure 8-2 A sample FORTRAN card.

no means for correcting errors. Naturally a hole, once punched, cannot be refilled in a "strike-over" fashion. Thus a computer card with an error in any of its 80 columns must be discarded and a new, corrected card must be punched.

Specific groups of columns on each card are reserved for specific information. For this reason it becomes important to punch the proper information precisely into the proper column of the card. To help with this process, the programmer can utilize specially printed FORTRAN coding sheets or may make his own, using paper with vertically ruled lines. An example of specially printed computer cards for FORTRAN programming is shown in Figure 8-2.

Statement numbers.   Some types of FORTRAN statements can be identified by a statement number at the option of the programmer. The statement number must be one of the digits between 1 and 99999 and is punched in columns 1 through 5 inclusive. This number, if shorter than five digits, may be placed anywhere in the field since leading and trailing blanks are ignored by the compiler. Statement numbers label a particular FORTRAN statement so that the programmer may refer to it at some other point in his program. If this type of identification is not required to satisfy the logic of the program, it is wise to omit the statement number. Unnecessary statement numbers can decrease the efficiency of compilation and thus waste valuable computer time.

FORTRAN statements.   The text of a FORTRAN statement is written in columns 7 through 72. If a statement is too long to fit this space, the statement may be continued on up to five additional cards by placing a character, other than a blank or zero, in card column 6 on each of the extra cards. In FORTRAN statements, blank columns may be used to enhance the readability of a statement since blanks are ignored by the compiler.

Comments.   Narrative information to explain a program may be included in a FORTRAN program. Such information is usually included in all engineering programs since it allows the programmer to explain how the program works, to document what the form of the inputs and outputs will be, and to specify what the units and dimensions of the inputs and outputs will be. Comments are identified with a C in column 1, and the comment text is listed in columns 2 through 72. Since comment cards are not processed by the FORTRAN compiler, they may be included anywhere in a program except after the END statement or before a continuation line.

Card sequencing. Columns 73 through 80 are not scanned by the FORTRAN compiler and are thus available for numerical or alphabetical identification. If numbers are used to sequence the card deck, a deck that is inadvertently dropped or otherwise shuffled may be reassembled in the proper order by hand or by means of a sorting machine. Sequencing is especially important when there are a large number of cards in a deck.

8.2 FORTRAN constants and variables

Within a FORTRAN program there will be symbolic quantities which may assume different values as the program progresses. These are called variables. There will also be exact numbers, which are called constants. For example, in the expression A = 3.1415926 + B/2., A and B are variables and 3.1415926 and 2. are constants. Variables and constants can be further classified as either integer (fixed point) or real (floating point). The rationale for this distinction comes from the fact that certain engineering quantities will always be represented as discrete values or whole numbers (e.g., the number of teeth on a gear, the number of bolts on a pipe flange, the number of passengers on a bus, and so on). Other quantities are best represented as continuously variable, real numbers (e.g., the magnitude of the distance between two points, the mass of an object, and so on). Considering all combinations of type and form, we could get integer constants, real constants, integer variables, and real variables. We will discuss each of these separately.

Integer constants. An integer constant in FORTRAN is a number that does not contain a decimal point. (The decimal point is assumed to be after the last digit specified.) The maximum allowable number of digits in an integer constant will depend on the fixed-point word size for the particular computer being used. An integer constant may have a sign, but commas are not permitted within the constant. A space within the constant will be read as zero. Some examples of valid integer constants are:

$$0$$
$$1$$
$$20$$
$$-36$$
$$+2389$$

The following representations are not valid integer constants:

1.0	(Contains a decimal point)
5,280	(Contains a comma)

Real constants. The FORTRAN compiler understands any constant that contains a decimal point to be real. The maximum number of usable significant digits in a real constant will depend on the word size of the particular computer being used. Real constants may not contain a comma. In a manner similar to the familiar scientific notation (i.e., $30. \times 10^6$), a real constant may be written as a decimal value followed by the letter E followed by a one- or two-digit integer constant to indicate the power of ten. Some examples of valid real constants are:

0.0	
3.1415926	
30.E06	$(30. \times 10^6)$
30.E6	$(30. \times 10^6)$
−1.9	

The following representations are not valid real constants:

35	(no decimal point)
30.E	(no exponent)
30E06	(no decimal point)
30.E006	(exponent too long)

Variables. A FORTRAN variable is a specially addressed storage location into which computed values can be placed and from which these values can be recalled later. The recall process is accomplished through the use of the name of the variable. A variable name consists of from one to six (for some machines from one to five) alphabetic or numeric characters, the first of which must be alphabetic. The first letter of a variable name serves to identify the variable as either real or integer.

The variable type may be specified either implicitly or explicitly. An implicit specification is automatically made by means of two fundamental rules that are inherent in the FORTRAN compiler. These are:

1. If the first character of a variable name is I, J, K, L, M, or N, the variable is assumed to be integer.
2. All other first letter alphabetic characters are assumed to identify real variables.

Examples of valid integer variable names might be:

ITIME, N, M52, IXY, I3XYZ4.

Examples of valid real variable names might be:

X, Y, DIRT, FNCT, X34, XIMJ4.

Examples of invalid variable names might be:

3ABC	(first character must be alphabetic)
A3 + B	(improper symbol [+])
XYZIJKL	(too many characters).

In variable names, blank spaces are ignored and mathematical symbols are not permissible characters. If the programmer chooses explicitly to override the implicit rules, he may do so by means of a type statement listing those variables that are exceptions to the rule. Such statements take the form:

REAL ITEM, NCOUNT, J6

or

INTEGER X, DGRE, ALFA

This type specification statement is placed at the first part of a FORTRAN program so that the compiler will encounter it before encountering any FORTRAN statements or expressions containing these special variable names.

Since there is a substantial difference between the storage mode for integer and real variables, it is important that the engineer understand when to use the appropriate type. With care and a bit of imagination, variable names can be selected to clarify the meaning and form of the parameters they describe in a program. For example, an angle alfa expressed in degrees might be stored under the name ALFDEG. The same angle in radians might be ALFRAD. Usually, engineering parameters can be abbreviated or modified in order to provide a FORTRAN variable name that is both descriptive and of the proper form. For example, the variable IYEAR would be an integer variable that might contain a four-digit number corresponding to the year in a date. XMASS could be used as the name of a real variable that could represent the value of a mass in kilograms.

Arrays. In engineering computations it is often convenient to use a single variable name to describe a whole set of quantities. The individual elements of the set are distinguished by means of subscripts. For example, the seven coefficients of a sixth-order polynomial might be represented as a_j in the expression:

$$0 = \sum_{j=0}^{6} a_j x^j$$

The components of a vector might be described in terms of the same name in the form $\mathbf{V} = V_1 \mathbf{i} + V_2 \mathbf{j} + V_3 \mathbf{k}$. The state of a stress field or the temperature distribution in a problem might be described in terms of a matrix of the form:

$$\begin{bmatrix} S_{11} & S_{12} & S_{13} \\ S_{21} & S_{22} & S_{23} \\ S_{31} & S_{32} & S_{33} \end{bmatrix}$$

The FORTRAN compiler is equipped to handle such variable names with subscripts. These subscripted variables in FORTRAN are called arrays.

An array variable is a group of associated storage spaces reserved in an ordered way, into which a group of computed values may be placed and from which this group can later be recalled. An individual element in the array is identified by an integer subscript denoting its position in the array. For example, if the following five values were stored in an integer array named MASS,

$$20, 31, 45, 3, 20$$

then the third element, having a value of 45, would be referred to in mathematical form as $MASS_3$. Since characters in FORTRAN must all be placed at the same level (subscripts and superscripts are not available), we identify the subscript by placing it in parentheses as MASS(3) in order to distinguish it from the new variable name MASS3. Thus, the elements and their values in this example array would be written as:

```
MASS(1) = 20
MASS(2) = 31
MASS(3) = 45
MASS(4) = 3
MASS(5) = 20
```

In FORTRAN programs it is sometimes convenient to use an integer variable name rather than a constant as the subscript for an array. For example, the program could utilize MASS(I) where *I* could equal any value between 1 and 5. Just as before, the first letter of an array name will identify the type of array variable as either real or integer. It should be kept in mind that the value of the subscript always must be a positive integer. Simple mathematical expressions can be used as subscripts. Such expressions must be of the form:

$$ICONS1 * IVAR \pm ICONS2$$

where ICONS1 and ICONS2 are unsigned integer constants and IVAR is an unsigned integer variable. The sequential order of the variables in this expression must be maintained.

Thus the following representations are valid array variables and subscripts:

```
CX(I)
Y(3 * I + 1)
XZ(3)
JM(4 * J)
```

The following arrays do not have valid subscripts:

AX(−I)	(the variable subscript must be unsigned)
Y(−3∗J)	(the constant subscript must be unsigned)
C3Z(2.5)	(the subscript must be an integer)
I(2+K)	(the order of the subscript expression is wrong; the correct form is K+2.).

In order to represent a matrix, an array having two subscripts must be used. For example, in the stress matrix:

$$
S = \begin{bmatrix} 1.2 & 3.0 & 4.8 \\ 3.0 & -2.5 & 1.4 \\ 3.6 & 4.5 & -1.4 \end{bmatrix} \begin{matrix} \text{Row 1} \\ \text{Row 2} \\ \text{Row 3} \end{matrix}
$$

with Column 1, Column 2, Column 3 labeling the columns.

the element in the first row of the third column would be denoted $S(1, 3)$ and has a value of 4.8. FORTRAN allows the programmer to utilize arrays of up to three subscripts.

In order to tell the FORTRAN compiler how much storage space is to be reserved for a given array, the programmer must specify the dimensions of that array. This is done at the beginning of the program by means of the following statement:

```
DIMENSION M(3,2), V(4), X(2,4,4)
```

Such a statement tells the compiler that three arrays are being used. The first is a two-dimensional integer array (a matrix) with three rows and two columns (a total of six elements). The second is a singly subscripted real array with four elements. The third array, $X(I, J, K)$, is a three-dimensional real array where the maximum value of I is 2, the maximum value of J is 4, and the maximum value of K is 5 (a total of $2 \times 4 \times 5 = 40$ individual elements.)

The type of an array variable name can be changed from the standard notation by means of the explicit declaration mentioned previously. If this option is used, the dimension declaration for that variable can be specified at the same time. For example:

```
INTEGER XMAX, YG(30), Z
```

This would eliminate the need for a separate dimension statement unless, of course, there were other variables that also need dimensioning.

8.3 FORTRAN expressions

In FORTRAN, arithmetic expressions can be found on the right-hand side of arithmetic statements. The fundamental form of a FORTRAN expression is:

$$A = expression$$

where A is a subscripted or nonsubscripted variable and *expression* is an arithmetic expression containing constants, variables, function names, and arithmetic operation symbols. Although a FORTRAN statement closely resembles a conventional algebraic equality, it should be kept in mind that the equals sign signifies a replacement. Thus the expression is evaluated and the result replaces the current value of the variable A in storage.

Operation symbols. The five basic arithmetic operation symbols used in FORTRAN are:

+	addition
−	subtraction
*	multiplication
/	division
**	exponentiation

These symbols are combined with variables, constants, and functions to make FORTRAN expressions, subject to the following guidelines:

1. No two operational characters may be adjacent. For example, X + −Y is invalid. The correct form would be X + (−Y) or X − Y.
2. No operation symbol will be assumed. For example, 2X will not mean 2. ∗ X.

Operation rules.   The statement "two times three plus five" can be interpreted in two different ways. These are:

$$2.*(3. + 5.) = 16.$$
$$2.*3. + 5.\ \ = 11.$$

In order to avoid such ambiguities when writing FORTRAN expressions a special set of rules is used.

1. Parentheses can be used to specify and to clarify the mathematical meaning of an expression. Parentheses group terms and do not imply multiplication. Expressions in parentheses enter the computational process with the same status as a variable or constant. Unnecessary parentheses are allowed. If they are used properly, they have no effect. For example, A ∗ B is the same as A ∗ (B).
2. If the order of operations to be performed is not explicitly stated by means of parentheses, the following order of priorities prevails:
   (a) Expressions enclosed in parentheses
   (b) Evaluation of functions
   (c) Exponentiation
   (d) The process of forming negative values of positive quantities
   (e) Multiplication and division (left to right)
   (f) Addition and subtraction (left to right).

With a little practice, these rules can become almost second nature to the engineering programmer. It is, of course, as important to be able to convert engineering formulae into FORTRAN expressions as it is to be able to use a FORTRAN expression to compute a value. For example, if A = 1.0,   B = 2.0,   and   C = 3.0,   then   the   expression   D = (A + B) ∗ C ∗∗ 2/B would have a value of 13.5. The mathematical expression:

$$X = Y^2 + Z^2 - \frac{1}{Y + Z^{1/3}}$$

could be written in FORTRAN as:

$$X = Y**2 + Z*Z - 1./(Y + Z**(1./3.))$$

Mode of an expression. The mode of an expression is said to be integer or real depending on whether its variables and constants are of integer or real type. If the expression contains both integer and real parts, the mode is said to be mixed. Examples of these expressions are:

Expression	Mode
3	Integer
I+3	Integer
3.+A	Real
3. + A * J	Mixed

In a mixed mode expression, the parts of the expression involving pure integer operations are computed in the integer mode. These integer results are then converted to real values and the computation is completed in the real mode. For example, in the expression:

$$G+(I*A)+(I/J)+K**4$$

I/J and K $**$ 4 are computed in the integer mode and the resulting integer values are converted to real values. For the part I*A, the I value is converted before the real multiplication takes place.

This characteristic of the FORTRAN system can cause difficulties if the engineering programmer is not careful. In integer division, the integer result is always rounded down to the nearest whole number. Thus, for example, if J = 3/2 the result is stored in integer form as "1". Since integer subparts of mixed mode expressions are done by integer mathematics, this behavior can cause trouble. For example, A = 3/2 + 1.0 would give A = 2.0 since the 3/2 is stored as integer "1" before being converted to a real value. (It is wise to use 3./2. for the value 1.5 if this is what is intended.)

In exponentiation, if the exponent is an integer, the exponentiation is done by repeated multiplication. If the exponent is real, the result is computed by logarithmic means. Thus, for example, A $**$ 1000 would require 1000 multiplications of A by itself. One would expect the computational process to go much faster by use of $A ** 1000$. Of course with exponents that are not whole numbers, the logarithmic process is required. Care should always be exercised when using real exponents with variable arguments, since a negative argument in this situation can give trouble. This is best illustrated by considering the problem of $A^{2.5}$ where $A = -1.0$. What will be the sign of the result? (We know that $(-1.)^2 = 1.0$ and $(-1.)^3 = -1.$ but $(-1.)^{2.5}$ is indeterminate.)

Library functions. Certain mathematical functions occur frequently in engineering problems. To help with the evaluation of these, the FORTRAN compiler contains a modest library of function subprograms. A list of the most commonly used of these is shown in Table 8-1. They may be included in a FORTRAN expression as in the following example:

$$A = 3.0 * SIN(X) + SQRT(ABS(Y))$$

Note that it is possible to use the output of one function as an argument to another function. There is, of course, no danger of mistaking a function with an integer argument for an array variable since the name would not appear

Table 8-1   FORTRAN Supplied Functions (FORTRAN IV)

Name	Function Performed	Type of Argument	Type of Output
SIN(X)	Trigonometric sine (Argument in radians)	Real	Real
COS(X)	Trigonometric cosine (argument in radians)	Real	Real
ALOG(X)	Natural logarithm	Real	Real
EXP(X)	Argument power of *e* (i.e., e^x)	Real	Real
SQRT(X)	Square root	Real	Real
ATAN(X)	Arctangent	Real	Real
ABS(X)	Absolute value	Real	Real
IABS(J)	Absolute value	Integer	Integer
FLOAT(J)	Convert integer argument to real	Integer	Real
IFIX(X)	Convert real to integer	Real	Integer

in the dimension statement list. The prudent programmer will avoid selecting array variable names that resemble library function names. Special
functions that are desired but are not available in the library may be written
by the individual user. The procedure for this will be explained in Chapter
10.

8.4 Summary

The understanding of any field of scientific knowledge is based on the
careful application of a few fundamental principles or rules. The basic
information about FORTRAN variables and FORTRAN expressions presented in this chapter provides the foundation upon which the engineer can
build his ability as a programmer.

PROBLEMS **8.1** Conceive meaningful FORTRAN variable names for the following
integer variables:

(a) Number of bolts   (f) Page number
(b) Number of engineers   (g) Teeth per gear
(c) Month   (h) TV-channel
(d) Day   (i) θ
(e) Year   (j) $

8.2 Conceive meaningful FORTRAN variable names for the following real
variables:

(a) Time   (f) Velocity
(b) β (g) Threads per cm
(c) μ (h) Slope
(d) Resistance in ohms   (i) Volume in m^3
(e) Mass in kg   (j) Harold Evans' Lucky Points

8.3 State the value of A or I stored as a result of each of the following
arithmetic statements.

(a) A = 6. * 1./6.   (g) I = 6. * 1./6.
(b) A = 6. * (1./6.)   (h) A = 6. * (1/6)
(c) I = 6 * (1/6)   (i) I = 19/5 + 5/4
(d) A = (6. * 1.)/6.   (j) A = 3.0 * (1.0E + 4)/4.
(e) A = 6./1. * 6.   (k) A = 10./4. + 5./4.
(f) A = 6./(1. * 6.)   (l) I = 3. * 6 + 2

8.4 For each of the following arithmetic statements, show the mathematical equation it represents:
(a) Z = H ** 3 − 70./H + 6.
(b) Z = H ** 3 − 70./(H + 6.)
(c) Z = (H ** 3 − 70.)/(H + 6.)
(d) Z = H ** (3 − 70.)/H + 6.
(e) Z = H ** 3 − (70./H) + 6.

8.5 For each of the following mathematical equations, write the arithmetic FORTRAN statement needed for proper evaluation:

(a) $A = \dfrac{(x^2 + y^2)^{1/4}}{2 \sin 3x}$

(b) $B = \dfrac{x^{k+1}}{10^4}$

(c) $C = \dfrac{2.9L^2 W}{a^2 + b^2} + \tan^2 \theta$

(d) $D = \dfrac{\log_e (2x + H)}{\sqrt{Ax + 10^3}}$

8.6 Which of the following variable names are not valid? (State why they are not valid.)
(a) 3A6
(b) XYZ
(c) X36
(d) I + 4
(e) ABCX3
(f) ABCX35A
(g) +AB
(h) X+
(i) A * B
(j) R(3)

8.7 Which of the following are not valid integer constants?
(a) 3.4
(b) 4
(c) 3 × 10⁶
(d) I4
(e) 2
(f) 3 + 4
(g) 0.01
(h) I(4)
(i) 729684
(j) 86

8.8 Locate all errors in the following FORTRAN expressions.
(a) A = B + −C
(b) X(3) = 2 + Y(3) ** +5
(c) A ** 2 = B ** 2 + C ** 2
(d) C = 2Y + 4
(e) X = A(B) + C
(f) C = A123CDE + 9.

8.9 If $I = 2$, $J = 3$, $X = 2.5$, and $Y = 3.0$, what will be the value of the following FORTRAN expressions?

(a) 3.*X+2.*Y   (f) I*X/Y

(b) 3.**I   (g) I+J+X−Y

(c) 3.**I/J   (h) I/J + X

(d) 3.**(I/J)   (i) I/(J+X)

(e) X**Y   (j) (I/J)+X

8.10 What will be the mode of the following expressions? (Integer, real or mixed.)

(a) I+J   (f) X**2+4.

(b) IA+JB   (g) X+Y+J

(c) I+A   (h) AJ+BK

(d) X/I+4.   (i) AJ/BK

(e) X+Y   (j) A**X

REFERENCES

DICKSON, G., and H. SMITH. *Introduction to FORTRAN IV Programming, a Self-Paced Approach.* San Francisco, Calif.: Rinehart Press, 1972.

FORSYTHE, AIKEN, HUGHES, and ORGANICK. *Computer Science—Programming in FORTRAN IV with WATFOR and WATFIV.* New York: John Wiley & Sons, Inc., 1975.

FREIDMANN, J., P. GREENBERG, and A. HOFFBERG. *FORTRAN IV.* New York: John Wiley & Sons, Inc., 1975.

GOTTFRIED, B. *A Comparison of Programming Languages.* New York: Quantum Publishers, Inc., 1973.

KERNIGHAN and PLAUGER. *The Elements of Programming Style.* Whippany, N.J.: Bell Telephone Laboratories, Inc., 1974.

MAY, P. *Programming Business Applications in FORTRAN IV.* Boston, Mass.: Houghton Mifflin Co., 1973.

McCRACKEN, D. *A Guide to FORTRAN IV Programming.* Second Edition. New York: John Wiley & Sons, Inc., 1972.

McCUEN, R. *FORTRAN Programming for Civil Engineers.* Englewood Cliffs, N.J.: Prentice-Hall, Inc., 1975.

PASKUSZ, G. *Computers and Programming—a Self-Paced Study Guide.* Sarasota, Fla.: Omni-Press, Inc., 1975.

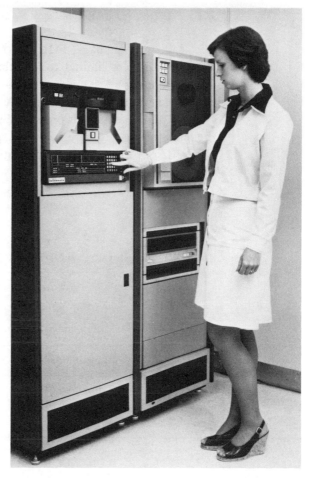

Computer program tape storage and control.
(*Courtesy* Interdata, Inc.)

FORTRAN statements and their use in programs

9

Like any language, FORTRAN has a special vocabulary. Fortunately this vocabulary is limited to less than two dozen unique statements. This limited number of statement types makes FORTRAN a language that is quickly learned and easily used. A summary of the most commonly used FORTRAN statements is presented in Table 9-1. This table may be used by the engineering programmer as a quick reference for the preparation of FORTRAN programs. The application of each of these statements will be discussed in detail in the following sections.

Table 9-1   A Summary of FORTRAN Statements

Type	Name	Form
Arithmetic Statement	Arithmetic Assignment	*v = arithmetic expression*
Control Statement	Unconditional GO TO	GO TO n
	Computed GO TO	GO TO $(n_1, n_2, .. n_k)$, iv
	Arithmetic IF	IF(*arithmetic expression*)n_1, n_2, n_3
	Logical IF	IF(*logical expression*) *statement*
	DO	DO n iv = i_1, i_2, i_3
		DO n iv = i_1, i_2
	CONTINUE	CONTINUE
	STOP	STOP
	END	END
Input/Output Statement	Read	READ(i,n) *variable list*
	Write	WRITE(i,n) *variable list*
	Format	n FORMAT($dcs_1, dcs_2, ...$)
Specification Statement	Real	REAL *variable list*
	Integer	INTEGER *variable list*
	Dimension	DIMENSION $v_1(k_1), v_2(k_2), ...$
	Equivalence	EQUIVALENCE $(v_1,v_2, ..), (v_4,v_5, ..), ..$
	Data	DATA $v_1, .. v_k/ic_1*c_1, .. ic_n*c_n/, ...$

Key: Uppercase letters are required. Lowercase letters are to be specified by the programmer.
    dcs—data conversion specification
    n—statement number
    iv—integer variable name
    ic—integer constant
    i—integer variable or constant
    v—general variable of any type
    c—general constant of any type

9.1 Arithmetic statements

The first class of FORTRAN statements, known as arithmetic statements, was discussed in detail in the previous chapter. It is worth repeating, however, that arithmetic statements cause values of arithmetic expressions to be assigned to program variables as the program is executed. Arithmetic statements may have statement numbers at the option of the programmer. Almost all calculations performed by a program will be accomplished through use of this class of statements.

Normally, FORTRAN statements are executed sequentially. This means that they are executed in the order in which they appear in the program. For example, the string of arithmetic statements:

```
10   A = 3.0
21   B = 2. + A
30   C = B*A
36   A = 2.
50   B - A*0.5
```

would be performed starting with statement 10 and proceeding through to statement 50. It is often desirable to modify this sequential procedure. The modification can be accomplished by means of control statements.

9.2 Control statements

This class of FORTRAN statements enables the programmer to control the course of the program. That is, the programmer can control the sequence of execution of program statements. Some types of control statements even permit the computer to make decisions based on the specific value of an expression at the time of execution of the control statement.

Unconditional GO TO statement. The unconditional GO TO statement of the form

GO TO n

interrupts the sequential execution and transfers control to statement n. The value of n must be an integer constant corresponding to an existing statement number. For example:

$$GO\ TO\ 21$$

would cause statement number 21 to be the next one executed, regardless of its position in the program.

Computed GO TO statement. The computed GO TO statement is of the form:

$$GO\ TO(n_1, n_2, n_3 \ldots n_k),\ iv$$

Like the GO TO statement, the computed GO TO statement transfers program control to a designated statement. The computed GO TO is more versatile, since the statement number to which the transfer is made may be altered during the execution process. In this statement, $n_1, n_2, \ldots n_k$ is a sequence of statement numbers and iv is a nonsubscripted variable whose value is in the range:

$$1 \le iv \le k$$

and whose value indicates which of the k statement numbers is to be used. Thus, if $iv = 3$, control is transferred to statement n_3. In the example,

$$INAME = 4$$
$$GO\ TO(36,21,30,50),\ INAME$$

control would be transferred to statement number 50 since the value of INAME indicates that the fourth statement number is the desired choice. This control statement should be used with care to be sure that the value of iv is within the allowable range. If:

$$iv > k \quad or \quad iv < 1$$

the results are unpredictable.

Arithmetic IF statement. The arithmetic IF statement of the form:

$$IF(arithmetic\ expression)\ n_1, n_2, n_3$$

allows the programmer to specify a conditional transfer to one of the three statements $n_1, n_2,$ or n_3 depending on whether the numerical value of the arithmetic expression is less than zero, equal to zero, or greater than zero, respectively. In this statement the arithmetic expression must be enclosed in parentheses and the three statement numbers must be separated by commas. In the example:

IF(C * 5.) 10, 40, 50

the conditional transfer depends on the value of the arithmetic expression C*5. If the expression is less than zero, control is transferred to statement number 10; if the expression is exactly equal to zero, control is transferred to statement number 40; and if the expression is greater than zero, control is transferred to statement number 50.

Logical IF statement. The logical IF statement is of the form:

IF(*logical expression*) statement

In this statement the logical expression has a value that is either true or false. When the logical expression is true, the statement to the right of the parentheses is executed before passing control to the next sequential statement in the program. When the logical expression is false, the statement that follows the parentheses is ignored. Logical expressions generally take the form of inequalities by combining arithmetic expressions and the logical operators shown in Table 9-2. In the statements:

```
        IF(STRESS.LE.SMAX) GO TO 30
    21  A = 3.56
    30  STRESS*C(1)*4.32
```

control is transferred to statement 30 if STRESS $\leq$ SMAX. Otherwise, control would be transferred to statement 21.

Table 9-2 Logical Operations

Operator	Meaning
.LE.	Less than or equal to ($\leq$)
.LT.	Less than ($<$)
.EQ.	Equal to ($=$)
.NE.	Not equal to ($\neq$)
.GT.	Greater than ($>$)
.GE.	Greater than or equal to ($\geq$)

DO statement.   Since the digital computer is particularly well suited for the solution of problems involving repeated calculations, it is often used for engineering computations that are iterative in nature. Such problems require that the computer repeatedly execute a group of statements.

As an example, suppose that the average value of all 1000 numbers stored in an array A(I) is to be determined. This value could be found by means of the following group of FORTRAN statements:

```
       •
       •
   C    THIS PART OF THE PROGRAM COMPUTES THE NUMERICAL AVERAGE
   C    OF THE 1000 VALUES STORED IN THE ARRAY A(I).
   C
    8  SUM = 0.0
    9  I = 1
   10  SUM=SUM+A(I)
   11  IF(I.EQ.1000)GO TO 20
   12  I=I+1
   13  GO TO 10
   20  AVG=SUM/1000
       •
       •
```

In this program segment, four separate statements are required to control the iterative process. These are statements 9, 11, 12, and 13. Statement 9 initializes the value of the array subscript; statement 12 increments the subscript value in steps of one unit; and statements 11 and 13 keep the summing process in operation until I exceeds 1000. By using the DO statement, these four control statements can be combined into a single statement. This streamlined version of the program segment would appear as follows:

```
       •
       •
   C    THIS PART OF THE PROGRAM COMPUTES THE NUMERICAL AVERAGE
   C    OF THE 1000 VALUES STORED IN THE ARRAY A(I).
    8  SUM = 0.
       DO 10 I=1,1000
   10  SUM=SUM+A(I)
   20  AVG=SUM/1000
       •
       •
```

The general form of the DO statement is

$$DO\ n\ iv = i_1, i_2, i_3$$

or

$$DO\ n\ iv = i_1, i_2$$

This DO statement causes the computer to repeatedly execute all statements from the DO statement up to and including statement *n*. This group of statements is often referred to as the "DO-loop." The first time this group of statements is executed the value of the *index variable*, *iv*, is set to the *initial value* i_1. In successive executions of the DO-loop, the index variable is increased by the *increment value* i_3. If the increment value is left unspecified, the value is assumed to be 1. The integer value i_2 is called the *test value* and is the value that the index variable must not exceed. Before the statements within the DO-loop are executed, the index variable value is compared with the test value. If the index variable exceeds the test value, the DO-loop statements are not executed, and control is transferred to the statement following statement *n*.

As the iterative process progresses, the value of the index variable may be used as a subscript or as an integer variable in calculations. It may not be changed in value, however, by a statement within the range of the DO-loop.

The last statement in a DO-loop must be an executable statement and may not be another control statement such as an IF, GO TO, or DO.

A transfer out of a DO-loop (other than the normal exit) may be accomplished at any time by means of a GO TO or IF statement. A transfer back into a DO-loop is permitted only if neither the index value, *iv*, nor any of the index parameters, i_1, i_2, and i_3 is changed outside of the loop. Although this type of transfer is permitted, it is wise to avoid doing it unless absolutely necessary.

It is sometimes convenient to include one or more DO-loops within the range of another DO-loop. This procedure is allowed as long as all statements in the range of an inner DO-loop are contained within the outer DO-loop and as long as each of the DO statements has a different index variable name. When this telescoping arrangement is satisfied, the loops are said to be *nested*. Most computers have a limit on the maximum depth of a single nest of DO's. Generally this will be on the order of twenty to thirty

DO-loops. An example of the structure for a valid set of nested DO-loops is as follows:

(Note that the brackets are used to indicate the range of the DO-loops.) The following structure would not be valid because of the overlap of the nested DO-loops.

CONTINUE statement. There are some circumstances under which it is convenient to end a DO-loop with an IF or GO TO statement. When such circumstances occur, it is desirable to have a method to circumvent the restriction against such statements at the end of the DO-loop. One way to circumvent the restriction, of course, would be to invent a "do-nothing" statement such as DUMMY=1.0 where the variable DUMMY has no meaning whatsoever in the program. Another, more efficient, way to accomplish this is to use the CONTINUE statement. The CONTINUE statement is a dummy statement which does not produce any calculated result. It merely indicates that the normal sequence of statements should be continued. The CONTINUE statement is principally used as the range limit for a DO-loop but can also be used anywhere in a program that the programmer finds convenient. An example of the use of the CONTINUE statement is as follows:

```
        DIMENSION A(1000)
        •
        •
C       THE PURPOSE OF THIS GROUP OF STATEMENTS IS TO SEARCH
C       THE A(I) ARRAY TO FIND THE FIRST POSITIVE VALUE.
        APOS1=0.0
        DO 7 I=1,1000
        IF(A(I))7,7,6
    6   IFIRST=I
        GO TO 8
    7   CONTINUE
        GO TO 9
    8   APOS1=A(IFIRST)
    9   CONTINUE
C       NOTE THAT UPON LEAVING THE DO-LOOP THE A(IFIRST) VALUE
C       HAS BEEN DISCOVERED TO BE THE FIRST POSITIVE VALUE.
C       IF NO POSITIVE VALUE HAS BEEN FOUND APOS1=0.0
        •
        •
        •
```

STOP statement.   The STOP statement is used to terminate the execution process of a program. Although more than one STOP statement may be placed in a program, the first one to be reached causes the program to terminate. Some computer systems are better equipped to terminate program execution through other types of statements, such as CALL EXIT.

END statement.   The END statement identifies the last FORTRAN statement of a program. It is placed after the last FORTRAN statement as a signal to the compiler that the last statement to be compiled has been reached. The END statement is not executed. Any statements that follow the END statement will not be compiled.

9.3   Input/output statements

Input/output (I/O) statements control the flow of information between the computer and the input/output equipment; that is, they provide communication links between the computer program and the peripheral equipment, such as card readers, line printers, and so on. Each of the peripheral pieces of equipment is designated by a logical unit number in the (I/O) statement. Three fundamental categories of I/O statements exist. These are the READ, WRITE, and FORMAT statements.

READ statements.   The READ statement is used to transmit information from an input unit to the computer. The most common form of input is through the medium of punched data cards. The READ statement has its general form as follows:

READ(i,n) variable list

In this statement *i* is an integer variable or constant that specifies the logical unit number to be used for the input data. This value differs from computer to computer, and the FORTRAN programmer must check the operations manual of the particular computer system being used in order to identify this number. The parameter *n* is a statement number of the FORMAT statement that specifies the form in which the data are to be understood by the read process. The *variable list* is a list of variable names in the order that they will be read. This list specifies the number of values to be read and identifies the named locations into which these values are to be placed.

For example, the FORTRAN statement:

READ(5,100)   A,B,I,K

would read four values from a card utilizing FORMAT statement 100. These four values would be stored in the named locations corresponding to A,B,I, and K. After the execution of this statement the values formerly stored in these four storage locations would be replaced by the newly read values. Any number of quantities may be read by the same READ statement. As the above example indicates, there is no restriction on mixing integer and real types of variables in the list.

When an array variable name appears in a read list in unsubscripted form, all of the quantities in the array are assumed to be transmitted. For example:

```
        DIMENSION A(1000)
        •
        •
        •
20      READ(5,101) A
        •
        •
```

would imply that all 1000 values of A(I) are to be read by the computer when it executes statement number 20.

Sometimes it is convenient to transmit only a portion of an array. Suppose, for example, that the programmer desires to transmit only the first 100 elements of the array A(I). This could be done by the following statements:

```
        DIMENSION A(1000)
        •
        •
        •
        DO 1 I=1,100
1       READ(5,101) A(I)
        •
        •
```

Since this situation occurs so frequently, the FORTRAN compiler allows a form of DO indexing to be used in the input list itself. This procedure saves the writing of the DO statement. Thus the above statements could be shortened to:

```
        DIMENSION A(1000)
        •
        •
        •
        READ(5,101)(A(I), I=1,100)
```

The reader will note that here the indexing is quite similar to the DO loop previously described. This type of read statement is known as an *implicit* DO.

The variable name list of a read statement may contain both normal variable names and implicit loops as long as the implicit loops are enclosed in parentheses. Indeed, multiple levels of indexing are possible as long as each level is enclosed in parentheses. For example:

READ(5,102) A,B,((D(I,J),I=1,30),J=1,10)

would read the single values of *A* and *B* as well as all 300 values of D(I,J) from D(1,1) to D(30,10).

WRITE statement.   The WRITE statement is used to transmit information from the computer to an output unit. The most common form of output is through the printed page. The WRITE statement is quite similar to the READ statement and has the general form

WRITE(i,n) *variable list*

In this statement *i* is an integer variable or constant that specifies the logical unit number to be used for the output. Naturally, this integer is different from the integer identifying the READ unit. Here again, the engineering programmer must consult the operations manual of the computer system being used in order to identify this number.

Some programmers prefer to use variable names such as IREAD and IWRITE in READ and WRITE statements for the logical unit numbers. The actual values of these variables are then specified by two arithmetic statements at the start of the program. In this way, a program written for use on one computer can be quickly converted for use on another by changing the two arithmetic statements to reflect the new values for IREAD and IWRITE. This technique eliminates the need to replace the many READ and WRITE statements that can appear in a complex program.

The parameter *n* in the WRITE statement is the statement number of the FORMAT statement specifying the form in which the data are to be written. The variable list is a list of variable names separated by commas and placed in the order that they are to be written. Thus the FORTRAN statement:

WRITE(6,100) A,B,I,K

would write the value of four variables in storage utilizing the FORMAT. statement number 100. When an array variable name appears in a write list in unsubscripted form, all of the elements of the array are transmitted. The "implicit DO" described previously is permitted as long as the implicit loops are enclosed in parentheses.

For example:

WRITE(5,104)IMAX,A,(B(I),I=1,10)

would write the present values of IMAX, A, and elements B(1) through B(10).

Most printers attached to FORTRAN systems take their cue regarding spacing of lines (carriage control) from the first character of each line. This character does not print. The allowable characters for carriage control and an explanation of their meaning is presented in Table 9-3.

Table 9-3 Allowable Characters for Carriage Control
Using the First Character in Each Line

Character	Result
blank	single spaces before the line is printed
0	double spaces before the line is printed
1	skips to the top of a new page before printing
+	causes all spacing or skipping to be suppressed before printing

Since the control of spacing is important to the readability of the output, the engineer should pay close attention to the proper use of these special characters. Forgetting the fact that the character in the first print space of a line does not print can provide misleading results. For example, if the five-digit integer 29654 is written in the first five spaces on a line the result would be 9654. For this reason, most programmers skip spaces by using an X field or other printout device to exercise control over the first character of a line, as discussed later in this chapter. This procedure is further illustrated in example programs at the end of this chapter.

FORMAT statement. In order for a FORTRAN program to transfer data either to or from the computer, it is necessary for the programmer to specify the form in which the data will be transmitted. The data conversion specification (*dcs*) explains the form in which the data are to be written or read. This is accomplished by means of the FORMAT statement. The general form of the FORMAT statement is as follows:

$$n \quad \text{FORMAT}(dcs_1, dcs_2, dcs_3, \ldots)$$

The statement number *n* is required because it is referred to in the READ and WRITE statements. The dcs_i elements represent data conversion specifications. The data conversion specification elements must be separated by commas, and the total list of elements must be enclosed in parentheses. The data conversion specifications are sometimes referred to as data *fields*. A summary table of acceptable data conversion specifications is presented in Table 9-4.

Since FORMAT statements perform no manipulative function by themselves, they may be placed at any convenient location in a FORTRAN program after the specification statements (to be defined in Section 9.4) and

Table 9-4 Summary of Acceptable Data Conversion Specifications

Specification	Use
Aw	transmits alphameric data utilizing either real or integer storage
Ew.d	transmits real numerical data in scientific notation form $w \geq d + 7$ is required
Fw.d	transmits real numerical data in normal decimal form $w \geq d + 3$ is required
wHalphameric characters	transmits a string of alphameric characters
Iw	transmits integer data
Tw	transmits information concerning the starting position of a record on a card or page
wX	specifies that w blanks will be skipped
'literal data'	transmits the string of alphameric and special characters enclosed in apostrophes
	specifies the beginning of a new record: in reading it skips to a new card, in printing it skips to a new line

Key: Uppercase letters are required. Lowercase letters represent values to be specified by the programmer.
w—represents the total width of the field.
d—represents the total number of decimal digits in a field.

before the END statement. A FORMAT statement need not appear adjacent to the READ or WRITE statement that it complements, although some programmers prefer to elect this option. A single FORMAT statement may be used by any number of different READ and/or WRITE statements. Since the FORMAT statement is not an executable statement it may not serve as the end of a DO-loop or as a transfer point from a GO TO or IF statement.

The numerical and alphameric data specifications in the FORMAT statement must have a one-to-one correspondence in type with the variable names in a READ or WRITE list. For example, the statements:

```
            READ(5,200)A,I
       200  FORMAT(F10.5,I5)
```

would be valid since the real variable A requires a real data conversion specification, and the integer variable I requires an integer data conversion specification. If the number of data conversion specifications in a FORMAT statement is less than the total number of variables being read, the specification list will be repeated as long as the data conversion specifications agree in type with the variables. Whenever a FORMAT specification list is repeated, the read or write process will start a new card or new print line. Data conversion specification elements within a list also may be repeated by placing an integer multiplier ahead of the individual specification. Thus the statements:

```
        READ(5,200) (A(I), I = 1,40)
   200  FORMAT(8F10.5)
```

would specify that eight values per card would be read using the conversion specification F10.5. In this example the specification list would have to be repeated five times in order to read all 40 values of A(I). Under no circumstances may the programmer specify a single string of data conversion specification elements that occupy more space than is allowable on the particular I/O device. Data cards can have, at most, 80 punch positions, and printer paper output usually has no more than 120 spaces to a line. A limited, one-level parenthetical expression is allowed in a FORMAT statement as a convenience to permit repetition of data conversion specification patterns. For example:

```
   201  FORMAT(2X,2(I5,2X,F10.5))
```

would be the same as writing:

201   FORMAT(2X,I5,2X,F10.5,I5,2X,F10.5)

"A" data conversion specification. Many engineering quantities are labeled with an identifying name. For this reason it becomes important to be able to read, write, and manipulate alphameric characters in a FORTRAN program. The specification Aw is used to read or write w characters. For example, the FORTRAN statements:

100   FORMAT(A3)
      READ(5,100) FLUID

would read three alphameric characters and store them under the single variable name FLUID. A suitable data card for these statements is shown in the accompanying figure. If the number of alphameric characters read is less than the field width, the remaining characters are assumed to be blanks. If the number of characters read is greater than the field width, the excess characters are left out.

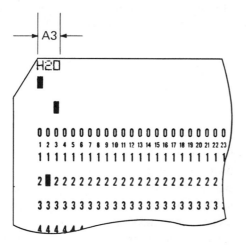

In using this type of field the programmer should keep in mind that only a limited number of alphameric characters can be stored in a single computer storage space. This number depends on whether real or integer storage names are being used as well as on the particular computer system.

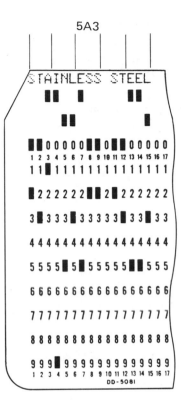

For example, if only three characters are allowed for each storage location, the data card shown, having fourteen characters, could not be read into a single storage location. The information could be read into five locations using five A3 fields. Rather than write A3 five times this data conversion specification string can be written as 5A3. Thus the statements:

```
        READ(5,100)(X(I),I=1,5)
100     FORMAT(5A3)
```

would perform the task.

"E" data conversion specification. Real engineering quantities are often specified in scientific notation. The E-conversion allows transmission of these quantities in scientific form. For example, the number $+0.234\ 56 \times 10^{-24}$ may be written in E-conversion form as $+0.23456E$-24. The E field is specified as Ew.d where w denotes the total width of the field and d specifies the number of decimal digits desired. Since spaces are required for the sign, zero, decimal, E, exponent sign, and two-digit exponent, the value of w must not be less than d+7. If w is greater than d+7, leading blanks are assumed. An example data card using the FORMAT statement:

20 FORMAT(A3,E15.5)

is shown in the following figure.

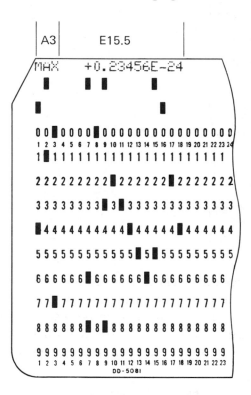

"F" data conversion specification. The most common way to transmit real numbers is by the F-conversion of the form Fw.d. Here w is the total width of the field and d is the number of decimal digits desired. The total field length should provide sufficient positions for the sign, a whole-number digit, the decimal point, and the decimal portion of the number. Thus, $w \geq d + 3$ is required. If insufficient positions are reserved by d, the fractional part is truncated. For example, the number +10.392 156 98 written in F10.6 would be +10.392156. It is important to note that truncation is different from rounding off in that this number would be rounded to six decimal digits as +10.392 157. If excess positions are reserved by d, zeros are added to fill the field. For example, 18. written in F10.3 would be 18.000.

If insufficient field width is provided to accommodate the whole-number portion of a real variable, the computer will print an error code to alert the programmer that the output cannot fit into the field specified. Thus, for instance, the number 9 546.3 has too many whole number digits to be written in F10.8 since there are insufficient positions to the left of the decimal. An error code that is commonly used is a string of asterisks equal in number to the width of the field. Thus an error code for the field F10.5 might be **********.

When using the F-conversion for input data, the user may punch the decimal point at any position within the limits of the field and the value will be properly interpreted by the computer, as long as it is contained within the limits of the field. If the programmer chooses not to punch a decimal point, an implied decimal point is automatically understood to be placed so that the last d card columns in the field represent the decimal digits. Thus the number 3.14159 could be transmitted using the FORMAT statement:

30   FORMAT(F10.5)

and either of the two cards shown.

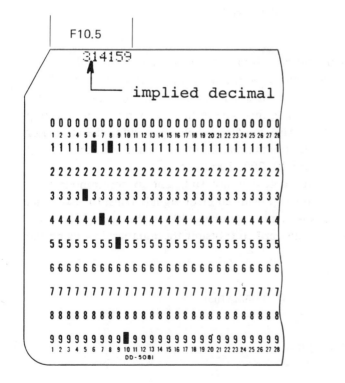

"H" data conversion specification. The H-conversion provides a way to transmit a string of literal alphameric data. This conversion field might be used to write titles on a page or headings on columns of numbers. In this specification the integer constant to the left of the H specifies the total number of alphameric characters to be transmitted. Blank spaces are counted as characters. The most frequent error made by programmers using this type of field is in miscounting the number of characters. An example of the use of this field would be as follows:

```
          A=3.14
          WRITE(6,101) A
    101   FORMAT(3H A=,F10.5)
```

This set of statements would cause the output pages to have the following printed:

```
          bA=bbb3.14000
```

Here the lowercase *b*s represent blank spaces.

"I" data conversion specification. I-conversion is used to transmit integer data. In this conversion, written as Iw, the w specifies the width of the field. Integer values for input and output are right justified. The most frequent error made by programmers using this type of field for input is in punching the integer data in the wrong card column. When this is done the computer automatically assumes that the trailing blanks are zeros and thus the value 2 can be misinterpreted to mean 20, 200, 2000, etc.

If the width of an output field is not sufficient to accommodate an integer variable, the computer will print an error signal. Thus, for example, if the programmer attempts to write a number 3496 in the field I3, an error code will result. A correct data card to transmit the number 354 using the FORMAT statement:

```
    41   FORMAT(I5)
```

is shown in the following figure.

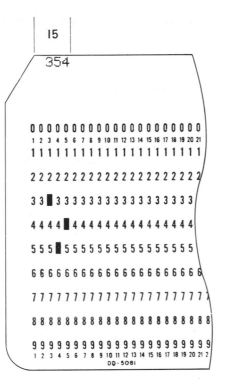

"T" data conversion specification. T-conversion allows the user to begin transmitting data at any position on a page or card. For example, the FORTRAN statements:

```
          A=10.
          WRITE(6,104) A
     104  FORMAT(T40,F10.5)
```

would begin the F10.5 field at position 40 on the page. Since the first character of each line does not print, this would correspond to the thirty-ninth print position.

"X" data conversion specification. The X field is used to skip spaces in an output or input record. The number of spaces to be skipped is specified as an integer that precedes the X. Thus the data conversion specification 5X would skip five spaces. The skip field is often used to add readability to a printed page by providing blank spaces between columns of numbers. For example:

202   FORMAT(11X,12H STRAIN DATA)

Literal data in apostrophes.   Literal data of the form of alphameric and special characters may be transmitted by placing the string of characters in apostrophes. An apostrophe character within such a string is represented by two successive apostrophes in order to distinguish it from the apostrophe signifying the end of the string. H format and literal format may be used interchangeably. Examples of valid literal data strings in FORMAT statements are:

205   FORMAT(' STRESS ANALYSIS SUMMARY')
206   FORMAT(' ITEMS THAT HAVEN''T BEEN SPECIFIED')
207   FORMAT(24H STRESS ANALYSIS SUMMARY)

9.4   Specification statements

Specification statements are special nonexecutable statements that provide information to the compiler. This information deals with the nature of variables and with the allocation of storage space. All specification statements must precede any executable statements in the source program. Specification statements should appear in the following order:

Type Statements (REAL, INTEGER)

DIMENSION
COMMON (to be discussed in the next chapter)
EQUIVALENCE
STATEMENT FUNCTION (to be discussed in the next chapter)
DATA

first executable statement

(Other specification statements that relate to subroutine and function sub-programs will be discussed in the next chapter.)

Type statement. Type statements of the form:

REAL   *variable list*

INTEGER   *variable list*

are used to override the default rule that determines the type of a named variable according to the first letter of the variable name. The use of these two statements was discussed in the previous chapter.

DIMENSION statement. The DIMENSION statement provides information regarding the allocation of storage space for array variables (unless this information is already specified in a Type statement). The general form of the DIMENSION statement is:

DIMENSION $v_1(k_1), \ldots v_n(k_n)$

where $v_1 \ldots v_n$ are array names and the $k_1 \ldots k_n$ are each composed of 1 or more unsigned integer constants that specify the maximum value of subscripts. An example of the DIMENSION statement would be:

DIMENSION A(100), B(200), X(20,10,3)

EQUIVALENCE statement. In most FORTRAN programs, each variable is assigned to a unique storage location. Occasionally, however, it is convenient to have two or more variables share the same storage location. This option is provided by the EQUIVALENCE statement of the general form:

EQUIVALENCE$(v_1, v_2, \ldots), (v_4, v_5, \ldots) \ldots \ldots$

Each pair of parentheses encloses a list of two or more variable names that refer to the same location. For example, suppose that it is desired to make the ultimate stress "SULT" and the yield point stress "SYP" equal for one particular run of a stress analysis program. This could be accomplished by the single statement:

EQUIVALENCE (SULT,SYP)

The program could be converted to its previous (unshared) state simply by removing this EQUIVALENCE statement.

DATA statement. The DATA statement is used to set initial numerical values of variables. Although arithmetic assignment statements could be used to initialize variables, to do so would require a separate statement for each value initialized. The DATA statement can perform all desired initialization in a single statement. The general form of the DATA statement is:

$$\text{DATA } v_1, \ldots v_k / ic_1 * c_1, \ldots ic_n * c_n /, \ldots$$

In this statement the v_i values are variable or subscripted array names and the c_i values are data constants that may be real, integer, or alphameric depending on the type of variable to which they are assigned. The ic_i values are optional unsigned integer constants that indicate how many variables are to be assigned the value they precede. A slash is used to separate and to enclose the data constants. As an illustration of the use of the DATA statement, consider the following example:

DATA A,B/2.4,3.5/

In this statement the variable A is set to 2.4 and the variable B is set to 3.5. In the example:

DATA C(1),D/2*0./

both $C(1)$ and D are set to zero. If an array name is listed in a DATA statement in unsubscripted form, the constants are assigned starting from the first element and proceeding toward the end of the array. For example:

DIMENSION F(5)
DATA F/2 * 1.0,1 * 2.0,2 * 10./,A/'YES'/

In this statement the five element values of the array F are assigned as follows:

F(1) = 1.0
F(2) = 1.0
F(3) = 2.0
F(4) = 10
F(5) = 10

The variable A in this statement is assigned the literal value 'Yes'.

9.5   The engineering approach to programming

Good programming practice requires that the engineer follow a systematic approach in preparing the FORTRAN statements to solve a given problem. Some important rules to follow when preparing FORTRAN programs are:

Rule 1:   *Be sure that you understand the problem to be solved.* The lack of a clear understanding of the problem can lead to considerable frustration and waste of time for the programmer.

Rule 2:   *Decide what inputs and outputs will be necessary for the program.* Be sure to keep in mind the importance of dimensional units for the input and output quantities.

Rule 3:   *Select a method to solve the problem.* An *algorithm*, or step-by-step plan for solving the problem, may be selected in whatever way seems most efficient to the programmer. Beginning programmers often find it helpful to use *flowcharts* to diagram the calculation/decision process. Sample flowchart symbols are presented in Figure 9-1. As the programmer becomes more proficient he will find that the "logical flow" process will become automatic, and it may not be necessary to draw a flowchart diagram.

It should be noted that the selection of a particular program algorithm is a personal matter. A complex problem may be approached in many different ways. The FORTRAN language provides sufficient versatility so that a variety of different algorithms can often be used to solve a given problem. When preparing a FORTRAN program it is wise to anticipate where difficulties in the input, output, or algorithm may occur. Sufficient

Element	Diagram Symbol	Remarks
START	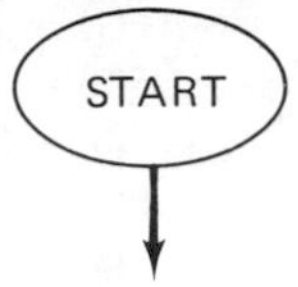 START	Identifies the point where computation begins.
READ	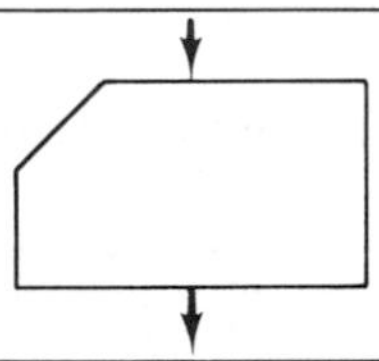	Identifies a point where a READ occurs. The variable names to be read are listed in the diagram symbol block.
WRITE	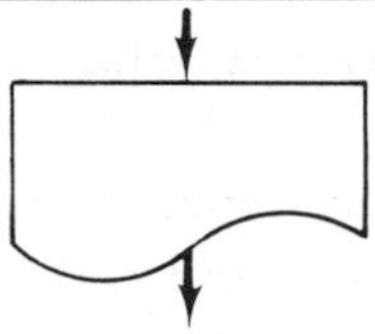	Identifies a point where a WRITE occurs. The variable names to be written are listed in the diagram block.
DECISION	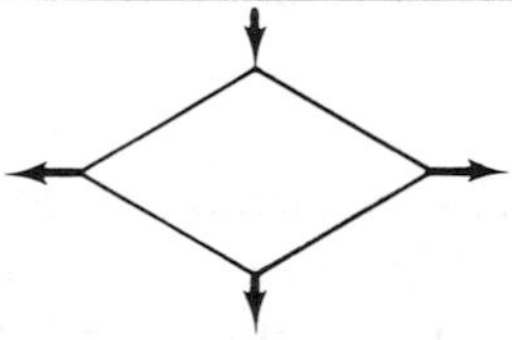	Identifies a point where a decision occurs. The question to be asked is placed in the block. The 3 branches are alternatives.
ARITHMETIC OPERATION	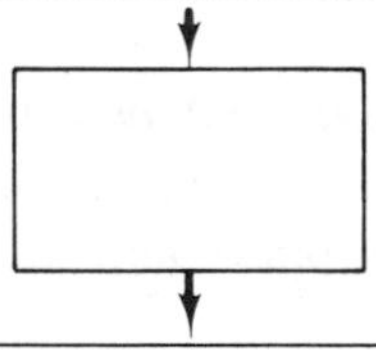	Identifies a point where an arithmetic operation occurs. The arithmetic statement is placed in the block.
DO-LOOP	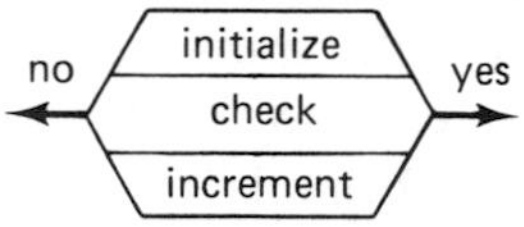 no / initialize \ yes check \ increment /	Identifies a point where a repeated loop begins.
TRANSFER POINT	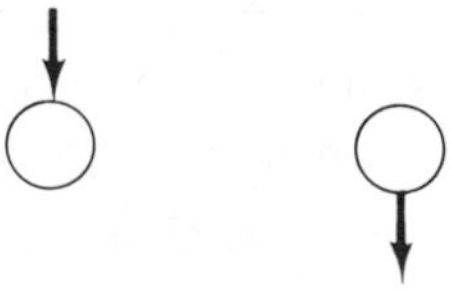	Identifies points of transfer to or from other points in the diagram. The points are identified by number.
STOP	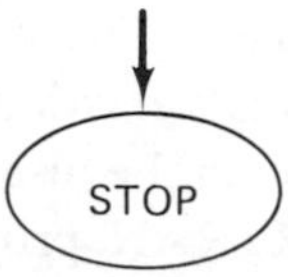 STOP	Identifies the point where computation stops.

Figure 9-1 Sample flowchart symbols. The symbols are placed end to end and are connected with lines to make a flow diagram according to the required logic flow of the program.

checks (IF statements, etc.) may be included in a program to safeguard against faulty input or algorithm breakdown.

Rule 4: *Write and keypunch the program.* This phase of program preparation actually converts the algorithm into FORTRAN statements. In doing this, the programmer should make generous use of comment cards to document what the program does, how it works, who wrote the program (including the date), what the input and output quantities are (including appropriate units), what the limitations or restrictions on the use of the program are, and so on. Since a useful computer program can be shared with other engineers and/or retained for reuse in the future, it is extremely important to make the program "self-documenting." A poorly documented program is difficult for another engineer or even for the programmer himself to rerun and/or modify after the programmer has forgotten how the program works. Documentation is also extremely important on the output page since the output often is separated from the program listing. The output, by itself, will have meaning only if the programmer has used literal write statements to provide titles, headings, and dimensional units on the output page.

Rule 5: *"Debug" the program.* This process utilizes the compiler to check for syntax errors in the FORTRAN statements as well as minor errors in the logical flow process. Even the most careful programmer can make FORTRAN syntax errors in writing a program.

Rule 6: *"Check Run" the program.* Whenever a program is first written, it should be run with at least one set of input data for which the answers are known. In this way the program can be checked to make sure that the algorithm is operating correctly. The check run should attempt to exercise every loop of the program to safeguard against hidden errors that might occur later.

9.6 Example applications

The best way to learn to write programs is through actual experience. A number of practice programming problems are suggested at the end of this chapter for the engineering programmer to try. Some sample programs are also presented.

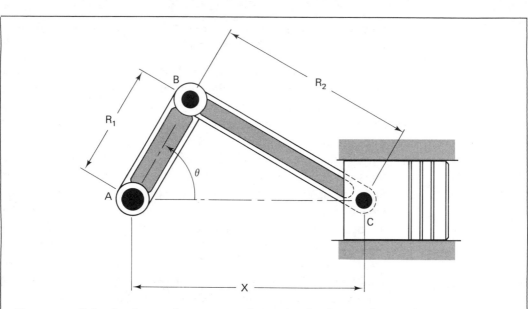

EXAMPLE 9-1   In the engine system shown in the figure above, the crank rotates
with a constant angular velocity of 10 rad/s counterclockwise. It is
desired to generate data for use in plotting the displacement, the
velocity, and acceleration of the piston for 10-degree positions of
the crank. The program must be capable of reading the crank and
coupler lengths, R_1 and R_2, from punched cards and should check
to make sure that R_2 is longer than R_1 for proper operation.

From the law of cosines for the triangle ABC the engineer can find:

$$x^2 - 2R_1 x \cos \theta + R_1^2 - R_2^2 = 0$$

Thus for the positive root of this quadratic:

$$\text{displacement} = x = R_1 \cos \theta + \sqrt{R_2^2 - R_1^2 \sin^2 \theta}$$

Taking derivatives gives:

$$\text{velocity} = \dot{x} = \frac{\dot{\theta} R_1 x \sin \theta}{R_1 \cos \theta - x}$$

$$\text{acceleration} = \ddot{x} = \frac{\dot{x}^2 + 2R_1 \dot{x}\dot{\theta} \sin \theta + R_1 x \dot{\theta}^2 \cos \theta}{R_1 \cos \theta - x}$$

A sample flowchart, FORTRAN program, and resulting output for
solution of this example problem are shown on the following pages.

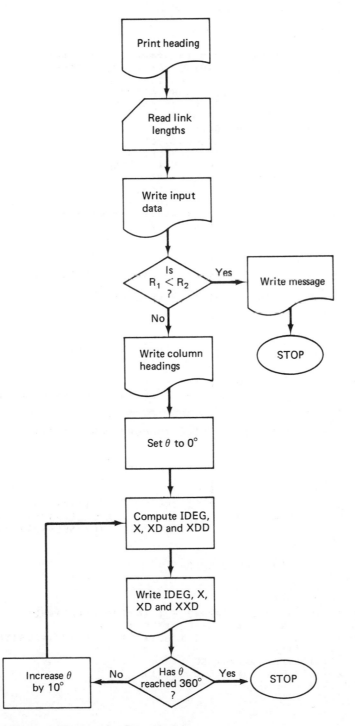

Logic flow diagram for Example 9-1.

Computer program for Example 9-1.

```
C
C       ****************************************************
C       THIS PROGRAM ANALYZES AN ENGINE CRANK AND PISTON
C       MECHANISM FOR DISPLACEMENT, VELOCITY, AND
C       ACCELERATION AT TEN DEGREE CRANK INTERVALS.
C       THE CRANK ROTATES AT A RATE OF 10.RAD/SEC.
C                              T. E. SHOUP 9/75
C       NOTATION USED IN THIS PROGRAM-
C                    X     - DISPLACEMENT (CM.)
C                    XD    - VELOCITY (CM/SEC.)
C                    XDD   - ACCELERATION (CM/SEC**2)
C                    THETA - CRANK ANGLE (RADIANS)
C                    R1    - CRANK LENGTH (CM)
C                    R2    - COUPLER LENGTH (CM.)
C       ****************************************************
        DATA IREAD,IWRIT/5,6/,PI/3.1415926/
C
C       PRINT HEADINGS FOR THE PAGE
        WRITE(IWRIT,100)
  100 FORMAT('1KINEMATIC ANALYSIS OF AN ENGINE RUNNING AT 10.RAD/SEC')
C
C       READ THE LINK LENGTHS AND WRITE THEIR VALUES
        READ(IREAD,101)R1,R2
  101 FORMAT(2F10.5)
        WRITE(IWRIT,102)R1,R2
  102 FORMAT(' CRANK LENGTH   R1 = ',F10.5,/,
     1        ' COUPLER LENGTH R2 = ',F10.5,//)
C
C       CHECK TO BE SURE THAT R1.LT.R2
C       IF THIS IS NOT TRUE, PRINT A MESSAGE AND TERMINATE THE PROGRAM
        IF(R1.LT.R2) GO TO 1
        WRITE(IWRIT,103)
  103 FORMAT(' THESE PROPORTIONS GIVE IMPROPER OPERATION')
        STOP
C
C       PRINT HEADINGS ON THE PRINTOUT COLUMNS
    1   WRITE(IWRIT,104)
  104 FORMAT(1X,50('-'),/,
     1 ' CRANK         PISTON        PISTON         PISTON',/,
     2 ' ANGLE      DISPLACEMENT     VELOCITY     ACCELERATION',/,
     3 ' (DEG)         (CM)         (CM/SEC)      (CM/SEC**2)',/,
     4 1X,50('-'))
C
C       CALCULATE AND PRINT THE VALUES
        DO 2 I=1,37
        IDEG = 10*(I-1)
        THETA = IDEG*PI/180.
        X = R1*COS(THETA) + SQRT(R2**2 - (SIN(THETA)*R1)**2)
        XD = 10.*R1*X*SIN(THETA)/(R1*COS(THETA)-X)
        XDD =(XD*XD + 2.*R1*XD*10.*SIN(THETA) + R1*X*100.*COS(THETA))/
     1    (R1*COS(THETA)-X)
    2   WRITE(IWRIT,105)IDEG,X,XD,XDD
  105 FORMAT(2X,I3,5X,F8.3,5X,2(E10.3,5X))
        WRITE(IWRIT,106)
  106 FORMAT(1X,50('-'))
        STOP
        END
```

Output for Example 9-1.

```
KINEMATIC ANALYSIS OF AN ENGINE RUNNING AT 10.RAD/SEC
CRANK LENGTH    R1 =    1.00000
COUPLER LENGTH R2 =     2.00000
```

CRANK ANGLE (DEG)	PISTON DISPLACEMENT (CM)	PISTON VELOCITY (CM/SEC)	PISTON ACCELERATION (CM/SEC**2)
0	3.000	.000	-.150+03
10	2.977	-.259+01	-.146+03
20	2.910	-.505+01	-.134+03
30	2.803	-.724+01	-.115+03
40	2.660	-.903+01	-.893+02
50	2.490	-.103+02	-.587+02
60	2.303	-.111+02	-.255+02
70	2.108	-.112+02	.731+01
80	1.914	-.108+02	.361+02
90	1.732	-.100+02	.577+02
100	1.567	-.887+01	.708+02
110	1.423	-.758+01	.757+02
120	1.303	-.626+01	.745+02
130	1.205	-.500+01	.698+02
140	1.128	-.383+01	.639+02
150	1.070	-.276+01	.582+02
160	1.031	-.179+01	.537+02
170	1.008	-.878+00	.509+02
180	1.000	-.457-06	.500+02
190	1.008	.878+00	.509+02
200	1.031	.179+01	.537+02
210	1.070	.276+01	.582+02
220	1.128	.383+01	.639+02
230	1.205	.500+01	.698+02
240	1.303	.626+01	.745+02
250	1.423	.758+01	.757+02
260	1.567	.887+01	.708+02
270	1.732	.100+02	.577+02
280	1.914	.108+02	.361+02
290	2.108	.112+02	.731+01
300	2.303	.111+02	-.255+02
310	2.490	.103+02	-.587+02
320	2.660	.903+01	-.893+02
330	2.803	.724+01	-.115+03
340	2.910	.505+01	-.134+03
350	2.977	.259+01	-.146+03
360	3.000	.274-05	-.150+03

EXAMPLE 9-2   A new type of vehicle race has been suggested in which the objective is to drive from 100 to 500 miles with minimum fuel consumption. Prepare a computer program that will read the name, number of miles driven, and number of gallons used for each of ten entries. The program must compute the number of miles per gallon and select the winner of the race. Any driver who does not drive the required range of miles must be disqualified. The input data will be given in the form of one set per card as follows:

(NAME(I,J),I=1,5),DIST(J),GAL(J)
100   FORMAT(5A3,2F5.1)

The program that performs the solution to this example problem is presented below. A sample of the program output is also presented.

Computer program for Example 9-2.

```
C       ********************************************************************
C       THIS PROGRAM COMPUTES THE RESULTS OF AN ENERGY EFFICIENCY RACE
C       IN WHICH 10 VEHICLES WILL COMPETE.  THE RACE IS OVER A
C       DISTANCE OF 100 TO 500 MILES AND THE WINNER WILL BE THE
C       PERSON WHO HAS THE BEST MILES PER GALLON FUEL CONSUMPTION.
C       A DRIVER WHO DOES NOT DRIVE THE REQUIRED DISTANCE RANGE IS
C       DISQUALIFIED.
C                                        T. E. SHOUP 9/75
C       NOTATION USED IN THIS PROGRAM -
C               NAME(I,J) - AN ARRAY CONTAINING THE DRIVER'S NAME
C               DIST(J)   - AN ARRAY CONTAINING THE DISTANCE DRIVEN
C               GAL(J)    - AN ARRAY CONTAINING THE NUMBER OF GALLONS USED
C       ********************************************************************
        REAL MPG(10),NAME(5,10)
        DIMENSION DIST(10),GAL(10)
C
C       WRITE THE TITLE AND HEADINGS ON THE PAGE
        WRITE(5,98)
   98   FORMAT('1AUTO FUEL EFFICIENCY CONTEST RESULTS',/,1X,76('-'),/
       1 ' NAME OF DRIVER',7X,'MILES',4X,'GALLONS',4X,'MPG',10X,
       2 'COMMENTS',/,76('-'))
C
```

```
C       READ THE DATA CARDS AND COMPUTE MPG
        DO 1 J=1,10
        READ(2,100)(NAME(I,J),I=1,5),DIST(J),GAL(J)
  100 FORMAT(5A3,2F5.1)
    1   MPG(J) = DIST(J)/GAL(J)
C
C       FIND THE WINNER AND DISQUALIFY THOSE WHO VIOLAT  THE RULES
        BEST = 0.
        DO 2 J=1,10
        IF(DIST(J).GT.500.) GO TO 2
        IF(DIST(J).LT.100.) GO TO 2
        IF(MPG(J).LE.BEST) GO TO 2
        IBEST = J
        BEST = MPG(J)
    2   CONTINUE
C
C       WRITE THE DATA AND RESULTS
        DO 3 J=1,10
        WRITE(5,101)(NAME(I,J),I=1,5),DIST(J),GAL(J),MPG(J)
  101 FORMAT(1X,5A3,2(5X,F5.1),5X,F5.2)
        IF(J.EQ.IBEST) WRITE(5,102)
        IF(DIST(J).GT.500.) WRITE(5,103)
        IF(DIST(J).LT.100.) WRITE(5,104)
  102 FORMAT('+',T48,'***THE WINNER***')
  103 FORMAT('+',T48,'DISQUALIFIED - TOO MANY MILES')
  104 FORMAT('+',T48,'DISQUALIFIED - TOO FEW MILES')
    3   CONTINUE
        WRITE(5,105)
  105 FORMAT(1X,76('-'))
        CALL EXIT
        END
```

Output for Example 9-2.

```
AUTO FUEL EFFICIENCY CONTEST RESULTS
----------------------------------------------------------------------------
NAME OF DRIVER        MILES     GALLONS     MPG      COMMENTS
-----------           ------    -------    -----
GOMER MILES           980.0      35.0      28.00 DISQUALIFIED - TOO MANY MILES
ETHYL STINGE          301.0       8.6      35.00 ***THE WINNER***
MILES MISER            99.0       5.4      18.33 DISQUALIFIED - TOO FEW MILES
AUTO GUZZLEGAS        208.0      20.0      10.40
IMA SAVER             406.0      12.0      33.83
RHODA MOTORBIKE       150.0       7.4      20.27
RONDA CIRCLE          170.0      12.4      13.70
HADA WRECK            105.0       8.2      12.80
RENTA CAR             101.0       7.1      14.22
RITA WRONGSIGN        499.0      21.0      23.76
----------------------------------------------------------------------------
```

9.7 Summary

Once the engineer knows the basic vocabulary of the FORTRAN language, he or she can build a vast variety of programs to exploit the speed and accuracy advantages of the digital computer. As the engineer becomes more proficient at program preparation, he or she may find that some advanced FORTRAN techniques are quite useful in implementing problem solution methods. The most commonly used of these advanced techniques is the FORTRAN subprogram. This important topic will be discussed in the next chapter.

PROBLEMS   **9.1** Identify the errors or difficulties associated with the following FORTRAN statements.

(a)		DO 3, I=1,10
(b)		IF(A) GO TO 7
(c)		IF(A) 3,45
(d)		WRITE(5,600) (A,B,C)
(e)		IF(B.LT.7.) 7,6,6
(f)		READ(6,700) D,E,F(I),I=1,7
(g)		A+B=C
(h)	100	FORMAT(E6.4,2X,A3)
(i)	50	FORMAT(3X.F7.9)
(j)	44	FORMAT(2X,I6.4)
(k)		DO 4 J=10,2
(l)	60	FORMAT(10HSTRESS RESULT)
(m)		GO TO, 4
(n)		EQUIVALENCE(A)
(o)		DIMENSION A(10),B,C(40)
(p)		DATA A,B/3.0/
(q)		DATA A,I/2*3.4/
(r)		FORMAT(2F10.5)
(s)		READ(A,100) B,C
(t)		GO TO I6

9.2 A program contains the following statements:

> DATA A,B,I,J/−3.0,2.56,−1,7/
> •
> •
> WRITE(6,105) A,I,B,J
> •

Indicate the form and spacing of the output for the following different FORMAT statements:

> (a) 105   FORMAT(2(2X,F10.5,2X,I5))
> (b) 105   FORMAT(' A = ',F5.2,/,'I = 'I5,/,
> 1   ' B=',F5.2,/,' J=',I5)
> (c) 105   FORMAT(' VALUES OF A,I,B AND J ARE',//,
> 1   2(F10.8,/,I6,/))
> (d) 105   FORMAT(2X,E15.6,2X,I3)
> (e) 105   FORMAT(T2,F10.5,T30,I5.T40,F10.5,T70,I5)
> (f) 105   FORMAT(12H ANSWERS ARE,/,2(1X,F6.2,/,I5,/))

(If you are unsure of one or more of these you may wish to write a simple program to check the result.)

9.3 Give five examples of the types of engineering decisions that would be programmed using the IF statement.

9.4 Give five examples of the types of engineering calculations that are iterative and would thus require the use of the DO statement.

9.5 Write a FORTRAN program that will print a table of the form:

x	x^2	$x^{1/2}$	x^3	$x^{1/3}$
1.				
2.				
3.				
.				
.				
10.				

You may use whatever format output form you wish; however, keep in mind that each column should be labeled.

9.6   Write a FORTRAN program that will:

(a) read an integer N (I10)
(b) read N cards containing 1 number each (F10.5)
(c) compute the average value of the N numbers, and
(d) print the numbers and the final average value.

9.7   Write a FORTRAN program that will print a set of tables of the form:

θ (degrees)	sin (θ)	cos (θ)	tan (θ)
0.	.	.	.
1.	.	.	.
2.	.	.	.
.	.	.	.
.	.	.	.
90.	.	.	.

You may use whatever format form you wish; however, keep in mind that each column should be labeled.

9.8   Prepare a general program that will:

(a) Read a card containing an explanation of the data set. Use 20A4.
(b) Read the engineering data set x_i where $i = 1, 2, \ldots n$. Use F10.5 and an array X(i).
(c) Stop reading values when a blank card is encountered.
(d) Compute the mean $\bar{x}$ and standard deviation σ for the data

$$\bar{x} = \frac{1}{n} \sum_{i=1}^{n} x_i$$

$$\sigma = \frac{1}{n} \sum_{i=1}^{n} (x_i - \bar{x})^2$$

for a set of as many as 100 data points. In addition to the above, your program should:

(i) Write a title on the output page. This should include the information contained on the first data card.
(ii) Print the input data as a list.
(iii) Write the mean and standard deviation with the appropriate annotation.

9.9 Write a FORTRAN program that will read three numbers A(1), A(2), and A(3) from a card using the field 3F10.7. Sort the numbers and write them on the output page in order from the smallest to the largest.

9.10 An engineering firm is planning to make a machine that will accept and recognize the correct change for $1.00 and will return a paper dollar. Write a program that will list all correct combinations of nickels, dimes, quarters, and half-dollars that total one dollar.

9.11 The exponential function e^x can be expressed as the series:

$$e^x = 1 + x + \frac{x^2}{2!} + \frac{x^3}{3!} + \frac{x^4}{4!} + \cdots .$$

Write a FORTRAN program that will read a value of x in the range $0 \le x \le 1$ and will compute e^x accurate to ± 0.001.

9.12 The cost of manufacturing a product is found to be a function of three design variables x, y, and z. The cost is:

$$\text{cost} (x, y, z) = x^2 + x^y + y\sqrt{z^2 + x^2} + \frac{1}{xyz}$$

It is desired to minimize the cost of manufacture on the range.

$$0 \le x \le 1$$

$$0 \le y \le 1$$

$$0 \le z \le 1$$

Write a FORTRAN program that will search for the minimum cost to the nearest 0.1.

9.13 Write a FORTRAN program that will read ten numbers $N(I)$ from a set of ten cards using the field I5. Sort the numbers according to whether they are odd or even and print all of the even numbers in order from the smallest to the largest.

9.14 Write a FORTRAN program to print a table of 30 Fibonacci numbers defined by:

$$F_0 = 1$$

$$F_1 = 1$$

$$F_K = F_{K-1} + F_{K-2}$$

9.15 Write a program that will list the first seven prime numbers. (A prime number can be divided by no other whole number than itself or 1.)

9.16 Draw a logic flow diagram for the program for Example 9.2.

9.17 The following data values were gathered in an engineering experiment.

x	y
1.0	2.3
2.0	4.5
3.0	6.7
4.0	8.2
5.0	9.8

Write a computer program that will read these data, store the data, and use linear interpolation to find the y value corresponding to any value $1.0 \le x \le 5.0$ read on a card using the format F10.5.

9.18 Write a FORTRAN program that will find roots of the equation:

$$x^3 + 6x^2 + 11x + 6 = 0$$

by Newton's method of iteration. (You may need to consult a mathematics book to learn about Newton's method.)

9.19 Write a FORTRAN program that will find the value of the integral:

$$\int_1^2 \left[3x^2 + \frac{2 \sin x}{\sqrt{x + 4}} \right] dx$$

using ten trapezoidal segments.

9.20 It is desired to design a new type of clock that will divide a 24-hour day into 10 parts (decihours) and the decihours into 100 deciminutes. Write a FORTRAN program that will print a conversion table between traditional times for the hours and their equivalent values in the new system. Your output should take the form:

Traditional Time (Hr)	Decihour	Deciminute
0000	. . . .	. . . .
0100	. . . .	. . . .
.	.	.
.	.	.
.	.	.
2400	. . . .	. . . .

REFERENCES

FARINA, M. V. *FORTRAN IV Self-Taught.* Englewood Cliffs, N.J.: Prentice-Hall, Inc., 1966.

LEDLEY, R. S. *FORTRAN IV Programming.* New York: McGraw Hill Book Company, Inc., 1966.

MANNING, W. A., and R. S. GARNERO, *FORTRAN IV Problem Solving.* New York: McGraw Hill Book Company, Inc., 1970.

MCCRACKEN, D. *A Guide to FORTRAN IV Programming*, Second Edition. New York: John Wiley & Sons, Inc., 1972.

NOLAN, R. L. *FORTRAN IV Computing and Applications.* Reading Mass.: Addison-Wesley Publishing Co., 1971.

RULE, W. P., R. G. FINEKENAUR, and F. G. PATRICK. *FORTRAN IV Programming.* Boston, Mass.: Prindle, Weber & Schmidt, Inc., 1973.

Data analysis. (*Courtesy* NASA.)

Preparation and use of subprograms in FORTRAN

10

We live in a modular world. The technological evidence of this fact surrounds us every day. Civil engineers design and utilize whole sections of buildings and structures that are prefabricated before assembly. Electrical engineers utilize subcircuits consisting of removable, interchangeable printed circuit boards. Mechanical engineers design and use subassemblies in the construction of the automobile and many other mechanical systems. The usefulness of the modular concept is clear. Use of modules simplifies complex design; the use of modules allows testing and improvement of a module apart from the whole system; and the use of modules provides considerable time saving in the analysis, construction, and maintenance phases of product design, since modules are readily interchangeable.

In the FORTRAN language the modular concept, with its many advantages, can be applied to the assembly and debugging phases of the programming process. In the FORTRAN language, whole *subprograms* can be called to execution by means of a single statement or a portion of a single statement. The modules used in FORTRAN programming, in order of

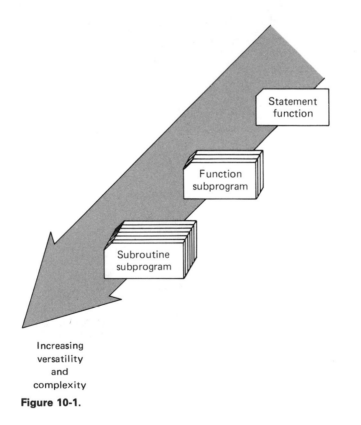

Increasing
versatility
and
complexity

Figure 10-1.

increasing complexity, are: the statement function, the function subprogram, and the subroutine subprogram (Figure 10-1). As the complexity of these modules increases so does the programming versatility.

10.1 Function subprograms

The use of special FORTRAN-supplied functions such as SIN(X), ATAN(Y), ALOG(Z), and so on, was discussed in Chapter 8. The FORTRAN language also allows the programmer to specify his own function to meet special computational needs not satisfied by library routines. In order to use a function in FORTRAN, the programmer must first define the function. This means that the function must be assigned a unique name by which it can be called. The parameters or arguments necessary to evaluate the function must be stated, and the mathematical and/or logical procedures for evaluating the function must be clearly explained.

The FUNCTION subprogram is a separately written program which is executed whenever its name appears in the main program. The general form for each FUNCTION subprogram definition would be as follows:

```
FUNCTION name (argument list)
•   (FORTRAN statements)
•
•
RETURN
END  .
```

The parameter *name* is the calling name of the FUNCTION, and will consist of a string of up to six alphameric characters, the first of which will be alphabetic. An example of a valid function name might be CAT1. One of the FORTRAN arithmetic statements in the FUNCTION subprogram must be of the form:

name = arithmetic expression

to set the function value. Thus, for the example name given, this statement could be CAT1 = 3. + A + 4. * B. The one or more RETURN statements in the FUNCTION return control to the main program. Since the FUNCTION subprogram is completely separate from the main program, it is separately compiled and has its own END statement to signal that the last FORTRAN statement of the FUNCTION has been reached.

The *argument list* of a FUNCTION will consist of a string of variable names or array names that will be replaced at the time of execution by corresponding variable or array values from the main program. The elements in the argument list must be enclosed in parentheses and must be separated by commas. Variables and arrays used in an argument list are often called "dummy" variables or "dummy" arrays since there is no need for the same names to be used in the main program. The order in these two lists, however, is of great importance. The first variable named in the calling program argument list will be understood to be the same as the first variable named in the FUNCTION argument list; the second variable in the calling program argument list will be understood to be the same as the second variable in the FUNCTION argument list, and so on. For this reason, dummy argument names in the FUNCTION argument list must always agree in type and in number with the main program argument list.

The concept of communication between subprogram and main program through a dummy argument list may be viewed as a set of post-office boxes. On the open, back side of the boxes (the main program side) the post-office workers have a label corresponding to the box number. On the front side of the boxes (the FUNCTION subprogram side) the owner has placed his own name. Neither the box owner nor the post-office worker cares about the labeling discrepancy so long as the proper mail gets into the proper box. In the example:

Main Program	FUNCTION Subprogram
DIMENSION X(5), Y(50)	FUNCTION SUM1(A)
•	
•	DIMENSION A(50)
•	SUM1 = 0.0
•	DO 1 I = 1,50
AVGX=SUM1(X)/50.	1 SUM1=SUM1+A(I)
•	RETURN
AVGY=SUM1(Y)/50.	END
•	

the FUNCTION SUM1 will compute the numerical sum of all 50 elements in any array that it is supplied. In the example main program above, SUM1 is called upon to compute the sum for the X-array and later the sum for the

Y-array. Indeed, the FUNCTION will form the sum for any 50-element array that is supplied in the argument list. It is important to note that since the variable A in the FUNCTION is an array, a DIMENSION statement is required in the FUNCTION subprogram.

The FUNCTION subprogram itself may contain any FORTRAN statement except another FUNCTION statement or a SUBROUTINE STATEMENT. One FUNCTION subprogram may call another subprogram. Since the FUNCTION is an independent subprogram, its variables (other than those in the argument list) and its statement numbers do not relate to the main program. Values of the dummy arguments must not be altered in the FUNCTION subprogram. This means that they may not appear on the left side of an equal sign in an arithmetic statement, in the variable list of a read statement, or as the index of a DO-loop.

Although the type of the output variable of a FUNCTION may be implicitly specified by the first letter of the FUNCTION name (i.e., REAL A–H and O–Z, INTEGER I–M), it is possible to explicitly override this rule by including the word REAL or INTEGER before the word FUNCTION. Thus, for example:

```
INTEGER FUNCTION COUNT(A,B,C)
•
•
RETURN
END
```

would cause the output value COUNT to be stored as an integer, and

```
REAL FUNCTION MASS(X,I,N)
•
•
RETURN
END
```

would cause the output value MASS to be stored as a real variable. When the type of the FUNCTION name is explicitly specified in this way, the type of the FUNCTION name must also be specified in the main program by including the name in the variable list of a REAL or INTEGER type statement. For example:

```
INTEGER X,XC,COUNT
```

or

```
REAL IFIX,MASS
```

10.2   Statement functions

Some engineering functions are sufficiently simple to be expressed by a single equality expression. For this situation the function may be defined without a separate subprogram. The special FORTRAN statement used in this case is called a STATEMENT FUNCTION and has the general form:

NAME(argument list) = *expression*

Thus, for example:

CAT1(A,B) = 3. + A + 4. * B

The STATEMENT FUNCTION must be placed after the specification statements in a main program and before the first executable statement. The argument list is a list of dummy variables. Those variables in the expression that are not listed in the dummy argument list are ordinary variables that appear elsewhere in the main source program. The dummy arguments in the STATEMENT FUNCTION must not be subscripted variables. An example application of the use of the STATEMENT FUNCTION is as follows:

```
C  THIS PROGRAM CALCULATES THE PROFIT AND OVERHEAD
   REAL I
   DIMENSION X(10)
C  THIS STATEMENT FUNCTION COMPUTES COST
   COST(DOL,CENTS)=100.*DOL + CENTS + PROFIT
      .
      .
      .
   A = 5.
   B = 3.
   PROFIT = 0.5*A
   OVHEAD = 0.005*COST(A,B)
      .
      .
      .
```

10.3   The COMMON statement

Although the usual method of communication between a subprogram and a main program is through the argument list, an alternate mechanism does exist. This is the COMMON statement. Through the use of this special specification statement, variables and arrays that appear in the main program may be made to share the same "common" storage locations with variables or arrays in the subprogram. The general form of the COMMON statement is:

COMMON *variable name list*

If a main program contains the common specification statement:

COMMON A,B,C,I

and the subprogram contains a specification statement of the form:

COMMON X, Y, Z, J

then the variables A, B, C, and I will share the same storage locations with X, Y, Z, and J.

Whenever a pair of COMMON statements is used, the variable name list of each must have a one to one correspondence in type, number, and size. Thus, for example, the pair of statements:

(main program)   COMMON A,B,I
(subprogram)   COMMON X,I,J

would not be valid since the type of the variable *B* and *I* do not agree. The COMMON statement pair:

(main program)   DIMENSION B(3)
                   COMMON B,J
(subprogram)   COMMON X,Y,Z,I

would of course be valid since the *B*-array contains three storage spaces.

In engineering programs the COMMON statement is frequently used to transmit large amounts of data to or from a subroutine in order to eliminate the need for a lengthy argument list each time the subroutine is called. In this way large tables of information such as steam tables and thermocouple conversion tables can be made available to the computational process.

10.4 SUBROUTINE subprograms

The SUBROUTINE subprogram is similar to the FUNCTION subprogram in many ways. Both are used to perform a set of commonly used computations; both require a RETURN and an END statement; both utilize dummy arguments; and both have identifying names. There are, however, two basic differences. Unlike the FUNCTION subprogram, the SUBROUTINE is not restricted to a single output result. This means that a single SUBROUTINE can produce any number of results. For example, the engineering programmer might wish to call a SUBROUTINE that will compute the mean, standard deviation, and variance for a set of data values stored in an array. Or perhaps the engineering programmer might wish to have the output value of a routine specified in the units of several different dimensional systems. Thus, an output for mass may be given in kilograms, grams, milligrams, and so on.

The second important difference between SUBROUTINEs and FUNCTIONs is that a SUBROUTINE is permitted to alter the value of any parameter in the argument list.

The SUBROUTINE subprogram is defined as an independent group of FORTRAN statements in a way quite similar to the FUNCTION subprogram. Its general form is:

```
SUBROUTINE NAME (argument name list)
   •
   •
   •
   •
RETURN
END
```

NAME is the identifying term that consists of from one to six alphameric characters, the first of which must be alphabetic. The argument list will consist of a string of variable names or unsubscripted array names, each separated by commas. At least one RETURN statement must be presented in the SUBROUTINE although many more could be used if desired. The

SUBROUTINE may contain any FORTRAN statement except a FUNC-TION statement or another SUBROUTINE statement. Since the SUB-ROUTINE is a separate subprogram it must have an END statement last. Its statement numbers and variable names (with the exception of those in the argument list or a COMMON list) do not relate to any other variables or statement numbers in the main program.

Unlike the FUNCTION subprogram, the SUBROUTINE cannot be called in an arithmetic expression. It must be called by a separate FOR-TRAN statement of the form:

CALL *NAME (argument list)*

In this statement the name must correspond to an existing subprogram name, and the argument list must have a one to one correspondence in type and number of variables with the SUBROUTINE itself. Upon return from the SUBROUTINE the next executable statement following the CALL statement is given control.

In the example:

Main Program	Subprogram
DIMENSION B(100),C(100)	SUBROUTINE CALC(SUM,PROD,A)
•	DIMENSION A(100)
•	SUM=0.
CALL CALC(X1,Y1,B)	PROD=1.0
•	DO 1, I = 1, 100
•	SUM = SUM + A(I)
CALL CALC(X2,Y2,C)	1 PROD=PROD*A(I)
•	RETURN
•	END

the subroutine CALC is used to calculate both the sum and the product of all elements in an array of 100 variables. The calculation procedure can be repeated as often as necessary for different arrays by means of the sub-routine call. This procedure eliminates the necessity of repeating the calcula-tion statements wherever they are needed. It should be kept in mind that careful attention to the self-documentation of subroutines will enhance their utility.

EXAMPLE 10-1 Suppose that it is desired to write a FORTRAN SUBROUTINE to calculate the maximum deflection and end slopes for the simply supported beam shown. The general formulas for this beam can be found to be*:

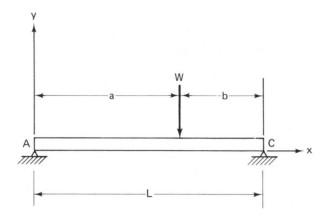

$$Y_{max} = \frac{-Wab}{27EIL}(a + 2b)\sqrt{3a(a + 2b)}$$

$$\Theta_A = \frac{-W}{6EI}(bL + b^3/L)$$

$$\Theta_C = \frac{+W}{6EI}(2bL + b^3/L - 3b^2)$$

The FORTRAN SUBROUTINE is presented below. The reader will note that the self-documentation of this subroutine makes it useful without any supplementary writeup.

* Roark, R. J. *Formulas for Stress and Strain*, Fourth Edition, New York: McGraw Hill Book Company, 1965.

FORTRAN SUBROUTINE for Example 10-1.

```
C
C     ........................................................
C
C         SUBROUTINE SSBEAM
C
C     PURPOSE
C         TO COMPUTE THE MAXIMUM DEFLECTION AND END SLOPES FOR A
C         SIMPLY SUPPORTED BEAM WITH A SINGLE INTERMEDIATE LOAD.
C         THE BEAM IS OF THE FORM--
C
C              Y                               W
C              I                               I
C              I--------------A----------------I----B-----I
C              I                               I         I
C              I                               I         I
C              I                               V         I
C              ***************************************************
C              ***************************************----------X
C              O                                         O
C              A                                         C
C
C     USAGE
C         CALL SSBEAM(A,B,L,W,EI,YMAX,ATHETA,CTHETA)
C
C     DESCRIPTION OF INPUT PARAMETERS
C         A           - LENGTH OF THE LONGER SEGMENT OF THE BEAM(IN)
C         B           - LENGTH OF THE SHORTER SEGMENT OF THE BEAM(IN)
C         L           - TOTAL LENGTH OF THE BEAM (IN)
C         W           - THE APPLIED LOAD (LB)
C         EI          - FLEXURAL RIGIDITY OF THE BEAM (LB*IN*IN)
C
C     DESCRIPTION OF OUTPUT PARAMETERS
C         YMAX        - MAXIMUM DEFLECTION OF THE BEAM (IN)
C         ATHETA      - THE SLOPE OF THE BEAM AT THE LEFT END
C         CTHETA      - THE SLOPE OF THE BEAM AT THE RIGHT END
C
C     METHOD
C         THIS SUBROUTINE  IS AN ADAPTATION OF FORMULAS FOUND ON
C         PAGE 106 OF THE BOOK 'FORMULAS FOR STRESS AND STRAIN'
C         BY RAYMOND J. ROARK, MCGRAW HILL 1965.
C
C         T. E. SHOUP    10/75
C
C     ........................................................
C
      SUBROUTINE SSBEAM(A,B,L,W,EI,YMAX,ATHETA,CTHETA)
      REAL L
C
C     CHECK FOR IMPROPER INPUT DATA
      IF(A+B.NE.L)RETURN
C
C     APPLY THE FORMULAS TO THE DATA
      YMAX=-W*A*B*(A+2.*B)*SQRT(3.*A*(A+2.*B))/(27.*EI*L)
      ATHETA=-W*(B*L-B**3/L)/(6.*EI)
      CTHETA=+W*(2.*B*L+B**3/L-3.*B*B)/(6.*EI)
      RETURN
      END
```

249

10.5 Subroutine libraries

Before the engineering programmer undertakes the lengthy process of writing and debugging a new program to perform a particular computational task, it is worthwhile to make a careful search for programs or subroutines that are already written to do the job. Such prewritten packages can save considerable time and effort on the part of the engineering programmer. Prewritten packages to solve a variety of engineering problems are available both as complete programs and as callable subprograms. Possible sources for prepackaged software could include: computer manufacturers, software companies, user groups, and the government. The software from these sources may be free or may be available for a fee, depending on the type of organization that has developed them.

Computer manufacturers. Every computer equipment manufacturer provides a variety of different software systems for use on its particular machines. Perhaps the best known example of this type of software package is the IBM Scientific Subroutine Package. This package is a collection of over 300 FORTRAN subprograms specifically prepared to meet the needs of engineering programmers.

Software companies. In the past two decades a new type of service organization known as the software company has appeared. These companies offer prepackaged programs for a fee. Often these organizations will develop special purpose programs to meet a particular user need. Some of these companies offer both the software and the computer hardware in the form of timeshare or batch-processing terminals (Figure 10-2). Such computer arrangements are well suited for the small engineering organization that cannot afford to purchase and/or operate a computer of its own. The present generation of small, typewriter-like time-share terminals makes it possible for the engineer to have a communication link with the computer right beside his desk.

User groups. In the United States a number of computer user groups have been formed to allow sharing of computer software for the benefit of all members. One of the best known of these is the SHARE group made up of IBM users. In most cases, computer programs and subroutines obtained through these groups are free.

Figure 10-2 A general purpose computer terminal. (*Courtesy* of Interdata, Inc.)

Government.   A number of the agencies of the U.S. Government provide software to interested users. The Computer Software Management and Information Center (COSMIC) was established in 1966 to disseminate computer software produced by NASA, the Department of Defense, and parts of the Atomic Energy Commission. COSMIC charges a nominal fee for its programs. Another useful resource for programs within the U.S. Government is the Clearinghouse for Federal Scientific and Technical Information in Springfield, Virginia.

10.6 Summary

Through the modular concept provided by FORTRAN subprograms, the engineering programmer can assemble complex programs in a simple fashion.

Other, more advanced FORTRAN techniques, not discussed in this text, are available for the advanced engineering programmer. For a discussion of these, the interested reader should consult the references at the end of this and the previous chapter.

PROBLEMS **10.1** Prepare a FORTRAN STATEMENT FUNCTION to perform the following computational tasks:
(a) Convert degrees Fahrenheit to degrees Centigrade.
(b) Convert a length in feet to a length in meters.
(c) Convert an angle in degrees into an angle in radians.
(d) Compute the quadratic formula with "+" square root term.

10.2 Prepare a FUNCTION subprogram to perform the following task: Given the sine of an angle ($S1$) and the cosine of the same angle ($C1$) find the value of the angle and be sure that its value is placed in the proper quadrant.

10.3 Prepare a SUBROUTINE to perform the following task: Using an array of I elements ($I \le 100$), compute the mean and standard deviation, and transmit this information back to the main program using an argument list of the form (ARRAY,I,XMEAN,STDEV).

10.4 Identify which of the following pairs of COMMON statements will work together:

(a) COMMON A,B,C,J,X
    COMMON G,F,D,K,Y
(b) COMMON I,J,K,M,N
    COMMON A,B,C,D,E
(c) DIMENSION A(5)
    COMMON A,J
    COMMON B,X,Y,Z,W,K
(d) COMMON ITEM,XRAY
    COMMON COUNT, WANE

10.5 Write a FORTRAN SUBROUTINE that will find an approximation to the derivative of a function at a point x using the formula:

$$\text{derivative} = \frac{F(x + h) - F(x)}{h}$$

where $h = 0.01 * x$ and where $F(z)$ is a given STATEMENT FUNCTION.

10.6 Under what circumstances would it be better to use a COMMON statement rather than an argument list to pass values to a FORTRAN SUBROUTINE?

10.7 Write a FORTRAN STATEMENT FUNCTION that will round a real variable value to the nearest even integer.

10.8 Write a FORTRAN STATEMENT FUNCTION that will extract the sign (±1) of a real valued variable.

10.9 Prepare a FORTRAN SUBROUTINE that will convert an angular velocity in rpm to its equivalent in rad/s and rad/hr.

10.10 Write a FORTRAN SUBROUTINE that will sort an array $A(I)$ of I values and will store them in ascending order in an array $B(I)$.

10.11 Under what circumstances might one use a FORTRAN SUB-ROUTINE that has no arguments named in its argument list? Can you think of an engineering application of this?

10.12 Write a FORTRAN SUBROUTINE that will compute the surface area and volume of a right circular cone of height H and base diameter D.

10.13 Given a FORTRAN SUBROUTINE: SUBROUTINE SAMPL-(X,Y,I,J), which of the following subroutine calls are not valid, and why?

(a) CALL SAMPL(X,Z,I,K)
(b) CALL SAMPL(X,Y,I,K)
(c) CALL SAMPL(3,Z,2,K)
(d) CALL SAMPL(X,Z,Y,M)
(e) CALL SAMPL(I,Y,I,J)
(f) CALL SAMPL(X,Y,Z,I,M)

10.14 Prepare a FORTRAN SUBROUTINE: SUBROUTINE CONVRT-(ADEG,AMIN,RAD) that will convert an angle in degrees and minutes into its equivalent in radians.

REFERENCES

LaFara, Robert L. *Computer Methods for Science and Engineering.* Rochelle Park, N.J., Hayden Book Company, Inc., 1973.

"The Computer as a Design Tool." Reprinted from *Machine Design.* Cleveland, Ohio: Penton Publishing Co., 1966.

System/360 Scientific Subroutine Package Programmer's Manual. White Plains, N.Y.: International Business Machine Corp., 1969.

Mischke, C. R. *An Introduction to Computer-Aided Design.* Englewood Cliffs, N.J.: Prentice-Hall, Inc., 1968.

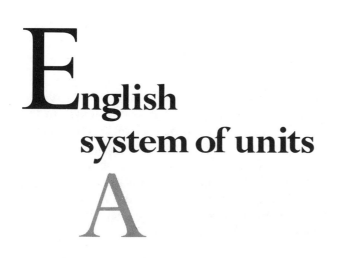

English
system of units
A

The English System of Units, long used by American engineers, differs from the International System of Units (SI) in several ways. In the English system, the particular unit used to measure a given quantity often depends upon the magnitude of the quantity being measured. Further, the basic dimensions of the English system include force as well as length, mass, and time. The force unit is based on the gravitational system, i.e., the force resulting from gravity.

A.1 Primary units

The primary units used in the English system of units are listed in Table A-1. These units may be described as follows:

Table A-1   Primary Units—English System

Quantity	Unit of Measure	Abbreviation
length	foot	ft
mass	pounds mass	lb_m
mass	slug	$lb_f sec^2/ft$
force	pounds force	lb_f
time	second	sec
thermodynamic temperature	Fahrenheit	°F
absolute thermodynamic temperature	Rankine	°R
electric current	ampere	amp
amount of substance	mole	mol
light or luminous intensity	candela	cd
plane angle	degree	°
plane angle	radian	rad
solid angle	steradian	sr

Length or distance.   Units of length in the English system vary with the magnitude of the quantity being measured. The basic unit of length in this system is the *foot*, but larger or smaller measurements usually are made in terms of other units which are related to the foot by no consistent factor. For example, there are 5 280 feet or 1 760 yards in one mile; there are three feet in one yard, 12 inches per foot, and the inch is divided into $\frac{1}{8}$, $\frac{1}{16}$, $\frac{1}{32}$, $\frac{1}{64}$, etc. As a result, use of length measurements in the English system requires considerably more memory and constant conversion of the various units than the SI system does.

Mass. The mass of an object in the English system is measured in *pounds mass* (lb_m) or *slugs* ($lb_f sec^2/ft$) and reflects the quantity of the object. The mass of an object does not vary with gravitational acceleration or location.

Force. The force unit in the English system is determined by means of Newton's second principle, and is designated the *pound force* (lb_f). The unit of force results from standard gravitational acceleration acting on a unit of mass called the slug. The slug is that unit of mass which can be accelerated 1 ft/sec^2 by a 1 pound force (i.e., $1\ lb_f = 1\ slug \cdot ft/sec^2$). The standard value for acceleration resulting from gravity (g_0) is 32.173 98 ft/sec^2 at sea-level conditions. The actual acceleration at the point of force action depends on local gravitational acceleration, which varies with both altitude and location. The pound mass, then, is equal in magnitude to the pound force only at sea-level conditions.

In order to use the pound force term easily in engineering expressions, it has been necessary to develop a conversion constant for use with Newton's second principle such that

$$F = \frac{ma}{g_c}$$

where F is in pounds force (lb_f), m in pounds mass (lb_m), and a in ft/sec^2. The conversion constant, g_c, is

$$g_c = 32.174 \frac{lb_m\ ft}{lb_f\ sec^2}$$

Many engineering problems may involve units of lb_m and lb_f, and the constant g_c must be used to convert between the two.

Time. The unit of time, the *second*, is universal in that it applies to all aspects of the English system as well as the International System.

Temperature. In the English system, temperature is measured in degrees *Fahrenheit*. The *Rankine* scale is the "absolute temperature scale" of the English system and is used for many engineering calculations. The Fahrenheit and Rankine scales are related such that 0°R is −459.69°F and 32.00°F (freezing point of water) is 491.69°R (see Table 2-3).

The relationship between the increments of temperature on the English scales and International scales are as follows:

$$1°C = 1.8°F \qquad 1K = 1.8°R$$

The magnitudes may be calculated by

$$°F = \tfrac{9}{5}(°C) + 32 \qquad °R = \tfrac{9}{5}(K) + 32$$

and in reverse,

$$°C = \tfrac{5}{9}(°F - 32) \qquad K = \tfrac{5}{9}(°R - 32)$$

Conversion between these temperature scales often is necessary in engineering calculations.

Electric current. The *ampere* is used as the measure of the rate of flow of charge in the English system as it is in the International System.

Table A-2   Derived Units—English System

Quantity	Unit of Measure	Abbreviation
acceleration	feet per second per second	ft/sec^2
angular acceleration	radians per second per second	rad/sec^2
angular velocity	radians per second	rad/sec
area	square feet	ft^2
concentration	mole per cubic foot	mol/ft^3
density	pounds mass per cubic foot	lb_m/ft^3
energy	foot pounds or Btu	$ft\ lb_f$, Btu
enthalpy	British Thermal Units per pound mass	Btu/lb_m
heat	foot pounds or Btu	$ft\ lb_f$, Btu
moment	foot pounds	$ft\ lb_f$
power	foot pounds per second	$ft\ lb_f/sec$
pressure	pounds force per square foot	lb_f/ft^2
specific heat	Btu per pound mass °Fahrenheit	$Btu/lb_m°F$
stress	pounds force per square foot	lb_f/ft^2
velocity	feet per second	ft/sec
volume	cubic feet	ft^3
work	foot pounds or Btu	$ft\ lb_f$, Btu

A.2 Derived units

In addition to the primary units, there are a number of derived units in the English system. Selected quantities are listed in Table A-2. These derived units are functions of the basic units and are often used in engineering problem solving. To assist in the use of these units in problem solutions, factors for conversion between the English system and the International System are listed in Appendix B.

SI constants
and conversion factors
B

Table B-1   Physical Constants*

Quantity	Symbol	Value	×	Unit
Speed of light in vacuum	c	2.997 925	$\times 10^8$	$m\,s^{-1}$
Gravitational constant	G	6.673 2	$\times 10^{-11}$	$N\,m^2\,kg^{-2}$
Avogadro constant	N_A	6.022 169	$\times 10^{26}$	$kmol^{-1}$
Boltzmann constant	k	1.380 622	$\times 10^{-23}$	$J\,K^{-1}$
Gas constant	R	8.314 34	$\times 10^3$	$J\,kmol^{-1}\,K^{-1}$
Faraday constant	F	9.648 670	$\times 10^7$	$C\,kmol^{-1}$
Planck constant	h	6.626 196	$\times 10^{-34}$	$J\,s$
Electron charge	e	1.602 191 7	$\times 10^{-19}$	C
Electron rest mass	m_e	9.109 558	$\times 10^{-31}$	kg
Proton rest mass	m_p	1.672 614	$\times 10^{-27}$	kg
Neutron rest mass	m_n	1.674 920	$\times 10^{-27}$	kg
Stefan-Boltzmann constant	σ	5.669 61	$\times 10^{-8}$	$W\,m^{-2}\,K^{-4}$
Rydberg constant	R_∞	1.097 373 12	$\times 10^7$	m^{-1}
Classical electron radius	r_e	2.817 939	$\times 10^{-15}$	m
Standard acceleration of free fall	g	9.806 65		m/s^2
Standard atmosphere	atm	101 325		Pa

*NASA SP-7012.

Table B-2   Conversion Factors†. (An asterisk follows each number which expresses an exact definition).

ALPHABETICAL LISTING

To convert from	to	multiply by
abampere	ampere	$1.00* \times 10$
abcoulomb	coulomb	$1.00* \times 10$
abfarad	farad	$1.00* \times 10^9$
abhenry	henry	$1.00* \times 10^{-9}$
abmho	siemens	$1.00* \times 10^9$
abohm	ohm	$1.00* \times 10^{-9}$
abvolt	volt	$1.00* \times 10^{-8}$
acre	meter²	$4.046\ 856\ 422\ 4* \times 10^3$
angstrom	meter	$1.00* \times 10^{-10}$
are	meter²	$1.00* \times 10^2$
astronomical unit (IAU)	meter	$1.496\ 00 \times 10^{11}$
astronomical unit (radio)	meter	$1.495\ 978\ 9 \times 10^{11}$
atmosphere	newton/meter²	$1.013\ 25* \times 10^5$

† NASA SP-7012, pp. 11–20.

Table B-2 (*continued*)

To convert from	to	multiply by
bar	newton/meter^2	$1.00* \times 10^5$
barn	meter^2	$1.00* \times 10^{-28}$
barrel (petroleum, 42 gallons)	meter^3	$1.589\,873 \times 10^{-1}$
barye	newton/meter^2	$1.00* \times 10^{-1}$
board foot ($1' \times 1' \times 1''$)	meter^3	$2.359\,737\,216* \times 10^{-3}$
British thermal unit:		
(IST before 1956)	joule	$1.055\,04 \times 10^3$
(IST after 1956)	joule	$1.055\,056 \times 10^3$
British thermal unit (mean)	joule	$1.055\,87 \times 10^3$
British thermal unit (thermochemical)	joule	$1.054\,350 \times 10^3$
British thermal unit (39° F)	joule	$1.059\,67 \times 10^3$
British thermal unit (60° F)	joule	$1.054\,68 \times 10^3$
bushel (U.S.)	meter^3	$3.523\,907\,016\,688* \times 10^{-2}$
cable	meter	$2.194\,56* \times 10^2$
caliber	meter	$2.54* \times 10^{-4}$
calorie (International Steam Table)	joule	4.1868
calorie (mean)	joule	$4.190\,02$
calorie (thermochemical)	joule	$4.184*$
calorie (15° C)	joule	$4.185\,80$
calorie (20° C)	joule	$4.181\,90$
calorie (kilogram, International Steam Table)	joule	4.1868×10^3
calorie (kilogram, mean)	joule	$4.190\,02 \times 10^3$
calorie (kilogram, thermochemical)	joule	$4.184* \times 10^3$
carat (metric)	kilogram	$2.00* \times 10^{-4}$
Celsius (temperature)	kelvin	$t_K = t_C + 273.15$
centimeter of mercury (0° C)	newton/meter^2	$1.333\,22 \times 10^3$
centimeter of water (4° C)	newton/meter^2	$9.806\,38 \times 10$
chain (engineer or ramden)	meter	$3.048* \times 10$
chain (surveyor or gunter)	meter	$2.011\,68* \times 10$
circular mil	meter^2	$5.067\,074\,8 \times 10^{-10}$
cord	meter^3	$3.624\,556\,3$
cubit	meter	$4.572* \times 10^{-1}$
cup	meter^3	$2.365\,882\,365* \times 10^{-4}$
curie	disintegration/second	$3.70* \times 10^{10}$
day (mean solar)	second (mean solar)	$8.64* \times 10^4$
day (sidereal)	second (mean solar)	$8.616\,409\,0 \times 10^4$
degree (angle)	radian	$1.745\,329\,251\,994\,3 \times 10^{-2}$
denier (international)	kilogram/meter	$1.00* \times 10^{-7}$
dram (avoirdupois)	kilogram	$1.771\,845\,195\,312\,5* \times 10^{-3}$
dram (troy or apothecary)	kilogram	$3.887\,934\,6* \times 10^{-3}$
dram (U.S. fluid)	meter^3	$3.696\,691\,195\,312\,5* \times 10^{-6}$
dyne	newton	$1.00* \times 10^{-5}$
electron volt	joule	$1.602\,191\,7 \times 10^{-19}$
erg	joule	$1.00* \times 10^{-7}$

Table B-2   (*continued*)

To convert from	to	multiply by
Fahrenheit (temperature)	kelvin	$t_K = (5/9)(t_F + 459.67)$
Fahrenheit (temperature)	Celsius	$t_C = (5/9)(t_F - 32)$
faraday (based on carbon 12)	coulomb	$9.648\ 70 \times 10^4$
faraday (chemical)	coulomb	$9.649\ 57 \times 10^4$
faraday (physical)	coulomb	$9.652\ 19 \times 10^4$
fathom	meter	$1.828\ 8*$
fermi (femtometer)	meter	$1.00* \times 10^{-15}$
fluid ounce (U.S.)	meter^3	$2.957\ 352\ 956\ 25* \times 10^{-5}$
foot	meter	$3.048* \times 10^{-1}$
foot (U.S. survey)	meter	$1200/3937*$
foot (U.S. survey)	meter	$3.048\ 006\ 096 \times 10^{-1}$
foot of water (39.2° F)	newton/meter^2	$2.988\ 98 \times 10^3$
footcandle	lumen/meter^2	$1.076\ 391\ 0 \times 10^1$
footlambert	candela/meter^2	$3.426\ 259$
free fall, standard	meter/second^2	$9.806\ 65*$
furlong	meter	$2.011\ 68* \times 10^2$
gal (galileo)	meter/second^2	$1.00* \times 10^{-2}$
gallon (U.K. liquid)	meter^3	$4.546\ 087 \times 10^{-3}$
gallon (U.S. dry)	meter^3	$4.404\ 883\ 770\ 86* \times 10^{-3}$
gallon (U.S. liquid)	meter^3	$3.785\ 411\ 784* \times 10^{-3}$
gamma	tesla	$1.00* \times 10^{-9}$
gauss	tesla	$1.00* \times 10^{-4}$
gilbert	ampere turn	$7.957\ 747\ 2 \times 10^{-1}$
gill (U.K.)	meter^3	$1.420\ 652 \times 10^{-4}$
gill (U.S.)	meter^3	$1.182\ 941\ 2 \times 10^{-4}$
grad	degree (angular)	$9.00* \times 10^{-1}$
grad	radian	$1.570\ 796\ 3 \times 10^{-2}$
grain	kilogram	$6.479\ 891* \times 10^{-5}$
gram	kilogram	$1.00* \times 10^{-3}$
hand	meter	$1.016* \times 10^{-1}$
hectare	meter^2	$1.00* \times 10^4$
hogshead (U.S.)	meter^3	$2.384\ 809\ 423\ 92* \times 10^{-1}$
horsepower (550 foot lbf/second)	watt	$7.456\ 998\ 7 \times 10^2$
horsepower (boiler)	watt	$9.809\ 50 \times 10^3$
horsepower (electric)	watt	$7.46* \times 10^2$
horsepower (metric)	watt	$7.354\ 99 \times 10^2$
horsepower (U.K.)	watt	7.457×10^2
horsepower (water)	watt	$7.460\ 43 \times 10^2$
hour (mean solar)	second (mean solar)	$3.60* \times 10^3$
hour (sidereal)	second (mean solar)	$3.590\ 170\ 4 \times 10^3$
hundredweight (long)	kilogram	$5.080\ 234\ 544* \times 10$
hundredweight (short)	kilogram	$4.535\ 923\ 7* \times 10$
inch	meter	$2.54* \times 10^{-2}$
inch of mercury (32° F)	newton/meter^2	$3.386\ 389 \times 10^3$

Table B-2   (*continued*)

To convert from	to	multiply by
inch of mercury (60° F)	newton/meter^2	$3.376\ 85 \times 10^3$
inch of water (39.2° F)	newton/meter^2	$2.490\ 82 \times 10^2$
inch of water (60° F)	newton/meter^2	2.4884×10^2
kayser	1/meter	$1.00* \times 10^2$
kilocalorie (International Steam Table)	joule	$4.186\ 8 \times 10^3$
kilocalorie (mean)	joule	$4.190\ 02 \times 10^3$
kilocalorie (thermochemical)	joule	$4.184* \times 10^3$
kilogram mass	kilogram	$1.00*$
kilogram force (kgf)	newton	$9.806\ 65*$
kilopound force	newton	$9.806\ 65*$
kip	newton	$4.448\ 221\ 615\ 260\ 5* \times 10^3$
knot (international)	meter/second	$5.144\ 444\ 444 \times 10^{-1}$
lambert	candela/meter^2	$1/\pi* \times 10^4$
lambert	candela/meter^2	$3.183\ 098\ 8 \times 10^3$
langley	joule/meter^2	$4.184* \times 10^4$
lbf (pound force, avoirdupois)	newton	$4.448\ 221\ 615\ 260\ 5*$
lbm (pound mass, avoirdupois)	kilogram	$4.535\ 923\ 7* \times 10^{-1}$
league (U.K. nautical)	meter	$5.559\ 552* \times 10^3$
league (international nautical)	meter	$5.556* \times 10^3$
league (statute)	meter	$4.828\ 032* \times 10^3$
light year	meter	$9.460\ 55 \times 10^{15}$
link (engineer or ramden)	meter	$3.048* \times 10^{-1}$
link (surveyor or gunter)	meter	$2.011\ 68* \times 10^{-1}$
liter	meter^3	$1.00* \times 10^{-3}$
lux	lumen/meter^2	$1.00*$
maxwell	weber	$1.00* \times 10^{-8}$
meter	wavelengths Kr 86	$1.650\ 763\ 73* \times 10^6$
micron	meter	$1.00* \times 10^{-6}$
mil	meter	$2.54* \times 10^{-5}$
mile (U.S. statute)	meter	$1.609\ 344* \times 10^3$
mile (U.K. nautical)	meter	$1.853\ 184* \times 10^3$
mile (international nautical)	meter	$1.852* \times 10^3$
mile (U.S. nautical)	meter	$1.852* \times 10^3$
millibar	newton/meter^2	$1.00* \times 10^2$
millimeter of mercury (0° C)	newton/meter^2	$1.333\ 224 \times 10^2$
minute (angle)	radian	$2.908\ 882\ 086\ 66 \times 10^{-4}$
minute (mean solar)	second (mean solar)	$6.00* \times 10$
minute (sidereal)	second (mean solar)	$5.983\ 617\ 4 \times 10$
month (mean calendar)	second (mean solar)	$2.628* \times 10^6$
nautical mile (international)	meter	$1.852* \times 10^3$
nautical mile (U.S.)	meter	$1.852* \times 10^3$
nautical mile (U.K.)	meter	$1.853\ 184* \times 10^3$

Table B-2   *(continued)*

To convert from	*to*	*multiply by*
oersted	ampere/meter	$7.957\ 747\ 2 \times 10$
ounce force (avoirdupois)	newton	$2.780\ 138\ 5 \times 10^{-1}$
ounce mass (avoirdupois)	kilogram	$2.834\ 952\ 312\ 5^* \times 10^{-2}$
ounce mass (troy or apothecary)	kilogram	$3.110\ 347\ 68^* \times 10^{-2}$
ounce (U.S. fluid)	meter³	$2.957\ 352\ 956\ 25^* \times 10^{-5}$
pace	meter	$7.62^* \times 10^{-1}$
parsec (IAU)	meter	$3.085\ 7 \times 10^{16}$
pascal	newton/meter²	1.00^*
peck (U.S.)	meter³	$8.809\ 767\ 541\ 72^* \times 10^{-3}$
pennyweight	kilogram	$1.555\ 173\ 84^* \times 10^{-3}$
perch	meter	5.0292^*
phot	lumen/meter²	1.00×10^4
pica (printers)	meter	$4.217\ 517\ 6^* \times 10^{-3}$
pint (U.S. dry)	meter³	$5.506\ 104\ 713\ 575^* \times 10^{-4}$
pint (U.S. liquid)	meter³	$4.731\ 764\ 73^* \times 10^{-4}$
point (printers)	meter	$3.514\ 598^* \times 10^{-4}$
poise	newton second/meter²	$1.00^* \times 10^{-1}$
pole	meter	5.0292^*
pound force (lbf avoirdupois)	newton	$4.448\ 221\ 615\ 260\ 5^*$
pound mass (lbm avoirdupois)	kilogram	$4.535\ 923\ 7^* \times 10^{-1}$
pound mass (troy or apothecary)	kilogram	$3.732\ 417\ 216^* \times 10^{-1}$
poundal	newton	$1.382\ 549\ 543\ 76^* \times 10^{-1}$
quart (U.S. dry)	meter³	$1.101\ 220\ 942\ 715^* \times 10^{-3}$
quart (U.S. liquid)	meter³	$9.463\ 592\ 5 \times 10^{-4}$
rad (radiation dose absorbed)	joule/kilogram	$1.00^* \times 10^{-2}$
Rankine (temperature)	kelvin	$t_K = (5/9)t_R$
rayleigh (rate of photon emission)	1/second meter²	$1.00^* \times 10^{10}$
rhe	meter²/newton second	$1.00^* \times 10$
rod	meter	5.0292^*
roentgen	coulomb/kilogram	$2.579\ 76^* \times 10^{-4}$
rutherford	disintegration/second	$1.00^* \times 10^6$
second (angle)	radian	$4.848\ 136\ 811 \times 10^{-6}$
second (ephemeris)	second	$1.000\ 000\ 000$
second (mean solar)	second (ephemeris)	Consult American Ephemer and Nautical Almanac
second (sidereal)	second (mean solar)	$9.972\ 695\ 7 \times 10^{-1}$
section	meter²	$2.589\ 988\ 110\ 336^* \times 10^6$
scruple (apothecary)	kilogram	$1.295\ 978\ 2^* \times 10^{-3}$
shake	second	1.00×10^{-8}
skein	meter	$1.097\ 28^* \times 10^2$
slug	kilogram	$1.459\ 390\ 29 \times 10$
span	meter	$2.286^* \times 10^{-1}$
statampere	ampere	$3.335\ 640 \times 10^{-10}$

Table B-2   *(continued)*

To convert from	*to*	*multiply by*
statcoulomb	coulomb	$3.335\,640 \times 10^{-10}$
statfarad	farad	$1.112\,650 \times 10^{-12}$
stathenry	henry	$8.987\,554 \times 10^{11}$
statohm	ohm	$8.987\,554 \times 10^{11}$
statute mile (U.S.)	meter	$1.609\,344* \times 10^{3}$
statvolt	volt	$2.997\,925 \times 10^{2}$
stere	meter³	$1.00*$
stilb	candela/meter²	1.00×10^{4}
stoke	meter²/second	$1.00* \times 10^{-4}$
tablespoon	meter³	$1.478\,676\,478\,125* \times 10^{-5}$
teaspoon	meter³	$4.928\,921\,593\,75* \times 10^{-6}$
ton (assay)	kilogram	$2.916\,666\,6 \times 10^{-2}$
ton (long)	kilogram	$1.016\,046\,908\,8* \times 10^{3}$
ton (metric)	kilogram	$1.00* \times 10^{3}$
ton (nuclear equivalent of TNT)	joule	4.20×10^{9}
ton (register)	meter³	$2.831\,684\,659\,2*$
ton (short, 2000 pound)	kilogram	$9.071\,847\,4* \times 10^{2}$
tonne	kilogram	$1.00* \times 10^{3}$
torr (0° C)	newton/meter²	$1.333\,22 \times 10^{2}$
township	meter²	$9.323\,957\,2 \times 10^{7}$
unit pole	weber	$1.256\,637 \times 10^{-7}$
yard	meter	$9.144* \times 10^{-1}$
year (calendar)	second (mean solar)	$3.1536* \times 10^{7}$
year (sidereal)	second (mean solar)	$3.155\,815\,0 \times 10^{7}$
year (tropical)	second (mean solar)	$3.155\,692\,6 \times 10^{7}$
year 1900, tropical, Jan., day 0, hour 12	second (ephemeris)	$3.155\,692\,597\,47* \times 10^{7}$
year 1900, tropical, Jan., day 0, hour 12	second	$3.155\,692\,597\,47 \times 10^{7}$

LISTING BY PHYSICAL QUANTITY

ACCELERATION

foot/second²	meter/second²	$3.048* \times 10^{-1}$
free fall, standard	meter/second²	$9.806\,65*$
gal (galileo)	meter/second²	$1.00* \times 10^{-2}$
inch/second²	meter/second²	$2.54* \times 10^{-2}$

AREA

acre	meter²	$4.046\,856\,422\,4* \times 10^{3}$
are	meter²	$1.00* \times 10^{2}$

Table B-2   *(continued)*

To convert from	to	multiply by
barn	meter^2	$1.00* \times 10^{-28}$
circular mil	meter^2	$5.067\ 074\ 8 \times 10^{-10}$
foot^2	meter^2	$9.290\ 304* \times 10^{-2}$
hectare	meter^2	$1.00* \times 10^4$
inch^2	meter^2	$6.4516* \times 10^{-4}$
mile^2 (U.S. statute)	meter^2	$2.589\ 988\ 110\ 336* \times 10^6$
section	meter^2	$2.589\ 988\ 110\ 336* \times 10^6$
township	meter^2	$9.323\ 957\ 2 \times 10^7$
yard^2	meter^2	$8.361\ 273\ 6* \times 10^{-1}$

DENSITY

gram/centimeter^3	kilogram/meter^3	$1.00* \times 10^3$
lbm/inch^3	kilogram/meter^3	$2.767\ 990\ 5 \times 10^4$
lbm/foot^3	kilogram/meter^3	$1.601\ 846\ 3 \times 10$
slug/foot^3	kilogram/meter^3	$5.153\ 79 \times 10^2$

ENERGY

British thermal unit:		
(IST before 1956)	joule	$1.055\ 04 \times 10^3$
(IST after 1956)	joule	$1.055\ 056 \times 10^3$
British thermal unit (mean)	joule	$1.055\ 87 \times 10^3$
British thermal unit (thermochemical)	joule	$1.054\ 350 \times 10^3$
British thermal unit (39° F)	joule	$1.059\ 67 \times 10^3$
British thermal unit (60° F)	joule	$1.054\ 68 \times 10^3$
calorie (International Steam Table)	joule	4.1868
calorie (mean)	joule	$4.190\ 02$
calorie (thermochemical)	joule	$4.184*$
calorie (15° C)	joule	$4.185\ 80$
calorie (20° C)	joule	$4.181\ 90$
calorie (kilogram, International Steam Table)	joule	4.1868×10^3
calorie (kilogram, mean)	joule	$4.190\ 02 \times 10^3$
calorie (kilogram, thermochemical)	joule	$4.184* \times 10^3$
electron volt	joule	$1.602\ 191\ 7 \times 10^{-19}$
erg	joule	$1.00* \times 10^{-7}$
foot lbf	joule	$1.355\ 817\ 9$
foot poundal	joule	$4.214\ 011\ 0 \times 10^{-2}$
joule (international of 1948)	joule	$1.000\ 165$
kilocalorie (International Steam Table)	joule	4.1868×10^3
kilocalorie (mean)	joule	$4.190\ 02 \times 10^3$
kilocalorie (thermochemical)	joule	$4.184* \times 10^3$
kilowatt hour	joule	$3.60* \times 10^6$
kilowatt hour (international of 1948)	joule	$3.600\ 59 \times 10^6$
ton (nuclear equivalent of TNT)	joule	4.20×10^9
watt hour	joule	$3.60* \times 10^3$

Table B-2   (*continued*)

To convert from	*to*	*multiply by*

ENERGY/AREA TIME

To convert from	to	multiply by
Btu (thermochemical)/foot² second	watt/meter²	$1.134\ 893\ 1 \times 10^4$
Btu (thermochemical)/foot² minute	watt/meter²	$1.891\ 488\ 5 \times 10^2$
Btu (thermochemical)/foot² hour	watt/meter²	$3.152\ 480\ 8$
Btu (thermochemical)/inch² second	watt/meter²	$1.634\ 246\ 2 \times 10^6$
calorie (thermochemical)/cm² minute	watt/meter²	$6.973\ 333\ 3 \times 10^2$
erg/centimeter² second	watt/meter²	$1.00^* \times 10^{-3}$
watt/centimeter²	watt/meter²	$1.00^* \times 10^4$

FORCE

To convert from	to	multiply by
dyne	newton	$1.00^* \times 10^{-5}$
kilogram force (kgf)	newton	$9.806\ 65^*$
kilopond force	newton	$9.806\ 65^*$
kip	newton	$4.448\ 221\ 615\ 260\ 5^* \times 10^3$
lbf (pound force, avoirdupois)	newton	$4.448\ 221\ 615\ 260\ 5^*$
ounce force (avoirdupois)	newton	$2.780\ 138\ 5 \times 10^{-1}$
pound force, lbf (avoirdupois)	newton	$4.448\ 221\ 615\ 260\ 5^*$
poundal	newton	$1.382\ 549\ 543\ 76^* \times 10^{-1}$

LENGTH

To convert from	to	multiply by
angstrom	meter	$1.00^* \times 10^{-10}$
astronomical unit (IAU)	meter	$1.496\ 00 \times 10^{11}$
astronomical unit (radio)	meter	$1.495\ 978\ 9 \times 10^{11}$
cable	meter	$2.194\ 56^* \times 10^2$
caliber	meter	$2.54^* \times 10^{-4}$
chain (surveyor or gunter)	meter	$2.011\ 68^* \times 10$
chain (engineer or ramden)	meter	$3.048^* \times 10$
cubit	meter	$4.572^* \times 10^{-1}$
fathom	meter	1.8288^*
fermi (femtometer)	meter	$1.00^* \times 10^{-15}$
foot	meter	$3.048^* \times 10^{-1}$
foot (U.S. survey)	meter	$1200/3937^*$
foot (U.S. survey)	meter	$3.048\ 006\ 096 \times 10^{-1}$
furlong	meter	$2.011\ 68^* \times 10^2$
hand	meter	$1.016^* \times 10^{-1}$
inch	meter	$2.54^* \times 10^{-2}$
league (U.K. nautical)	meter	$5.559\ 552^* \times 10^3$
league (international nautical)	meter	$5.556^* \times 10^3$
league (statute)	meter	$4.828\ 032^* \times 10^3$
light year	meter	$9.460\ 55 \times 10^{15}$
link (engineer or ramden)	meter	$3.048^* \times 10^{-1}$
link (surveyor or gunter)	meter	$2.011\ 68^* \times 10^{-1}$

Table B-2   (*continued*)

To convert from	to	multiply by
meter	wavelengths Kr 86	$1.650\ 763\ 73* \times 10^6$
micron	meter	$1.00* \times 10^{-6}$
mil	meter	$2.54* \times 10^{-5}$
mile (U.S. statute)	meter	$1.609\ 344* \times 10^3$
mile (U.K. nautical)	meter	$1.853\ 184* \times 10^3$
mile (international nautical)	meter	$1.852* \times 10^3$
mile (U.S. nautical)	meter	$1.852* \times 10^3$
nautical mile (U.K.)	meter	$1.853\ 184* \times 10^3$
nautical mile (international)	meter	$1.852* \times 10^3$
nautical mile (U.S.)	meter	$1.852* \times 10^3$
pace	meter	$7.62* \times 10^{-1}$
parsec (IAU)	meter	$3.085\ 7 \times 10^{16}$
perch	meter	$5.0292*$
pica (printers)	meter	$4.217\ 517\ 6* \times 10^{-3}$
point (printers)	meter	$3.514\ 598* \times 10^{-4}$
pole	meter	$5.0292*$
rod	meter	$5.0292*$
skein	meter	$1.097\ 28* \times 10^2$
span	meter	$2.286* \times 10^{-1}$
statute mile (U.S.)	meter	$1.609\ 344* \times 10^3$
yard	meter	$9.144* \times 10^{-1}$

MASS

carat (metric)	kilogram	$2.00* \times 10^{-4}$
gram (avoirdupois)	kilogram	$1.771\ 845\ 195\ 312\ 5* \times 10$
gram (troy or apothecary)	kilogram	$3.887\ 934\ 6* \times 10^{-3}$
grain	kilogram	$6.479\ 891* \times 10^{-5}$
gram	kilogram	$1.00* \times 10^{-3}$
hundredweight (long)	kilogram	$5.080\ 234\ 544* \times 10$
hundredweight (short)	kilogram	$4.535\ 923\ 7* \times 10$
kgf second^2 meter (mass)	kilogram	$9.806\ 65*$
kilogram mass	kilogram	$1.00*$
lbm (pound mass, avoirdupois)	kilogram	$4.535\ 923\ 7* \times 10^{-1}$
ounce mass (avoirdupois)	kilogram	$2.834\ 952\ 312\ 5* \times 10^{-2}$
ounce mass (troy or apothecary)	kilogram	$3.110\ 347\ 68* \times 10^{-2}$
pennyweight	kilogram	$1.555\ 173\ 84* \times 10^{-3}$
pound mass, lbm (avoirdupois)	kilogram	$4.535\ 923\ 7* \times 10^{-1}$
pound mass (troy or apothecary)	kilogram	$3.732\ 417\ 216* \times 10^{-1}$
scruple (apothecary)	kilogram	$1.295\ 978\ 2* \times 10^{-3}$
slug	kilogram	$1.459\ 390\ 29 \times 10$
ton (assay)	kilogram	$2.916\ 666\ 6 \times 10^{-2}$
ton (long)	kilogram	$1.016\ 046\ 908\ 8* \times 10^3$
ton (metric)	kilogram	$1.00* \times 10^3$
ton (short, 2000 pound)	kilogram	$9.071\ 847\ 4* \times 10^2$
tonne	kilogram	$1.00* \times 10^3$

Table B-2 *(continued)*

To convert from	*to*	*multiply by*
POWER		
Btu (thermochemical)/second	watt	$1.054\ 350\ 264\ 488 \times 10^3$
Btu (thermochemical)/minute	watt	$1.757\ 250\ 4 \times 10$
calorie (thermochemical)/second	watt	$4.184*$
calorie (thermochemical)/minute	watt	$6.973\ 333\ 3 \times 10^{-2}$
foot lbf/hour	watt	$3.766\ 161\ 0 \times 10^{-4}$
foot lbf/minute	watt	$2.259\ 696\ 6 \times 10^{-2}$
foot lbf/second	watt	$1.355\ 817\ 9$
horsepower (550 foot lbf/second)	watt	$7.456\ 998\ 7 \times 10^2$
horsepower (boiler)	watt	$9.809\ 50 \times 10^3$
horsepower (electric)	watt	$7.46* \times 10^2$
horsepower (metric)	watt	$7.354\ 99 \times 10^2$
horsepower (U.K.)	watt	7.457×10^2
horsepower (water)	watt	$7.460\ 43 \times 10^2$
kilocalorie (thermochemical)/minute	watt	$6.973\ 333\ 3 \times 10$
kilocalorie (thermochemical)/second	watt	$4.184* \times 10^3$
watt (international of 1948)	watt	$1.000\ 165$
PRESSURE		
atmosphere	newton/meter²	$1.013\ 25* \times 10^5$
bar	newton/meter²	$1.00* \times 10^5$
barye	newton/meter²	$1.00* \times 10^{-1}$
centimeter of mercury (0° C)	newton/meter²	$1.333\ 22 \times 10^3$
centimeter of water (4° C)	newton/meter²	$9.806\ 38 \times 10$
dyne/centimeter²	newton/meter²	$1.00* \times 10^{-1}$
foot of water (39.2° F)	newton/meter²	$2.988\ 98 \times 10^3$
inch of mercury (32° F)	newton/meter²	$3.386\ 389 \times 10^3$
inch of mercury (60° F)	newton/meter²	$3.376\ 85 \times 10^3$
inch of water (39.2° F)	newton/meter²	$2.490\ 82 \times 10^2$
inch of water (60° F)	newton/meter²	2.4884×10^2
kgf/centimeter²	newton/meter²	$9.806\ 65* \times 10^4$
kgf/meter²	newton/meter²	$9.806\ 65*$
lbf/foot²	newton/meter²	$4.788\ 025\ 8 \times 10$
lbf/inch² (psi)	newton/meter²	$6.894\ 757\ 2 \times 10^3$
millibar	newton/meter²	$1.00* \times 10^2$
millimeter of mercury (0° C)	newton/meter²	$1.333\ 224 \times 10^2$
pascal	newton/meter²	$1.00*$
psi (lbf/inch²)	newton/meter²	$6.894\ 757\ 2 \times 10^3$
torr (0° C)	newton/meter²	$1.333\ 22 \times 10^2$
SPEED		
foot/hour	meter/second	$8.466\ 666\ 6 \times 10^{-5}$
foot/minute	meter/second	$5.08* \times 10^{-3}$
foot/second	meter/second	$3.048* \times 10^{-1}$
inch/second	meter/second	$2.54* \times 10^{-2}$

Table B-2 *(continued)*

To convert from	to	multiply by
kilometer/hour	meter/second	$2.777\ 777\ 8 \times 10^{-1}$
knot (international)	meter/second	$5.144\ 444\ 444 \times 10^{-1}$
mile/hour (U.S. statute)	meter/second	$4.4704^{*} \times 10^{-1}$
mile/minute (U.S. statute)	meter/second	$2.682\ 24^{*} \times 10$
mile/second (U.S. statute)	meter/second	$1.609\ 344^{*} \times 10^{3}$

TEMPERATURE

Celsius	kelvin	$t_K = t_C + 273.15$
Fahrenheit	kelvin	$t_K = (5/9)(t_F + 459.67)$
Fahrenheit	Celsius	$t_C = (5/9)(t_F - 32)$
Rankine	kelvin	$t_K = (5/9)t_R$

TIME

day (mean solar)	second (mean solar)	$8.64^{*} \times 10^{4}$
day (sidereal)	second (mean solar)	$8.616\ 409\ 0 \times 10^{4}$
hour (mean solar)	second (mean solar)	$3.60^{*} \times 10^{3}$
hour (sidereal)	second (mean solar)	$3.590\ 170\ 4 \times 10^{3}$
minute (mean solar)	second (mean solar)	$6.00^{*} \times 10^{1}$
minute (sidereal)	second (mean solar)	$5.983\ 617\ 4 \times 10^{1}$
month (mean calendar)	second (mean solar)	$2.628^{*} \times 10^{6}$
second (ephemeris)	second	$1.000\ 000\ 000$
second (mean solar)	second (ephemeris)	Consult American Ephemeris and Nautical Almanac
second (sidereal)	second (mean solar)	$9.972\ 695\ 7 \times 10^{-1}$
year (calendar)	second (mean solar)	$3.1536^{*} \times 10^{7}$
year (sidereal)	second (mean solar)	$3.155\ 815\ 0 \times 10^{7}$
year (tropical)	second (mean solar)	$3.155\ 692\ 6 \times 10^{7}$
year 1900, tropical, Jan., day 0, hour 12	second (ephemeris)	$3.155\ 692\ 597\ 47^{*} \times 10^{7}$
year 1900, tropical, Jan., day 0, hour 12	second	$3.155\ 692\ 597\ 47 \times 10^{7}$

VISCOSITY

centistoke	meter^2/second	$1.00^{*} \times 10^{-6}$
stoke	meter^2/second	$1.00^{*} \times 10^{-4}$
foot^2/second	meter^2/second	$9.290\ 304^{*} \times 10^{-2}$
centipoise	newton second/meter^2	$1.00^{*} \times 10^{-3}$
lbm/foot second	newton second/meter^2	$1.488\ 163\ 9$
lbf second/foot^2	newton second/meter^2	$4.788\ 025\ 8 \times 10$
poise	newton second/meter^2	$1.00^{*} \times 10^{-1}$
poundal second/foot^2	newton second/meter^2	$1.488\ 163\ 9$
slug/foot second	newton second/meter^2	$4.788\ 025\ 8 \times 10$
rhe	meter^2/newton second	$1.00^{*} \times 10$

Table B-2   (*continued*)

To convert from	to	multiply by
	VOLUME	
acre foot	meter³	$1.233\ 481\ 837\ 547\ 52* \times 10^3$
barrel (petroleum, 42 gallons)	meter³	$1.589\ 873 \times 10^{-1}$
board foot	meter³	$2.359\ 737\ 216* \times 10^{-3}$
bushel (U.S.)	meter³	$3.523\ 907\ 016\ 688* \times 10^{-2}$
cord	meter³	$3.624\ 556\ 3$
cup	meter³	$2.365\ 882\ 365* \times 10^{-4}$
dram (U.S. fluid)	meter³	$3.696\ 691\ 195\ 312\ 5* \times 10^{-6}$
fluid ounce (U.S.)	meter³	$2.957\ 352\ 956\ 25* \times 10^{-5}$
foot³	meter³	$2.831\ 684\ 659\ 2* \times 10^{-2}$
gallon (U.K. liquid)	meter³	$4.546\ 087 \times 10^{-3}$
gallon (U.S. dry)	meter³	$4.404\ 883\ 770\ 86* \times 10^{-3}$
gallon (U.S. liquid)	meter³	$3.785\ 411\ 784* \times 10^{-3}$
gill (U K.)	meter³	$1.420\ 652 \times 10^{-4}$
gill (U.S.)	meter³	$1.182\ 941\ 2 \times 10^{-4}$
hogshead (U.S.)	meter³	$2.384\ 809\ 423\ 92* \times 10^{-1}$
inch³	meter³	$1.638\ 706\ 4* \times 10^{-5}$
liter	meter³	$1.00* \times 10^{-3}$
ounce (U.S. fluid)	meter³	$2.957\ 352\ 956\ 25* \times 10^{-5}$
peck (U.S.)	meter³	$8.809\ 767\ 541\ 72* \times 10^{-3}$
pint (U.S. dry)	meter³	$5.506\ 104\ 713\ 575* \times 10^{-4}$
pint (U.S. liquid)	meter³	$4.731\ 764\ 73* \times 10^{-4}$
quart (U.S. dry)	meter³	$1.101\ 220\ 942\ 715* \times 10^{-3}$
quart (U.S. liquid)	meter³	$9.463\ 529\ 5 \times 10^{-4}$
stere	meter³	$1.00*$
tablespoon	meter³	$1.478\ 676\ 478\ 125* \times 10^{-5}$
teaspoon	meter³	$4.928\ 921\ 593\ 75* \times 10^{-6}$
ton (register)	meter³	$2.831\ 684\ 659\ 2*$
yard³	meter³	$7.645\ 548\ 579\ 84* \times 10^{-1}$

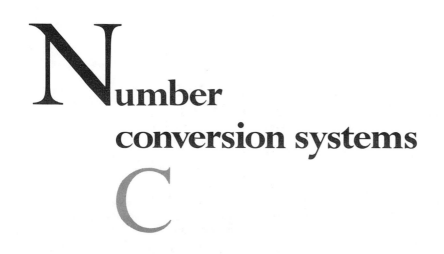

Number
conversion systems
C

C.1   Conversion of numbers into the base ten system

In order to understand the theory of number conversion from one base to another, it will be useful to look at the meaning of a number in the decimal system.

Each decimal digit in a number represents a coefficient to be multiplied by the appropriate power of ten, the base. The position of the coefficient in the number string indicates which power of ten is to be used in generating the products. The value of the number will be the sum of these products. Thus the number 125.64_{10} means:

$$1. \times 10^2 + 2. \times 10^1 + 5. \times 10^0 + 6. \times 10^{-1} + 4. \times 10^{-2}$$

Any number in any base can be converted to its base ten equivalent by summing the appropriate powers of the base, each multiplied by the proper coefficient. For example:

241.56_8 means:

$$2. \times 8^2 = 128.$$

$$+4. \times 8^1 = 32.$$

$$+1. \times 8^0 = 1.$$

$$+5. \times 8^{-1} = .625$$

$$+6. \times 8^{-2} = \underline{.093\ 75}$$

$$= 161.718\ 75_{10}$$

or

$C4.A_{16}$ means:

$$C(12.) \times 16^1 = 192.$$

$$+4. \times 16^0 = 4.$$

$$+A(10.) \times 16^{-1} = \frac{.625}{196.625_{10}}$$

or

110.101_2 means:

$$1 \times 2^2 = 4.$$

$$+1 \times 2^1 = 2.$$

$$+0 \times 2^0 = 0.$$

$$+1 \times 2^{-1} = \quad .5$$

$$+0 \times 2^{-2} = 0.$$

$$+1 \times 2^{-3} = \quad .125$$

$$\overline{\qquad 6.625_{10}}$$

C.2   Conversion from binary to base eight and base sixteen

Conversion from binary to octal can be accomplished by converting groups of three binary digits starting at the decimal point and working both ways using the conversion values found in Table 7.1. For example:

$$\underbrace{110}\underbrace{011} \cdot \underbrace{101}_2$$

$$6 \quad 3 \ \cdot \ 5_8$$

Conversion from binary to hexadecimal is accomplished in a similar manner except that bit groups of four digits are used rather than 3. For example:

$$\underbrace{11}\underbrace{0011} \cdot \underbrace{101}_2$$

$$3 \quad 3 \quad \cdot A_{16}$$

(In this process blanks are treated as zero.)

C.3 Conversion of base ten numbers into other base systems

Conversion from base ten into other new bases requires a two-part procedure. The first part of the procedure is used to convert the digits to the left of the radix point, i.e., the whole number part. This is done by first dividing the base ten number by the new base. This division may be accomplished using base ten mathematics. The division process will yield an answer in the form of a dividend and a remainder. The remainder becomes the first converted digit to the left of the radix point. Next, the dividend is divided by the new base to yield a second dividend and a new remainder which becomes the second converted digit. This process is repeated until the dividend is small enough to constitute only a remainder to become the final converted digit.

The conversion of 74_{10} to base eight would consist of:

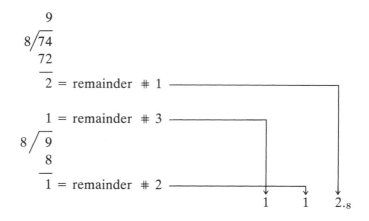

The second part of the conversion procedure is used to convert all the digits to the right of the decimal point, i.e., the fractional part. This conversion is done by multiplying the fractional part by the new base. The resulting product will be an integer plus a new fractional part. The integer is the first converted digit to the right of the decimal point, and the leftover fraction is used to generate the second converted digit by multiplying again by the new base. The result will be another integer plus a fractional part. This second integer is the second converted digit to the right of the decimal and this second, leftover fraction is used to generate the third converted digit. The procedure continues until the leftover fraction becomes zero or until the desired number of significant digits is achieved.

For example:

$.55_{10}$ converted to base 8 will be:

$$8 \times .55 = 4.40 \qquad \text{first digit} = 4$$

$$8 \times .40 = 3.20 \qquad \text{second digit} = 3$$

$$8 \times .20 = 1.60 \qquad \text{third digit} = 1$$

$$8 \times .60 = 4.80 \qquad \text{fourth digit} = 4$$

$$8 \times .80 = 6.40 \qquad \text{fifth digit} = 6$$

$$8 \times .40 = 3.20 \qquad \text{sixth digit} = 3$$

$$\vdots$$

so that $.55_{10} = .4314631463146\ldots\ldots\ldots_8$

repeating pattern

In this example we note that a repeating pattern appears. It is not always possible to find an exact equivalent for a fraction in two different base systems.

The main storage for a digital computer can only store a finite number of digits for a given fraction. It should also be mentioned that the digital computer does not round off answers in its printout. Rather, it is designed simply to truncate the values. Thus, if the number $.55_{10}$ is given to the computer, converted to base two, stored, retrieved from storage, and reconverted to base ten, the result may be truncated and printed as $.549999_{10}$.

Answers
to selected problems
D

Chapter 4

4.2 $J\,mol^{-1}\,K^{-1}$

4.6 dimensionless

4.10 $kg\,m^{-1}\,s^{-1}$

4.13 18.6 kg

4.17 55.5 Nm

4.21 3143 W

4.24 $5.59 \times 10^{-14}\,N$

Chapter 5

5.2 (a) 3.475×10^5 (f) 2.97×10^{-9}
    (b) 1.79×10^{-4} (g) $7.942\ 5 \times 10^{12}$
    (c) 9.4×10^7 (h) 1.478×10^0
    (d) $2.752\ 81 \times 10^2$ (i) 8.8×10^{-3}
    (e) 4.15×10^4 (j) 6.0×10^{-2}

5.5 $165 \pm 10\,N$; $165\,N \pm 6.1\%$

5.7 $\bar{x} = 5$; $\sigma = 2$

5.9 $\bar{x} = 79$; median $= 80$; $\sigma = 10$

5.13 1/6

5.15 $\bar{x} = 35.28$; $\sigma = 1.06$

5.20 $y = e^x$

5.22 $y = \sin x$

Chapter 6

6.1 (a) 23
    (b) −36
    (c) −152
    (d) 48.3
    (e) 502.0

6.5 0.636654

6.8 0.14 cm

6.11 2.60

6.14 0.92 m s^{-2}, 46.2 K

6.17 −73.3 K

6.22 10.0 N

Chapter 7

7.1 (a) 153.75$_{10}$ (d) 76800.$_{10}$
    (b) 2756.6875$_{10}$ (e) 0.0141904$_{10}$
    (c) 13.50$_{10}$ (f) 0.1875$_{10}$

7.3 (a) 1100100.0$\underline{1110101110000101000 1}_2$
               (the pattern repeats)
    (b) 100100110$_2$
    (c) 0.000$\underline{0000101000111101011 1}_2$
            (the pattern repeats)
    (d) 0.000001$_2$

7.5 (a) have
    (b) give

Chapter 8

8.1 (a) NBOLTS   (f) NPAGE
    (b) NENGRS   (g) NTEETH
    (c) MONTH   (h) NTVC
    (d) NDAY   (i) NTHETA
    (e) NYR   (j) NDOLLR
    (*Note*: Other answers are also possible)

8.3 (a) 1.0   (g) 1
    (b) 1.0   (h) 0.0
    (c) 0   (i) 4
    (d) 1.0   (j) 7500.
    (e) 36.   (k) 3.75
    (f) 1.0   (l) 20

8.6 (a) Not valid—starts with a number
    (b) valid
    (c) valid
    (d) Not valid—contains "+"
    (e) valid

(f) Not valid—contains too many characters
(g) Not valid—contains "+"
(h) Not valid—contains "+"
(i) Not valid—contains "*"
(j) valid

8.10 (a) integer   (f) real
     (b) integer   (g) mixed
     (c) mixed   (h) real
     (d) mixed   (i) real
     (e) real   (j) real

Chapter 9

9.1 (a) The comma after "3" should be omitted.
    (b) A comma is required after (A).
    (c) A comma is required after 4.
    (d) The parentheses around A,B,C should be removed.
    (e) The use of the logical expression (B.LT.7) is wrong.
    (f) A set of parentheses is missing.
    (g) A + B is not a valid variable name.
    (h) E6.4 is improper—E11.4 would be proper.
    (i) F7.9 is improper—F7.4 would be proper.
    (j) I6.4 is improper—I6 would be proper.
    (k) 10 is greater than 2.
    (l) The number of characters is 13 not 10.
    (m) The comma should be omitted.
    (n) The parentheses must contain more than one variable name.
    (o) The dimension on B is missing.
    (p) Two variables have been specified but only one data value is given.
    (q) I is an integer and cannot be assigned a real value 3.4.
    (r) The statement number is missing.
    (s) A is not an integer.
    (t) I6 should be a constant rather than a variable name.

9.14 The Fibonacci Numbers are as follows:

K	F_K
0	1
1	1
2	2
3	3
4	5
5	8
6	13
7	21
8	34
9	55
10	89
11	144
12	233
13	377
14	610
15	987
16	1597
17	2584
18	4181
19	6765
20	10946
21	17711
22	28657
23	46368
24	75025
25	121393
26	196418
27	317811
28	514229
29	832040
30	1346269

9.15 The first seven prime numbers are: 2, 3, 5, 7, 11, 13, and 17

9.18 The roots of the polynomial are -3, -1, and -2.

Chapter 10

10.1 (a) C(F) = (F − 32.)/1.8
(b) XMETER(F) = F*0.304801
(c) RAD(DEG) = DEG*0.0174533
(d) ROOT(A,B,C) = (−B+SQRT(B**2−4.*A*C))/(2.*A)

10.4 (a) will work
(b) Type conflict—will not work
(c) will work
(d) Type conflict—will not work

10.8 ISIGN(VAR) = VAR/SQRT(VAR**2)

10.13 (a) valid
(b) not valid—the name of the subroutine is wrong
(c) valid
(d) not valid—the third argument does not agree in type
(e) not valid—the first argument does not agree in type
(f) not valid—the number of arguments in the list is different

Index

A

A-field, 212, 214
Abacus, 120
Abscissa, 100
Accreditation, 6
  advanced level, 6
  basic level, 6
  engineering, 6
  engineering technology, 7
Accuracy, 53
Addition, 191
Aerospace engineering, 18
Agricultural engineering, 21
Air pollution, 10
ALGOL, 171
Amount of substance, 65
Ampere, 62
Analog computer, 174
Analysis:
  graphical, 99
  numerical, 107
  statistical, 90
Angle:
  plane, 66
  solid, 67
APL, 171
Arithmetic IF statement, 202
Arithmetic statement, 201
Array, 188
ASCII, 167
Assumptions, 50
Average, 90

B

Batch processing, 172
BASIC, 171
Bernoulli equation, 75
Bimodal, 94
Biot number, 76
BIT, 165
Buckingham theorem, 71
Burroughs, W. S., 121
Byte, 165

C

Calculators, 120
  basic function keys, 126
  data entry keys, 126
  decimal systems, 126
  electronic, 121
  four function, 124, 130
  multi-function, 124, 134
  overflow/underflow, 127
  pocket, 121
  programmable, 124, 142
  rounding errors, 127
  scientific, 124, 134
  special function keys, 126
Calculator logic, 127
  algebraic, 127
  algebraic operating system, 127
  algebraic with hierarchy, 127
  reverse polish, 127
Candela, 66
Card reader, 163
Card sequencing, 185
Carriage control, 211
Celsius, 63, 64
Centigrade, 63, 64
Chemical engineering, 4, 12
Chemical processes, 13
Civil engineering, 3, 8
COBAL, 171
Comments, 184
COMMON statement, 244
Communication systems, 15
Computational devices, 52
Computed GO TO statement, 202
Computer card, 182
Computer design, 16
Computer languages, 168
Constants, 185
CONTINUE statement, 206
Control statements, 201
Coordinate systems, 100
  cartesian, 100
  hyperbolic, 100

logarithmic, 100
polar, 100
rectangular, 100
semi-logarithmic, 100
Cores, 158
Coulomb, 62
CPU, 158
Current, 62
Curve fitting, 100

D

Data conversion specifications, 212
DATA statement, 222
Debug, 225
Decimal system, 59
Degree requirements:
  engineering, 6
  technology, 7
Design engineering, 28
Development engineering, 27
Deviation, 92
Digital computer, 156
DIMENSION statement, 221
Dimensions, 58
Disk pack, 161
Division, 1
DO loop, 204
DO statement, 204
Drag coefficient, 71
Drum storage, 162
DUMMY statement, 206

E

EBCDIC, 167
E-field, 212, 215
Electricity, 14
Electrical engineering, 4, 14
Electronics, 15
END, 207
Energy, 10, 20
Energy conversion, 10
Engineer, 5